OTHER SCHOOLS

AND OURS

Edmund J. King

King's College, University of London

OTHER SCHOOLS

AND OURS

REVISED EDITION

HOLT, RINEHART AND WINSTON, INC.
NEW YORK - CHICAGO - SAN FRANCISCO - TORONTO

August, 1965
Copyright © 1958, 1963, by EDMUND J. KING
Printed in the United States of America
Library of Congress Catalog Card Number 63-10252
24936-0213

To my wife, Margaret,
and our four children

Preface

This book is primarily intended to be read—that is, read rather than studied. I have therefore tried to keep the presentation lively and to select illustrative material that is interesting rather than merely documentary. Many types of people are keen to know how their neighbors live in cultures different from their own. Parents alert to their own family problems, citizens concerned with international understanding, and of course students, teachers, and professors very often feel the need for some straightforward introduction to other cultural assumptions. This book is intended to give them that. If no more than cursory attention can be given, *Other Schools and Ours* should nevertheless impart an understanding of the main patterns of thought and practice in homes and schools.

On the other hand, an increasing number of readers want something more penetrating than an introduction. This book is intended to provide that, too, for those who can afford the time to read critically. They should find not merely evidence to support or contradict their existing information, but plenty of deliberate challenge to the assumptions prevalent in their own country, no matter where that may be. I have tried to be provocative, believing that it is far better to stimulate enquiry and discussion than to hand out data or to solicit agreement. For this reason, though I have been at pains to ensure meticulous accuracy, I have tried to stimulate the serious reader to probe beyond the facts. This can be done either by challenging what is described here or by analyzing more thoroughly my presentation of the problem at hand. For this purpose I have included a graded bibliography.

Anyone interested in comparing social institutions, social and educational thought, or school systems should be able to use this book

[vii]

either as a basic textbook or as a supplementary source book. In any case, I recommend that readers make their way through it quickly—for enjoyment, if possible—and only later fasten onto particular problems for comparison and analysis. In comparative education and in the comparative study of social institutions generally, it is a mistake to suppose that we can easily find material to compare. Too often the things compared are incomparable. We should try first to see every system as a dynamic whole, a complex of answers to many interpenetrating human problems. Only after getting a global view should we settle down to discern and examine the constituent details. Even then, when we pull them apart, we must never forget that the apparently similar odds and ends we have gathered up from different places have lost their life and personality in the process. To see their real significance we must recognize them in their own context. We must always, as it were, honor that context. Hence the value of a sympathetic case study.

Nevertheless, it really is very important to study also the recurring themes in all these questions asked by statesmen, educators, and parents all over the world. Problems of economics, religious and racial factors, problems of class and of politics, troubles with language, and all the anxieties arising from social advance and technological reorganization constantly repeat themselves in varied social and educational contexts. When once we have our information about what actually goes on, we can properly proceed to the separate study of these factors. There has been no space or opportunity for such a study here. After analyzing the several social and educational factors in my *World Perspectives in Education* * or one of the other books recommended for this purpose, it should once more be possible to return to *Other Schools and Ours* for material on which to use the new criterion or perspective. In writing, I have borne this return in mind. That is one reason why each of the national case studies selected here is also highlighted to illustrate one or more universal problems.

Chapters 2 through 7 contain schematic diagrams of the six educational systems discussed. These diagrams are merely approximations, although close ones, because of the impossibility of depicting numerous exceptions. The diagrams, moreover, are not intended to show relative enrollments in the various types and levels of institution.

I wish to express my indebtedness to my colleagues, Professor Joseph

* London: Methuen & Co., and Indianapolis: The Bobbs-Merrill Company, Inc., 1962.

A. Lauwerys of the University of London Institute of Education and Dr. Nicholas Hans, formerly of the University of London King's College. From them I received my introduction to comparative education. I have also learned very much from professors, administrators, and (above all, perhaps) students from every part of the world. Some of them have come to London; others I have visited in their own universities and homes.

In the Revised Edition, extensive and sometimes deep reforms in the countries described have been reviewed and analyzed in terms of recent world trends of interest in education. The final chapter has been lengthened to include reference to several major problems at present affecting educational policy-making throughout the world. Realistic account has been taken not only of domestic debates on education but also of international considerations of security and prestige.

The book as it stands is a sufficient introduction to Comparative Education from the standpoint of case studies in which problems are pointed out for personal analysis or group review; but a much more explicit examination of recurring problems, with international examples, is now available in *World Perspectives in Education*, which was written to be a companion to the present volume.

EDMUND KING

University of London King's College, 1963

Contents

DIAGRAMS

OTHER SCHOOLS

AND OURS

Introduction

People who read introductions are really serious. They will want to know why certain countries have been chosen as case studies. It is not only because they are politically important, or significant for some great new idea in bringing up children. The real reason is that each national community chosen for study is faced with one or more problems like those familiar to us, but in accentuated form. Therefore we might say that each national survey in this book is in a special way the study of one main problem, or of one outstanding solution tried as a remedy for a complex of problems. Thus India is an ancient country undergoing rapid transformation since emancipation has set it on the road to industrialization; with meager resources it is trying to become very modern, while remaining true to itself. That is the main problem we examine when we read about India. But there are numerous others, too—those of language and religious differences, difficulties of a rapidly rising population, and so on. So our main theme is complicated from the beginning. In any country we select, the same is obviously true.

On the other hand, it does help if we simplify. Seeing the main outlines more clearly than they are found in nature is every beginner's way to a real picture of things. Therefore, some lines will be overdrawn here, perhaps, while others will be left indistinct. The serious readers of introductions who are dissatisfied with this treatment will be able to rectify matters by more detailed researches later.

Denmark has been chosen because it is a very small country, which with few resources and a short school life has achieved a standard of urbane civilization that others might envy. There education is not just in the school. That point is enough to make some teachers think twice. France is still the country of rationalism and intellectualism. With unerring logic it highlights the problems of academic purism, of rationalist secularism, of centralization. Some of our own ideas suffer in it their *reductio ad absurdum*. Yet if we look fairly we shall see that even now France is in many ways the land of truly gracious living. Britain is the home of cautious empiricism. British society has been revolutionized

[1]

but with regrets. The sort of class struggle that Marx expected to explode in violence is conducted through the schools in accordance with the rules of the game. Antique talismans are brandished no less than genuine standards; but it is a very serious and radical contest.

The United States is not only the country claimed for liberty; it is the land of luxury because it is the land of resources and machines. For many underdeveloped countries it represents one alternative "shape of things to come." If it is only the logical apex of industrialization and urbanization (as some people think), then it is hard to distinguish its material attractions from those of the other alternative—the Soviet Union's. Therefore it is vital for any observer to analyze the differences between the essential America and the essence of industrialized communism. The differences are not always those which Americans take for granted, and they are not always those most easy to maintain against the full logic of industrialized life.

The Soviet Union's achievements are colossal by any criterion. Many of them have been achieved through schools. It is as well to know what it is that makes the second power in the world tick—and sometimes creak. The eyes of more than half the people in the world are turned in its direction. Some gaze in admiration; some are dazzled by confusion. Too many (even in democratic countries) cannot distinguish between what is communistic and what is merely humane or scientific. We should make that distinction very clear, for then the hungry myriads of mankind and the vast underdeveloped regions of the earth may reach out for a better future without paying the price of communism. This book may help.

So we come back again to our basic reasons for looking at other people's children. Each one of us knows best, as the first chapter shows; but it is as well to have some comparative material. Here it is conveniently offered in a simplified form, made more vivid perhaps because we see other parents and teachers attempting to act out our drama.

chapter 1

We All Know Best

When it comes to bringing up our own children, we all know the best way. No one is going to teach us. But when we look around at the neighbors' children, we see that some parents do not succeed at the job, no matter how much theory they have behind them.

Is it just a case of failing to do the obvious thing? Or are the things we take for granted not quite so obvious after all? Get an Englisman into a corner, shake him, and ask him what education is for. With eyebrows still raised he will mumble that he supposes it is for the "training of character." He may add something about "a gentleman," or something else about a "full and useful life." His choice will depend in part upon his politics.

Get your American into a corner, shake him, and ask him the same question. He will confidently cry that education is for the development of individual qualities, for making first-class citizens who will have splendid careers and will be well-adjusted members of the community. He will make it quite clear he is thinking about girls as well as boys. He will go on to tell you about the usefulness of various offerings in American education for achieving these purposes. And because Americans are "sold" on education, he may go on to proclaim that it will advance the democratic and American way of life in a rather dubious world.

Get a Frenchman into a corner, and treat him likewise. With a gleam in his shrewd eye, he is ready with the answer. Education is for the sharpening of the intellect and for the transmission of *"culture gé-*

nérale." There are really no English words for this phrase as the
Frenchman means it. It means being steeped in the philosophical and
aesthetic values of the Western tradition by means of an extremely
thorough knowledge of the great books and of all the formal academic
disciplines. But the Frenchman does not feel any need to explain this.
His short, incisive sentence is supposed to be self-explanatory.

The American, the Englishman, and the Frenchman are neighbors.
Like good parents everywhere, the American and the Frenchman are
sure they are right. The Englishman feels fairly sure, and he acts as
though he just could not conceive of anything else. Is the difference
between these parents just one of emphasis? Will the results be much
the same in the end? You would not think so if you could go into the
schools of these three nations. They are as foreign to each other as can
possibly be imagined. If schools are nurseries for adults-to-be, or factories
for the future, it is amazing that the adult product is not more different
than we now see it is.

Differences between nations are plain to see. A French girl in Picca-
dilly or on Fifth Avenue is French to her elegant finger tips. Her walk,
her liveliness are Gallic. The keenness of her eye, the shape of her
mouth, and her eloquent changes of expressions are typical of France,
rather than of America or Britain. It is hard to be precise about the
difference; but few will doubt that a difference is usually there.

Similarly, it is easy to pick out most Americans in London. There is
no need of distinguishing features like cameras or clothes or hair styles.
Even when Americans have lived in Britain long enough to wear English clothes and have lost other outward signs, the natives still recognize the measured, flexible swing of the typical American walk. American girls seem to the English eye to have a frank, clear gaze, a confident
and somewhat boyish lift of the head, a rather large though attractive
mouth, and a general style of walking that could perhaps be described
as "liberated." How does it come about that Americans, being derived
from so many racial stocks that have not yet had time to amalgamate,
can be so typical? Not genetically, that is clear. Nor climatically, nor
through occupation or class. The answer can only be that looking
American, like being American and thinking American, is culturally
induced.

How does this come about? We begin to guess the answer when we
see how an Italian, for example, can pick out an Englishwoman abroad.
He does not rely on a tailored tweed suit, or shoes, or a schoolgirl complexion, though these things help. Something in her general bearing is

usually enough to indicate her nationality. But even if she is sitting still, her mouth may announce that she is English, even when seen from a distance. It looks like that because she habitually talks English with a British accent. An Italian friend, a professor with whom I was discussing comparative sociology, once picked out for me correctly most of the Englishwomen at an international conference, and claimed that he did this on the basis of mouth shape alone. He said they looked as though they spent the whole day saying nothing but "Mew, mew." Saying "Mew, mew" can evidently become part of your physiognomy. It is probably part of your character.

Happily, no two human beings are quite alike. No matter what the pressure toward standardization, there is a welcome range of personalities and appearances. No one would like his fellow countrymen to go about asking: "How typical can you get?" But no American is sorry that he looks American, for example. In general we can see that national habits and ways of talking or thinking become built into that outward self that is all that the world can see of me, you, or anyone else. In the long run it does not matter much what our racial origins are. Despite our race, and even despite our family background in many cases, Americanization goes on all over the United States and a similar kind of absorption goes on in England or any other country.

But how does this happen? Are French girls taught to be chic by French schools? Hardly. Do American schools teach boys to walk about as though they owned the earth? Do British schools teach boys to walk about as though they didn't care who owned it? Yes and no. There are no lessons in these accomplishments, yet all day and every day they are taught by the whole community. As the school is a sort of symptom of the community and its culture, so the child's mannerisms and states of mind can only be expected to reflect the community's scale of values and etiquette.

This is particularly true in the United States, where the school is conspicuously the folk institution par excellence. The school is both the servant of today's community and the parent of tomorrow's. It shoulders responsibilities that in other countries are reserved for the family or the church. It brings in the parents of its children to share its life. The social life of the school's great family often moves in an orbit round its varied assemblies and enthusiasms. The civic and vocational life of the community shows great concern for the efficiency and well-being of the school. New towns and cities plan schools before the layout of roads and houses is completed. The school is the shrine that houses the myth or prophecy of the future America. But not even in the United States does that sacred institution teach people, for example, to "walk American."

Who does, then? Children in the United States, like children everywhere else, copy the mannerisms and routine of their parents and their playmates. Without thinking about it, they value the same prestige groups and acquire the same order of priorities. Young children (though some harassed parents will doubt this) are passionate conformists, on the whole. Therefore their system of role rehearsal and their dreams of self-identification can hardly fail to be "typical." I mean that they will exemplify the myths and imaginary self-portraits that the community dreams up for itself. In a country like the United States, where geographic mobility and social mobility are probably greater than anywhere else in the world, an even greater need is felt to "identify" self with what is "normal" and "American." There is basically little need now for the conscious Americanization of the public school system. Children are almost too ready to learn that kind of lesson. Society (that is, the organized life of people) is teaching it already for all it is worth. In the United States you *live* American; that is, you eat, buy, play, and dream American. Your father-image, mother-image, ego, and superego are American. Educators overplay the role of the school in all this. The results they see do not arise from the treatment they hand out—at least, not to the extent they suppose. This can be shown by the fact that American-style schools in Japan or the Philippines continue to turn out Japanese and Filipinos.

It can also be indicated from evidence nearer home. I have already said that a European can often distinguish an American by his almost maritime style of walking. Americans themselves recognize a variation from the normal urban style in the swinging gait of the plainsman, cowboy, or hillbilly. Good-humored jokes are made about it. But they do not teach these things in school in the Midwest. Nor do Southern schools teach their young ladies to cultivate an alluring and ultrafeminine walk that somehow marks them off from their equally attractive but nevertheless different sisters in the North. Modes of life and superficial mannerisms are learned together, from region to region, class to class, and nation to nation. The schools play a part; but not even in the most community-conscious schools does their contribution preponderate. The same kind of schooling can be tried elsewhere with different results.

We must also notice that from country to country very different ideas prevail about the role the schools should play. In France, for example, it is only a few years since the public system of education was first called a system of "education." Before that it was called the public system of "teaching." Going back to the typical French definition of education given at the beginning of this chapter, we are not surprised to find that the school concerns itself primarily with teaching facts, or handing out the great ideas, or exercising children in very clear thinking. The children in these schools seem almost like young adults when contrasted with British or American youngsters, for example. Self-determination and community life are almost unconsidered, except in a few experimental schools which are untypical. The teachers enjoying the greatest esteem are those who teach for only fifteen hours a week in straight academic subjects and who do nothing else. Parents play no part in the life of the school, as a rule, except that they usually insist that junior complete the large amount of homework the teacher assigns. The emphasis is on work. Sports play a negligible part in the school's program, and many parents grudge the little time allotted to physical education. Every Frenchman and Frenchwoman sets great store by competition, and the educational system is full of it. Hence the French proverb: "A Frenchman—an individualist." Teachers have one clear job to do: to teach. As one of the most distinguished teachers of modern France put it to me, "They are priests of the intellect." There you have it—the asceticism, the austere withdrawal, the renunciation for school purposes of the devil, the world, and the flesh.

But no one supposes that the French man or woman grows up unaware of the dangers or delights of the devil, the world and the flesh. The French are proverbial for their *joie de vivre*, and their *bon vivant* is the prototype of the modern epicurean in any country. He does not, however, serve his apprenticeship to sensibility amid the austere exercises of the classroom—not officially, anyway.

Nor does the normal French curriculum yet seem to have close relation to the social and vocational needs of today, whether we consider the basic occupation of agriculture or the increasing tempo of industrialization. Many Frenchmen would like things changed in school to secure a greater realism. The emphasis is still overwhelmingly on quality, however, and quality of mind of a particular kind, so that it does not seem to matter much if vocational skill and life orientation are postponed or omitted. It does not cause public concern that about three-quarters of the French population do not qualify for the most valued secondary education, or that proposals for more "modern" alternatives still have a problematical future. The quality of those who do succeed is astonishingly high within the broad limits of the formal curriculum. To that extent the system is successful. It has been copied in many parts of the world. That is a sobering thought for the Briton or American who feels that the successful French scholar is learned rather than educated. The French system is the basis of many nations' school programs; the American system has hardly anywhere been willingly copied though individual aspects of it have been widely influential.

Of course, that fact tells us nothing about the real worth of the respective systems. But it does show very clearly that nations have ideas about the kind of schooling they want, and that those ideas are vastly different. No American or Briton can honestly declare that the "truths" in education are "self-evident." By seeing how other people reject our notions of how to bring up children we may come to a better appraisal of our current practice; we may alter it, or we may reinforce it. At least we may see ourselves as others see us.

Even if it were true that fifty million Frenchmen can't be wrong, as the saying has it, it is clear that their school system is very far from being the whole of their education. French life and French society are the educational matrix of the distinctive French character. Schools are an integral part, but a temporary part, of every French man or woman's scheme of living. They add something (it is hard to say what) to the chic turnout of our typical mademoiselle. She is as ready for life as our British or American miss, though her idiom is different; but she has had no formal schooling in the social arts or in personality adjustment. Her undoubted mastery of the essence of being French has been instilled into her by *living* French. So it goes for every nation or cultural community.

To this extent we can see that every nation or community is totalitarian. Paradoxically, this is true even of the most liberal regime. It enfolds us at birth; we are cradled in its relationships; we acquire its language of living, its special dialogue of communication, and its idiomatic scale of values. We cannot escape from it while waking, and if we cry out in dreams we speak our mother tongue. No matter how far or in what respect we wander, we have one home. Even in the secret things we take for granted, like love, there are national idioms. "What comes naturally" is very often learned.

So the "self-evident truths" of child-rearing are not obvious after all. Is our chief aim to be "character," or intellectual eminence, or the production of well-adjusted and prosperous citizens? If we choose one of these, or a harmony of several, how do we set about achieving it? Even those who seem to share our aims have a different family structure and different methods of teaching. Some who rely on our methods achieve very different results. You might have expected "human nature" to make it all simple and obvious; but it is all very confusing.

Though we privately know best, it may be of interest to see in greater detail what some of our neighbors are up to with their children. After all, their experiments can be seen as attempted answers to our own problems, especially in the contracting world of modern travel and instantaneous intercontinental communication—to say nothing of mass production and some standardization of expectation. Let us try to appreciate—indeed feel as sympathetically as we can—the intimacy of their context. That is the dynamic, ecological complex which educates them. It is frequently this conjunction of forces that solves the fundamental (and therefore usually unspoken) needs of civilized living.

But needs and expectations change; circumstances certainly change. Every new social situation produces new needs even as it copes with the old. Let us see our own homes and schools as merely passing expedients, evaluating them in the light of others' experiments and priorities.

chapter 2

DENMARK

Great and Small

The flags are almost certain to be flying today in Denmark. Soon after we see the green copper crowns of tower and steeple, and the clean warmth of brick and tile, our eyes pick out a multitude of cheerful flags. They flaunt the white cross on a scarlet background against a windy sky, which is nearly always of the palest blue or the palest gray. On as many occasions as possible the cheerful Danes fly their brilliant Dannebrog from public buildings, from houses, and even from the hundreds of tiny "community gardens" that cluster together near the apartment blocks in towns. Proud of their country, fond of the land, peaceful neighbors, and hard-workers, the Danes seem to have solved many of the problems of graceful living.

Yet Denmark is a naturally inhospitable land of heath and shallow soil. It consist of a peninsula north of Germany and about 125 islands between that peninsula and Sweden. Altogether, it is about half the size of Ireland or half the size of Maine. It is roughly one-fifth the size of Minnesota, extending to 16,576 square miles. Its population is less than 4,600,000, approximately the same as the small inner area of London governed by the London County Council, or half the population of New York City. The climate is rather harsh, being cold in winter and cool in summer. Nearly the whole of Denmark lies as far north as the northern half of Labrador.

There was a time when the Viking ancestors of the present Danes harried the seas and pillaged the coasts of northern Europe. They settled in Ireland, ruled England, and swept through the Mediterranean

EDUCATIONAL SYSTEM IN DENMARK

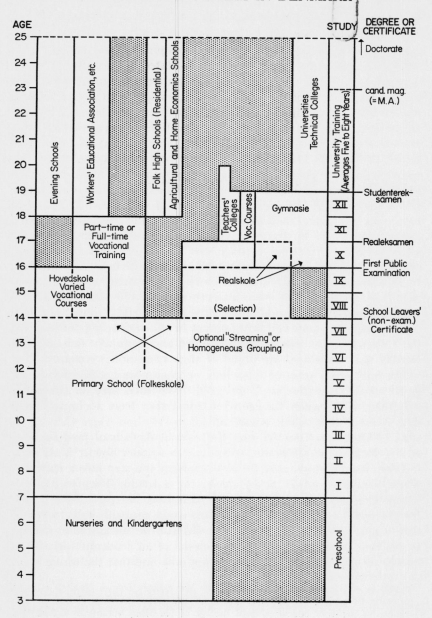

Sea. Until 1814, the king of Denmark was also king of Norway, Green-
land, and Iceland; but after Napoleon's defeat by the British the Danes
had to let Norway go. Then, though the population was no longer the
warlike scourge of the North, it mainly consisted of uncouth and brutal-
ized peasants eking out a hard life in scattered communities on the
sodden land. Many of the landlords were foreign in their sympathies if
not in blood. Yet amidst all these difficulties the Danes decided to
rescue their people and country by education. Compulsory schooling
was proclaimed in 1814. Within about three years it had effectively
begun. Today the Danes are among the best educated, cleanest, and
most civilized of all nations. They are probably the most democratic
of all. Differences of opportunity and wealth are very small. Community
life is very strong; but individual freedom is very great. Danes of all
categories get along well together at home, and are sure to give a
generous welcome to strangers. Though so proud of their country, its
language, and its cultural heritage, the Danes are great travelers and
quite at home in any community. All this achievement they attribute
to Danish education. Any stranger looking in on them is bound to support this testimony. Yet it has all been done in 150 years—the greater
part of it in less than a hundred years. During that time there have
been foreign invasions and near-famines in this naturally poor land; yet
the Danes are now materially prosperous and culturally rich. It is no
wonder that the Danes are proud of their educational system.

Yet only seven years of schooling are compulsory. Children do not
go to school until they are 7 years old. Even then they do not put in
a full day. They reach the age of 9 before they have a normal school
day. Most Danes leave school at 15 or 16, and then they go to
work.[1] When you consider that the normal day-school program ends
at 2 o'clock in the afternoon, you begin to wonder how it is all done.

There is even more cause for wonder when you step into a classroom
where youngsters of 13 or 14 are having a lesson. They will talk to
you in English—not perfect English, it is true, but perfectly adequate
for the job. If you were German, they could probably talk to you in
that language too. Some of them would also be successful in French.
If you were to sit in one of the top classes of an academic high school
having an English lesson, you would not only find that the whole lesson

---

[1] As will be shown later in this chapter, the law expects Danish children who are
   not already undergoing full-time instruction to attend evening classes or other
   centers of part-time education until the age of 18. Many voluntarily extend their
   formal education beyond this limit.

was conducted in excellent English but that the quality of the discussion would match anything in an American liberal arts college or the sixth form of an English "grammar school." It is quite uncanny. In a large town it is never necessary for the traveler to speak Danish. You are met not with the shopkeeper's or hotelkeeper's English of continental resorts, but with conversation and discussion. You will be welcomed into many homes; but you had better know what you are talking about. The Danes will be perfect hosts; but they will probably be a match for you in anything you discuss.

It must not be imagined that the schooling is all literary. The Danes are nothing if not practical. They live mainly by the export of dairy produce from a land that is naturally infertile except on one or two of the islands. They are great navigators and marine engineers. Their businessmen, technicians, and scientists range the world. If you go to the home of a typical farmer, owning his own lot of little more than 50 acres, you may find it as modern and comfortable as many a suburban house in Detroit or Wimbledon. It probably lacks a few gadgets that the city dwellings could well spare, but it probably has some refinements (such as music and singing) that they could benefit from. The farmer himself may have a Mercedes-Benz car or a good Volkswagen at least (and we must remember that cars are less familiar in Europe). In any case, the farmer's enterprises are skillfully linked up with magnificent sales organizations. His manures, foodstuffs, insurance policies, and mortgages are acquired on very favorable terms through his various cooperative schemes. His eggs and pigs form part of the great flow of exports although his hens and breeding animals are few. The most up-to-date cooperative dairies process his butter and cheese. In talking to such a farmer you are certainly talking to a businessman, and you do not always need an interpreter either.

Half of all the Danes live scattered over the countryside in villages, small townships, or on small islands. A quarter of the population lives in quaint little towns. The other quarter lives in Copenhagen. It is obvious that the task of providing fair opportunities for all in education, in communication, in urbane living is very great indeed. Denmark has no raw materials to speak of. There is no coal, no mineral wealth, no oil, no water power. With ingenuity and hard work, however, the Danes have made the effort necessary to supply the education they needed. With carefully educated skill and social engineering they have managed to pay for their schools and abundant social services. Their wealth has been won by exports. In a normal year, Denmark exports more butter and produces more bacon than any other country except the United States, which has nearly forty times its population and nearly two hundred times its area. This monumental achievement would have been impossible without a happy combination of individual enterprise and very close cooperation. The Danish way of education has served both endeavors and has been derived from them.

Let us look into a Danish home and see how Danish children grow up. Our visit will probably take us to a small apartment consisting of a living room-dining room, one or two compact bedrooms, a kitchenette, and a small bathroom and toilet. The main room may have a collapsible bed too. The apartment is warm and has plenty of hot water. It forms part of a block maintained by the municipality. Other apartment houses are established on a cooperative basis, being managed by the occupants. Some, of course, are privately managed. The rent is low.

To save space, much of the furniture is of simple but very elegant design, and is fitted close to the walls. An alcove or dining recess may be a feature of the room. The wallpaper is of a cheerful and modernistic pattern. Pastel shades predominate and brightly reflect the pale sunshine. Potted plants abound; some climb a trellis against the wall, others are dotted in front of the windows, and still others occupy the cool space between the double storm windows. As you have been invited for a meal, you have brought a gay bunch of flowers for your hostess. These are placed where they match the other flowers with which the room was decorated. Danes delight in floral decoration. Florists' shops are everywhere, and at all suitable seasons peddlers also sell flowers from pushcarts in the streets.

The street lies just below the window. There is no garden; but not far away the family has a "colony garden" or allotment on a communal piece of land. It has a small summerhouse where picnics are enjoyed. There are roses round the door, as in the song, and a trim hedge fends off the world from one Dane's castle. All kinds of flowers are grown, as in an old-world cottage garden, and so are herbs and some vegetables. Our hostess, in fact, has a pot of chervil and a pot of chives growing in her kitchen too. As we look out we are struck by the number of bicycles, and by the bright checks and cheerful patterns of the children's clothing as they play. In the cool air their cheeks glow healthily. No doubt their long woolen stockings, windproof jackets, and fur-trimmed caps keep them very warm. When they discard this outer clothing in the house or in the school's corridor-cloakroom, it looks like a festive bazaar. Their inner clothing is also warm, and also cheerfully colored. As far as color and individuality go, the scene resembles an American school, and is in marked contrast to many English schools.

At home the children are warmly welcomed. They treat their parents with affectionate respect. The parents in turn treat them with courtesy. The atmosphere seems to combine the old world of childhood and the new. As children do not begin to go to school before they are 7 (except in those urban areas where nurseries and kindergartens are provided for mothers who go out to work), a great deal of responsibility for the early stages of education falls on the family. It is not considered desirable that parents begin to teach their children the elements of reading, for example, although some do. The religious tradition among the Lutherans has always held that the home is the focus of a proper upbringing. Well over 90 percent of Danes are officially Lutherans, and though they wear their religion very lightly indeed, the habits of the old faith persist. Similarly, though a decreasing number of Danes are old-style farmers and craftsmen, there is a relic still of the time-honored notion that a significant part of a child's upbringing is experienced in the family's occupation. That is one reason why schools start at 7 years of age, and why they finish at 2 o'clock each day. It also helps to explain why there is no real antagonism to beginning work at 14 years of age. Schooling on a full-time basis may be temporarily discontinued then; but education is certainly not.

When little children go to school at first, they pass from one kind of parental atmosphere to another. The teacher is greatly respected. Even in the kindergartens, little girls coming in will curtsy to their teacher with a happy smile; little boys bow and shake hands. In the schools of an earlier period, the teacher was also the pastor, and the dignity remains to some extent. A higher proportion of teachers are men than we should find in Britain, and a much higher proportion than in the United States.

The full school day begins at 8 o'clock. There is an assembly at 9, after the first lesson. The school, especially if it is recently built, will be light and elegant. Yet economy has been carefully preserved in its construction, as it has been paid for out of the town's revenues. Great attention is given to soundproofing, and to good lighting with an absence of glare. The children troop along the light-painted corridors to the assembly hall. By the usual standards of Europe they seem very casual. Individualism prevails in hair styles as well as clothes. If the school is a *gymnasie* (academic high school) we may find that a few boys aged 17 or 18 are trying to grow mustaches or even beards. The head teacher comes in without much ceremony after the children are assembled, and greets them all. They wish him "Good morning" in return. There is a song or hymn, perhaps a short reading, an announcement or two—and that is all. There is no patriotic homage to a flag (none is on display), no declaration of allegiance, nothing solemn at all. Yet the Danes are passionately patriotic, keenly committed to education, and deeply respectful to authority, for all their liberty. After the assembly the children troop back to their classrooms. There are no prefects, no student government. The teacher is waiting for them, and the somewhat austere lessons begin again.

The teacher knows fairly definitely what each week's work, or even each day's work, will entail. There is not only a division of the day into regular periods, but even a fairly minute regulation of the whole study program. The principal teacher of the school is not, as in some countries, the chairman or leader of an almost autonomous band of teachers. He is an officer whose job it is to see that the government's regulations and other official interpretations are complied with. He is in fact called "Inspector." There is some local adjustment of the "school plan"; but the main direction comes from the Ministry downward.[2] This situation sometimes seems shocking to Britons and Americans, who cherish the idea of local autonomy; but we must bear in mind that it is possible for even an independent local authority (like the City of New York) to regulate public education very minutely, and to plan the teaching program more or less as is done in Denmark. The total number of Danes is not as great as the total population thus centrally governed in New York. In comparing school systems we have to get this kind of problem in perspective. It is noteworthy also that Danish teachers are more effectively able to influence the decisions of the local education authority than their counterparts in the United States or Britain, because they have representatives who possess considerable powers on the local education committee. Public opinion also accords high esteem to the teaching profession.

The day in a Danish school consists of six periods of 50 minutes, with a ten-minute break after each, except at 11 A.M. when it is longer. School is attended 6 days a week. The school year lasts from August

[2] The city of Copenhagen, where about one quarter of all the Danes live, enjoys a great measure of local autonomy in education; but the national pattern is closely followed, except in small details, and the city's education system is centralized just like the national system.

15 to June 24 approximately, with only 26 days' vacation during that time. Homework may take three or four hours a day after school. It seldom has much written content but usually consists of reading and understanding a text book assignment to be discussed next day. Competition is keen, and encouraged. There is now no charge for books, tuition, and medical or dental attention.

In the classroom it all adds up to a rather formal relationship between the teacher and the taught. There is much more talking by the teacher than would be considered proper in an English school, and much less activity and self-determination than is recommended by Americans. It seems incongruous, for example, to be present during a physics or chemistry lesson and find that the work is mainly done by dialogue between the teacher and the class, with a few visual illustrations and hardly any handling of anything. But the strongly verbal tendency in Danish education comes into its own in literary subjects and in anything that lends itself to discussion. Here there is very full class participation.

It is not surprising to find emphasis on the spoken word in an educational system that in times past was considered to be part and parcel of understanding the Word of God as set out in the Bible for interpretation among the faithful. In addition, the Danish educators of the early nineteenth century were greatly concerned to rescue the Danish language from the lowly status to which it had sunk. Therefore they encouraged a sense of nationhood and self-expression by the vigorous use of the mother tongue. To this day, the Danes are conspicuous for their eagerness to break into patriotic song on any excuse. It is all very happy and harmless. So far from being shut out, the visitor feels welcomed by it as by the gay flags that deck the streets on every possible occasion.

Yet it would be wrong to give the impression that Danish notions of education are bookish. What is done in school must be seen against the whole background of an education in society, at work, and in the home. Even in school, very close attention is given to self-expression in various manual forms of education. Many of our own notions about practical activities arise from the Scandinavian introduction of *sløjd* (*Sloyd*) woodwork in schools. Special teachers (wherever possible) give instruction in metalwork, home economics, music, and so on. Indeed, the public education authorities in towns of any size also conduct recreation centers where youngsters can pursue their hobbies in pottery, painting, and similar crafts under the supervision of paid teachers in the after-school hours of the afternoon and evening. These are very popular.

In addition, there is an ever-present interest in physical well-being. Towns make sure that doctors, dentists, nurses, and psychologists are available directly to schools. They may employ a nurse or a psychologist permanently on the staff of a large establishment. It is usual to make sure that the children have a Scandinavian sandwich meal (*smørrebrød*) with milk at about 11 o'clock. This balanced meal in miniature has not only improved the health of Danes in general; it has also taught generations the essentials of good nutrition. Under the name of the "Oslo breakfast" it has been widely recommended by physicians in many countries to impoverished or undernourished populations. As Americans have learned from its Swedish counterpart *smörgåsbord*, a sandwich meal can be very sumptuous. This is how you will find it in the more expensive cafés in Denmark too. It is interesting to see how what was once a part of social service has become a characteristic and delightful part of Danish living.

Children learn the elements of cleanliness in a practical way in many schools by having a bath at school once every two weeks. They are not, of course, allowed to suppose that this is enough! Either at school or after school they take an active part in games of all kinds. Because of the inclement climate, many games which visitors think of as outdoor games are played indoors in Denmark. Gymnasiums and indoor arenas are an important part of the educational provision. It is obvious that in a country as thrifty as Denmark the financial side of this accommodation may cause anxiety; but great public generosity is shown everywhere. Some of the folk high schools (about which more will be said later) are devoted mainly to physical culture, and teachers' training colleges make a strong feature of both fitness and readiness to teach physical education. This emphasis is particularly important when we remember that very many schools are small, and in country areas.

No matter what efforts are made to consolidate schools in one locality and provide a school bus system, a farming population thinly scattered throughout the islands must always rely heavily on the ingenuity of teachers in small schools. Partly because of the early religious associations of education, and also because of the undoubted devotion of teachers to their calling, the schoolmaster usually enjoys great prestige. It is significant that so many teachers are men; the normal word for "teacher" is masculine. In country schools especially, the teacher is a power in the community, as well as a factotum in the school. The schoolmaster with his violin (more mobile than a piano, and more personal) is a center of culture, an adviser, and often an organizer of adult education too.

To any people seeking emancipation or social mobility, education is seen as a ladder to greater things. The Danes are no exception. They have a fine feeling for the content of learning and for the humanities; but they are no fools when it comes to examinations. They love them —or (shall we say?) they love the certificates. Long after their formal day schooling has finished Danes seek professional certificates in this and that through the many opportunities available to them in further education. Their seriousness in this respect is exemplified for me in one fact. An apprentice between the ages of 16 and 18, undergoing a part-time course of evening instruction for a professional qualification, can actually bring a lawsuit against his teacher if he fails in his examination and can prove that his failure was due to the incompetence or incomplete teaching of his instructor!

In the light of this information, it is not surprising that the Danish system maintained selection by examination for the different kinds of secondary school career until August 1959. One school course prepared for academic and professionally useful examinations. The other was "examination-free." The different courses even then were always provided on the same premises until the age of 15. Since 1959 there has been a gradual adoption of a single type of comprehensive education for all children under the age of 14. A similar pattern has long prevailed in Norway.

Even after adoption of this new scheme in Denmark, children in their sixth and seventh years of common schooling pursue different courses in English, German, and mathematics. In schools with fourteen or more classes there may still be some division of the children into more academic and less academic programs, though the local authorities may insist on the maintenance of the comprehensive system even here. A big change under the new scheme is the introduction of a three-year *Realskole* preparing for commercial and similar vocations. This follows the ordinary school at the age of 14-plus. It offers a three-year course, especially in the countryside. The three years of the *Realskole* prepare for various opportunities or careers in commerce. At the end of the second year in the *Realskole* a public examination may be taken to decide whether pupils should or should not go on to a higher academic school for three or more years after the age of 16. This is the first public examination.

Thus there is no longer a formal examination at about eleven years of age to determine future careers, and in particular, to decide on various kinds of secondary schooling. Indications of this sort are still looked for —but in the ordinary framework of day-to-day school experience. The decision whether to enter a *Realskole* (which under the new arrangements comes at the end of compulsory schooling, still at 14 years of age) depends on the joint influence of parents' wishes and teachers' assessments. Therefore there is no doubt that children attending a *Realskole* are already considered to be of higher vocational or educational promise.

Further selection of children, this time of a much more formal kind, is undertaken in the first official examination just referred to. It comes during the *Realskole* career at about the age of 16, and selects on the basis of ordinary academic achievement in school subjects. Here we see something much more familiarly selective than the previous and more casual differentiation which took place according to parents' and teachers' assessments, or according to the child's previous indications by taking up such diagnostic preferences as a second foreign language or more difficult mathematics. The examination at the age of 16 helps in particular to distinguish between more strictly academic careers and those in commerce, the minor grades of public service, or at intermediate levels in industry.

Those children who seem to show most academic promise and go to a *gymnasie* after 16 follow a course very definitely "college preparatory" in American terminology, or "secondary grammar" in British terminology. It should be noted, however, that a child who starts a program that is less favored than the *gymnasie* is not automatically debarred from making the grade later. In fact, every inducement is given to the least academic group of children (i.e., those who do not pass into a *Realskole* at 14) to continue at school after the end of compulsory schooling, and to undertake vocational preparation of one kind or another either in a continuation of the ordinary school or in some special institution for craftsmen. Danish education is particularly well endowed with these. Vocational certificates have great economic importance in Denmark, as elsewhere; but in that country they very often have marked social importance too.

It should not be forgotten that in Denmark, as in other European countries, social etiquette requires a full recognition not just of doctorates and higher degrees but also of diplomas, certificates, and the like. They may be actually included in a person's title, as when you address a letter to him (or his wife), or introduce him to a third person. Although school examinations are not used for this purpose, some of the general pattern of academic appreciation attaches to them. Yet recognition of this sort does not make the Danes treat each other with snobbery. The impression you have is of difference rather than inequality. The most democratic citizens value their examination certificates, and often have opportunities to acquire qualifications of different types suited to their occupation. Indeed, the new Act requires that all schools shall provide vocational guidance from the seventh year upwards. It is realized that part of the educator's task is to make people acquainted with the world of work and its opportunities before leaving school. The Danes are reluctant to miss any chance of letting children make the most of themselves. Hence children may travel into towns by publicly provided bus or may, in a few cases, be boarders in residence at some special school.

The whole purpose of the 1959 innovations was to minimize the risk of early segregation, to facilitate transfer from one course of study to another wherever that seems appropriate, and to mitigate the accidental influence of environment or attendance at a particular school on the formal decision which used previously to depend so largely on "once-and-for-all" criteria. The Danes are very careful about the removal of all possible barriers and handicaps to progress. In particular, they try to minimize the disadvantages of isolation on an island or remote homestead. Before the new Act was introduced, village children living far from what was then called a "middle school with an examinations curriculum" could still continue their studies in an extension of the elementary school, with examinations in view; and they could be transferred to more urban opportunities later. Similar facilities exist now in the more remote areas.

To return to our children who have been lucky or bright enough to enter the *Realskole* at 14, in addition to the official selective examination at 16, they prepare for their first public *certificate* examination about the age of 17. The *Realeksamen*, as it is called, has long been highly esteemed for its vocational importance. It has traditionally been a school-leaving examination. Under the new dispensation it retains that character, but also includes the possibility of being followed by special technical courses after the age of 17. Danish agriculture has long been streamlined, and to a considerable extent mechanized with first-rate equipment; and in recent decades light engineering (and in particular marine engineering) has come very much to the fore.

A very much more difficult examination is the *Studentereksamen* taken in the *gymnasie* at about the age of 19 (or more) by those selected for academic and university careers at about the age of 16. The *Studentereksamen* entitles a student to register formally for university courses and eventually to present himself for university examinations. It covers a wide range of subjects and demands not only a highly developed intelligence but extreme diligence. As might be expected, *gymnasie* teachers doubt whether the high standards necessary for this examination can be maintained under the newer and more egalitarian school arrangements. A certain amount of professional partisanship no doubt colors their anxieties; but it must not be condemned for that.

Necessary though the new reforms were, teachers' anxieties are widely shared, at least to the extent that all Danes are eager to develop every child's potential abilities to the utmost. No one assumes that the highest standards are reached without constant effort. It is only through constant hard work, technical and professional skill, and business acumen that the Danes have built a prosperous nation. No Danish educator minimizes the need for the full development of different skills with all appropriate speed. As a nation dependent on exports, the Danes daily earn their living by their skills. The only real point of disagreement is over the need to broaden the basis of selection, and over the need to recognize different kinds of skill as professional in the sense that they can be taught as "liberalizing" ingredients of the ordinary school program. Outside the school program proper several such opportunities exist already.

Children who leave school before the age of 18 are expected to follow part-time courses of professional education until that age. A great many early leavers are still apprenticed to craftsmen whose responsibility it is to make sure that their boys and girls learn their trade properly. Trade schools in the larger towns provide evening and daytime courses as supplements to what is learned on the job. Provision is made for many skills; but hairdressing and fancy bakery seem specially popular. A particular feature of Denmark is the number of opportunities for the short-term residential study of agriculture, domestic science, and similar subjects likely to interest a rural population far removed from urban schools. There are many such opportunities for further education in commercial and professional pursuits also; but it is not necessary to provide such a high proportion of this training on a residential basis.

If Denmark had given nothing else to the world, it would be famous for its development of the folk high school. So much has been written about this type of education that the briefest mention will have to suffice here. From an extremely humble beginning in the 1840s, the folk high schools grew rapidly to provide farmers' sons with a general education based upon Danish literature, Danish history and sociology, religion and music. This was mainly offered then, as now, during the long winter months when the land was difficult or impossible to work. But in addition to the five or six winter months, some folk high schools offer a supplementary course of three months during the summer; and some which offer the longer course only to men make the shorter one available to women. The Danish word for "folk high school" means far more than the corresponding term in English. It carries the suggestion also of a *national* school and a *university*.

Especially as developed by Grundtvig and his admirers, folk high schools are strongly religious in atmosphere, though seldom so in formal worship nowadays. Their aim has always been to guide the moral and spiritual development both of persons and of the living Danish community, especially on the land. Yet the main emphasis in instruction at the schools is on formal lectures (again we see the influence of "the Word") followed by plenty of discussion. Continuous programs are personally tailored to suit students' own requirements and abilities. The principal or a tutor acts as personal guide to students in the preparation and elaboration of their work schemes. Individual reading and inquiry are strongly encouraged.

Living conditions at a folk high school are so harsh as to be almost forbidding. Rooms and food are plain in the extreme. Students are expected to do manual work for the community for at least an hour a day. Traditionally, folk high school students are from the laboring community, and the continuance of rustic near-rudeness in external treatment is a salutary experience for many who nowadays are more prosperous. The surprising thing is that in a folk high school you may find a banker's daughter and a ploughman on equal terms. The banker sends his daughter because he went to the same school and appreciates it. The system works. The students soon involve you in singing or whirl you into a merry folk dance. The intellectual fare is good; the society is good; and the opportunity for a kind of spiritual retreat from the daily preoccupations of a career is excellent.

Something like one-third of all Danish country and small-town dwellers passed through a folk high school in the years just before World War II, when students' enrollments were highest though the actual number of schools was less than in the early days of the century. Now the enrollments are fewer, and the schools' influence is on the decline.[3] Those who ought to know say that since the war folk high schools are only a shadow of their former selves. There can be no doubt, however, that they have contributed more to the Danish sense of democracy than any other type of schooling. Sometimes the actual work done in a folk high school has set students on the path to another profession. More often the experience of greatest significance is that of taking stock of one's life. The average age of attendance is about 23; but occasional students are considerably older, and some of the younger ones have had the advantage of a sound academic grounding. In no case is lack of money allowed to bar any serious candidate from entering. For tuition, residence, and food, students are charged only about $35 a month. Even this small sum may be reduced if a student earns a government grant, as the majority do. The schools themselves are private, a number being owned by their principals; but they may be helped directly or indirectly from public funds.

A number of folk high schools have a definitely vocational curriculum, a few of them concentrating on physical education but a greater number catering to farmers. There is the same Grundtvigian emphasis on personal regeneration; yet the curriculum itself is mainly technical. It includes Danish and arithmetic, because most of the students have left day school at about age 14; but the main bill of fare is agricultural science from a theoretical angle. These young men have had ten years' practical farming already, on an average. The agricultural folk high school brings them up to date in farming science. Hence Danish agriculture is highly organized, with the latest strains of crops and livestock, scientific manuring, and expert marketing. But in every sense the students' stay at the school is an experience of life in a home. The principal is a father or elder brother to them. His family life is identified with the school's. Danes, with their obvious love of children, have a remarkable knack of receiving you *en famille*. This observation is per-

---

[3] That is to say, their direct influence is on the decline. As schools for democracy, self-help, and civic dignity they have led to the founding of cooperative organizations, of social service schemes, and of many other practical schools of citizenship that are more in keeping with the modern temper than the semi-evangelical message of the folk high schools themselves. Also, the schools may well fade in direct influence as the causes they have fought for are recognized as having triumphed. Lastly, the appeal of the folk high school was primarily to a rural population, and Denmark is developing urban assumptions even faster than urban concentrations of population.

haps even more conspicuously true of the ordinary folk high school than of the vocational type.

A few folk high schools also welcome foreigners. This is difficult, because the whole emphasis is on "Danishness," and before an overseas student can participate it is usually necessary for him to spend three months or more with a Danish family, mastering the intricate language and its difficult pronunciation. That usually means working as a farm hand. Yet the pull exercised by the folk high school is such that at Askov I met middle-aged American women and students from the Far East. Askov, though still very Danish, is the largest folk high school; and for this reason and for its historic associations is a well-known showpiece. One folk high school, however, is intentionally international. This was established at Elsinore in 1921, to bring students of all origins together in mutual respect and understanding. Lectures and discussions are mainly in Danish and English, and sometimes in German. About 120 students can be accommodated at a time. Although this school is not really typical, it does give a taste of what the movement stands for, and both the founder-principal and the present principal are identified with the essence of the folk high school at its best.

On the whole, the folk high school movement has not affected the larger towns and cities directly, although a minority of students come from them. A few folk high schools, however, are associated with the Labor party and other left-wing organizations, and are understandably more urban in their enrollment. It is very interesting to visit such a college and see how, without essential loss of character, the almost religious atmosphere of personal conversion is made to promote a zest for political change. Grundtvig would have been aghast at some of the murals illustrating the march of the workers and at some of the blood-and-thunder songs; but he would have sympathized completely with the students' earnest self-examination. All the folk high schools impart a deep sense of personal and social commitment. No examinations are set. No certificates are issued. What people get out of it all is something they understand very well; but it is private to them.

The *mystique* or semievangelical enthusiasm associated with the Danish folk high school has inflamed its admirers in many lands— even where actual contact with Danes is almost nonexistent. But in Britain and the United States, to say the least, attempts to foster the cult in its specially Danish form are usually incongruous. Although we all need more person-to-person communication, and more time and opportunity to think over the great questions that come home to us in the sort of atmosphere the folk high schools achieve in Denmark, our context is quite different. The Danish movement triumphed because it was topical, intimate, and a real answer to the needs of a particular people in special circumstances. Anything that merits the same description for any other people is bound to be different.

Indirectly, the folk high school movement may be said to have prepared Danish farmers for the establishment of their many cooperative organizations during the terrible depression years of the later nineteenth century. Danish agriculture until then had relied mainly on the export of grain on a family or individualistic basis. It was soon faced with the need for radical reorganization of buying, producing, and selling on a cooperative foundation as the sole alternative to starvation. Now life in Denmark without cooperatives is almost unimaginable. The system, considered generally, combines the very best of private initiative with social safeguards for those needing help through no fault of their own. Although the cooperative ramifications of Danish life are in no literal sense a school system, there is no denying that the educational emphasis of Denmark's life would be totally altered without them. To think of it is like imagining the United States without a credit system or England without committees and "team spirit."

To pass from the folk high schools (whose name in Danish means nearly the same as "people's universities") and come to the universities proper is to make a great jump. The Scandinavian universities have all maintained a high standard of scholarship for centuries; and far from altering now, they seem to be making their courses tougher. After all his careful preparation in the *gymnasie* the student faces an arduous curriculum before he gets his first university degree. Admissions are severely restricted, yet even so a large number of admitted students fall by the wayside in their first or second years. To obtain a doctorate in Norway, Sweden, or Denmark is a far more grueling ordeal than in Germany, or even than in England. The American colleges requiring comparable excellence before conferring their highest awards could probably be counted on the fingers of one hand. This is no mean achievement for a small country of roughly four million inhabitants; yet even the universities are in some sense identified with the people. University lectures may be freely attended by anyone interested, though anyone who lacks the requisite examination qualifications will not be admitted to the university examinations. There is no tuition fee. The public can be present when a doctoral candidate defends his thesis. In essence there is no divorce between learning and living in Denmark. Though there are of course many things which progressive Danes wish to see altered (as happens in every country's stock-taking), Danish achievements can only be described as magnificent.

Our recognition of Danish success does not blind us, however, to some problems still unsolved or to newer reasons for disquiet. The crusading zest that was typical of the folk high school during the past century, for example, seems to be fading away from life in Denmark and Sweden. Neither of these countries suffered greatly in the recent war, in comparison with most European nations. Life is relatively easy; but the very absence of crying evils needing educational, social, or political remedies seems to have aggravated a kind of social fatigue or malaise. Most of the ordinary exigencies of life are prepared for by an adequate educational and political system, and most of the accidental perils of life are taken care of by social insurance and the welfare state. These safeguards are specially necessary in the precarious economy of tiny European nations so easily tossed about in the storms of international economics.

Yet welfare states must be re-earned every day, as the Danes maintain their economy by daily cooperation; and partnership in industrial, professional, and political roles must be continuously re-enacted with responsible understanding by every citizen. Many Scandinavians wonder if this is being done. Military conscription usurps the time and kills the enthusiasm once devoted to a period in the folk high school. Jobs— good jobs—are more easily won. People are glad to be at home rather than involved in community action; books, radio, and movies appeal to them separately. People claim to "live their own lives." This could be healthy; but drink is an increasing problem, and Denmark has a higher divorce rate than even the United States. New problems clearly need new solutions, and the Danes are anxiously seeking them.

In some ways Denmark, like Athens of old, has itself been a school for many of its contemporaries. The attention it has rightly earned has certainly not been won for it by its scholastic system in any narrow sense, though many of its excellent experiments challenge the professional observer. The Danish educational system is inseparable from the whole pattern of Danish living; it is identified with it.

This is a lesson we must learn when we look at any of our neighbors' ways of bringing up children. The absurd notion (presented in some American writing on Comparative Education) that you can compare the length of school life and the numbers of children involved, and thus reach a fair relative assessment of two educational systems, is

manifestly based upon a complete misunderstanding of what education
is. It ignores the fostering influence of individual families, the whole
social matrix that develops the maturing personality, and the vast range
of institutions or educational contacts that may be alternatives to the
influences at work in our own culture. It is no help to any serious parent
or student if a book or adviser uses clichés such as "a one-track system"
to recommend the American school provision because that is supposed
to be more "democratic" than any system which is not "one-track." It
is no help to use words that do not mean anything, and it is downright
misleading to ignore the facts. Danish schools are certainly not one-
track systems of education. Even after recent reforms they stress differences and perhaps make them. They may even be said to risk causing
inequality. But whatever we think about this, the results are far less
painful when society at large is full of lessons in equality and democracy.

Do we agree that in order to be democratic (and we have not settled
what that means!) we want all children to have exactly the same type
of schooling? If we do, then we must abolish elective subjects. We must
enforce attendance in exactly the same classes of all children, boys and
girls, slow and quick, "bookish" and "practical," of all income groups
and of all professional futures, in every single school in the country. We
shall rule out local and parental preferences. We shall prevent persons
or communities from providing anything better than what is offered to
the least privileged members of our society.

No one in a Western democratic society really wants this state of
affairs. In other words, no one simply because he is a democrat truly
wants a genuine "one-track" system. A democrat, or indeed any far-
sighted citizen of any free community, wants to provide children with
the best opportunities for self-development, social adjustment, and
community service. None of these things can be provided for by turning
mass-produced articles out of the same mold. We all want to see individual qualities encouraged—even by differentiated schooling. Though
we long for equality we want our community to be enriched socially and
professionally by different contributions; and at the same time we seek
a sympathy and harmony to be encouraged not just in the public school
system but in all the formative contacts of public life.

Teachers and parents must therefore be on their guard against misleading appeals on behalf of "one-track" or any other systems on the
automatic assumption that "we know best." We might indeed ask
ourselves if our own particular system is what it is alleged to be—either
"one-track" or "fair shares" or "democratic" or anything else. When

we put any system to the test we see that it is riddled with inequalities, inconsistencies, and educational superstitions. We also see that, if it works pretty well on the whole, its success depends not just on what is done formally by parents and teachers but on the whole complementary pattern of public life. In other words, for an educational system to be sound it is necessary to have home and school and work and public life helping one another in a realistic way. To be "real," the system must be true to its context; its idiom must suit the circumstances.

That is why it is wrong to expect other parents and teachers to see eye to eye with us, even though we are all asking the same fundamental questions about bringing up children. We live in different worlds of activity; we have different problems and opportunities; our value systems are as different as our idioms of language and dress and food.

Yet just as communication and clothing and nutrition are everywhere essential human needs, and just as we can appreciate the main theme better by studying the variations, so we can greatly profit our own families by looking at what happens to other people's children. Some small things we may copy outright for our own program. More often we may find our idioms challenged and needing greater clarification. We may need to rephrase our most pious proclamations, having learned to see the truth of our situation as we have never recognized it before. At least we may acknowledge that there is more than one way of doing a thing effectively.

Even if we think that our review of other people's educational practices and notions has done no more than show up our own family portrait in a sort of distorting mirror, or echo our pedagogic principles in some monstrous "double talk," we shall have begun to see ourselves as others see us. That is sometimes amusing. It is sometimes the beginning of wisdom.

chapter 3

FRANCE

The Central Light of Reason

La belle France!" There we have it; some countries are territories, some are nations, but France is a person—fair and feminine, inconstant and sometimes tempestuous, yet essentially true to character in all her moods. A French proverb puts it well: "The more we change, the more we stay the same."

Frenchmen of all factions think of their land as their love, their inspiration, and their joy. They are more radically divided than any other nation in politics, religion, and sympathies; but they are fanatically loyal to the France of their dreams. In the face of foreigners they close their ranks, and their quarrels are nearly all at home. Strangely enough, French discrepancies are all truly French in essence and expression. It would be hard to find any other country where national characteristics are so indelibly stamped on nationals' behavior. That was true centuries ago. History shows the essential France of today evolving recognizably through the past two thousand years or more, despite all the stormy changes that have taken place. What is more, this evolution has produced not only modern France; it has contributed to the free world a wealth of inspiring ideals.

In Britain and some other nations men have worked out empirical solutions to local problems, and their practice and institutions have sometimes been a great example to the world. But it is from France that we have received the great declarations of human rights in their most universal and radical form. Our liberal society and our enlightenment draw their inspiration from the almost intoxicating "universal

[30]

principles" which French *philosophes* and their international friends distilled from contemporary Europe (especially Britain) and the ancient world of Greece and Rome. The United States is probably more indebted to France for its democratic daydreams than to any other nation or culture. The American Declaration of Independence, the Bill of Rights, and so on, echo the very phrases (let alone the ideas) of the *philosophes*. The French Revolution's declaration of human rights owed much to the part played in its drafting by Benjamin Franklin and Thomas Paine; but those notions of natural law, natural rights, and self-evident truths were molded in their revolutionary form by French political theorists. "Freedom, equality, and brotherhood" has been a clarion call round the world for two centuries, and the note was first sounded in France.

How does it come about then that British and American achievements in democracy, industrialization, and learning are now so different from those of France? France is less than thirty miles from England; their capital cities are now less than an hour apart by air. Yet the daily idioms of the two countries could hardly be more different. Probably only the United States is more different from France than Britain is. If we had not been trained to notice the overwhelming influence of institutions and social background on our educational and political programs, we would have expected close similarity. Jefferson, for example, was much attracted to some French ideas on education. But both the United Kingdom and the United States have experienced the stimulation of French radical ideas without becoming more French. Why? Because the familiar institutions and practices of both the Anglo-Saxon countries are fundamentally different. It is these, rather than the rational ideas, that have so profoundly shaped their national character and aspirations.

What of France itself? France is a country of ideas; men fight over them as elsewhere they compete for money. This is especially true of her school system, but it is also true of her political structure and public life. What divides France is not differences of race or climate, occupation or class (though these differences are considerable); the sources of disagreement are nearly all of an intellectual origin. In other respects, France is remarkably united—from the vineyards above the Rhone to the rocky fisheries of Brittany, and from the dairies of Normandy to the parched coast of the Mediterranean. Thriftily and industriously, the Frenchman and his family enjoy their vivacious lives in characteristic fashion, remaining essentially Gallic no matter where they live or what their livelihood. French life is a rich and public thing, and the French

EDUCATIONAL SYSTEM IN FRANCE
Before Implementation of 1959–1969 Reforms

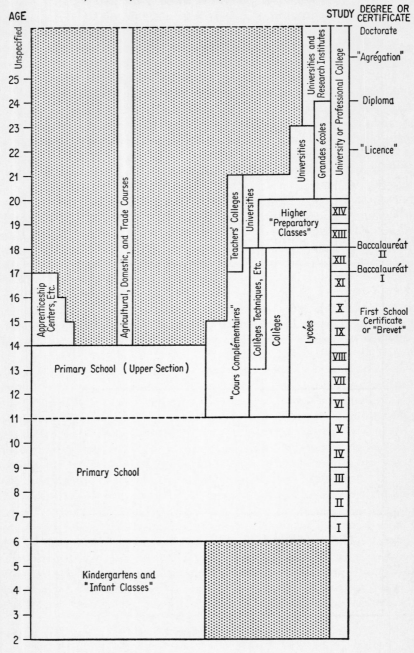

EDUCATIONAL SYSTEM IN FRANCE
In Transition 1959–1969

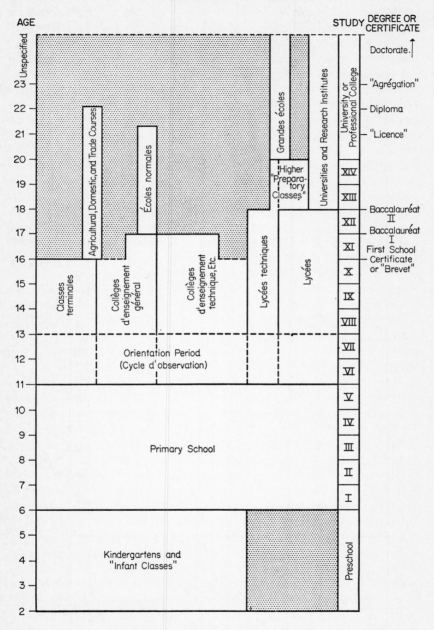

pursue it with passionate individuality. In France more than in most countries, the schools themselves play a great part in fomenting both unity and disunity. That is especially strange, because French schools are devoted to reason beyond all else. This paradox is itself a direct outcome of French religion, French politics, and French philosophical contributions to the world. Let us see how it works out.

Every child's first day at school is an impressive occasion; but if a French 6-year-old could stop to think about it he would find his first contact with school overwhelming. At 8 o'clock on September 16 every child in France, duly enrolled by the mayor of his town, begins the morning shift of three hours. That afternoon they will all begin another three hours at 1 o'clock. The term will last until the evening of December 23. The five-day week is arranged so as to leave Thursdays and Sundays (not Saturdays) free from school, so that any parents who so desire may have their children instructed in religious matters. All publicly provided schools are secular. Other holidays are fixed by the Order of February 11, 1939 and subsequent modifications. The choice of school subjects and the distribution of lessons are equally fixed by Article 19 of the Order of January 18, 1887, the Order of 1939 just referred to, and several other orders—all of which secure uniformity throughout the whole of France.

Boys are usually separated from the girls (except in experimental schools); but the program is almost identical. Only minute variations are allowed, and special permission must be secured for these. Everything is ordered. The teachers are all civil servants, selected on the basis of state qualifications that are the same for the whole of France; they are paid by the state according to a national scale, centrally directed and supervised, and charged with the execution of the educational laws. Though it is not quite true that every child in a given class in France is being taught the same thing at the same time, anyone examining the minutely regulated school programs might very well think so.

A growing number of nursery schools and classes (attended by more than half the children of France) are progressive and humane; but the compulsory primary schools for children over 6 are places for hard work. As the Circular of July 27, 1882, puts it: "The primary school's ideal is not to teach a great deal, but to teach it well. Children leave school with a limited knowledge, but what they have been taught they know thoroughly; their learning is restricted, but not superficial. They do not possess half-knowledge . . . for what makes any education complete . . . is not the amount of information imparted, but the manner in which it is imparted." This order seems to most foreign observers to err only on the side of understatement as far as French schools are concerned, for French children's "limited knowledge" would seem a very great amount to most British teachers and all Americans. It is duly examined and recorded at the end of school life on a formal certificate.

Yet French educators, for all their insistence on knowledge, are not primarily interested in factual learning; they insist that "the intellectual faculties shall be developed," and that children's minds shall be "trained, enriched, and broadened." That is what the law for elementary schools prescribes. The higher schools do the job much more thoroughly. The quick, alert eye of the French man or woman (or even the French child) pays testimony to the unsparing exercises of the French school. French meals are a delight to any connoisseur of food; but to the Frenchman they are leisurely occasions (very often lasting two hours, and nearly always one hour) where sparkling conversation is no less important than savory dishes and good wine. A visit to a village shop or café is very often an intellectual exercise, though an enjoyable one if your French is equal to it. You must also know very thoroughly whatever you are talking about, for the French do not bear fools gladly. Nearly everyone you meet in such circumstances has left school at the age of 14, when compulsory attendance ended, until the 1959 decrees provided for the gradual extension of compulsory attendance until 16 during the 1959–1969 decade. Exact figures are hard to come by, as there is so much uncertainty about what should be classified as "secondary" education; but as late as 1962, despite much voluntary extension of school life, only some 20–25 percent received secondary education. However, French wits have been very well sharpened without that for a very long time, and throughout the whole of France.

But is that what education is for? The average Frenchman is inclined to say "Yes." School is for intellectual matters. Parents support the school's aims with real conviction, and watch over their children's progress accordingly. They do not do so through American-style parents' associations (which, though encouraged, are negligible except in a few areas), but through real insistence on hard work at school and in homework. In 1957 an order was issued that made homework illegal for children under 11; but it will be some time before it can be effectively enforced. Until 1957 the only way to secure admission to secondary education in a *lycée* or *collège* (an academic high school) was through a selection examination, and it was not surprising that homework was officially and unofficially set to prepare children before the examination was taken about the age of 11. Between 1957 and 1959 children were selected for academic secondary education (or rejected) mainly on their previous teachers' recommendation, only those who were "uncertain" being required to take a written examination. (Those whose primary school was a private—usually Catholic—school were all officially "uncertain.")

Since September 1959 a new law has reconstructed French secondary education, envisaging changes which are to take place gradually until 1969. It incorporates many ideas from the Langevin-Wallon and similar proposals of the 1946–1947 period, which had a stormy passage then and have since repeatedly caused much legislation (even of a non-educational kind) to founder by their repercussions. Governments have been overthrown in consequence. It therefore remains to be seen how far some of the proposals will be implemented; and the first few years' experience of this process certainly induces caution in the observer, particularly as this has been the characteristic reaction of Frenchmen themselves.

The most important single feature of the new legislation is the requirement that most children between the ages of 11 and 15 shall have a period of "orientation" or observation, no matter what kind of secondary school they may happen to be in. Unfortunately, differences in curriculum of an extremely radical and diagnostic kind occur during this period, shaping the whole nature of a child's future career in life as well as at school. Not only do the existing schools continue to exist as separate institutions, with teachers recruited long ago, and of very different orders of esteem in the extremely sensitive hierarchy of republican France, but they also are closely geared to quite different examination prospects. The pace of progress no less than the complexion of subjects makes it more than doubtful whether any child for some years to come could have anything like the same prospect from an observation period in any two or three of the differing kinds of institution still in existence. More will be said later about the relative claims and merits of these. At the present moment we must simply note the dubious merits of the practice of "orientation" or observation as it now exists.

It may help in gaining a more realistic appreciation of the situation if we remember that the older, prestige-conferring *lycées* with the most exacting academic curriculum also have preparatory schools or departments for children below the age of 11. Officially these are public elementary schools charging no fees. Their teachers, however, are undoubtedly the most efficient in the whole district; their academic requirements and the pressure of parental anxiety combined contrive that (as late as 1962–1963) nearly all their children pass for "orientation" into the *lycée* of their choice, and commence such subjects as Latin in the January after their arrival. Supposing such preferential primary schools could be abolished, which is doubtful, and supposing that selection of children by curriculum attrition below the age of 11 could be eliminated, there would still remain the gravest doubts about equality of consideration and orientation from 11 to 15 as long as the present secondary schools enjoy their individuality and greatly differentiated prestige.

We are on much safer ground when we pass to the new proposals for programs after the age of 15. Five types of secondary schools have been established, all existing in some form or other before the 1959 reforms, but all now under different names. Three of these secondary schools give a "short" secondary education, and two "long." The latter are clearly the former *lycée* and the former *collège technique*, now called respectively *lycée* and *lycée technique*. More will be said about them later. The other three types of secondary opportunity henceforward exist in the *"classes terminales"* of the former elementary school (or *école primaire*); in the former *cours complémentaires* or supplementary secondary education of some larger towns, which are henceforward called *collèges d'enseignement général* (general education secondary schools); and a new comprehensive category of *collèges d'enseignement technique* (technical secondary schools). This last group is already gathering under its aegis a rather wide range of technical schools or apprenticeship training centers which enjoy special financial benefits under the French system of taxing industries for vocational training.

No doubt the ladder of opportunity will be strengthened and broadened, especially with the growth of the European common market and the rapid expansion of industry and commerce. Outsiders will note these developments with more appreciation than the traditional French academic—to say nothing of most employers and nearly all parents. The short courses lead to manual or intermediate commercial careers, skilled though they may be. But only the longer secondary education leads directly toward the university and professional careers. Therefore, for a generation to come (at least) we must suppose that European opinion will prefer the latter to the former in no uncertain way, and that anxiety and coaching the children *below* the age of "orientation" toward or away from various careers are likely to prevail.

Once admitted to orientation or *lycée*, the French child does a great deal of homework. Great concern has been expressed by doctors and parents since the war about the evil effects on children's physique, and even on their mental alertness. So educational reformers have taken steps to reduce the amount of homework by regulation, especially for the lower classes of secondary schools. It was not unusual for homework to last until nine, ten, or even eleven o'clock in the evening; and in the somewhat crowded family circumstances of many French homes the mere mechanics of doing it could be a real problem. It has become usual in many cases now to do the *devoir* at school after the end of formal lessons. Parents still take a keen interest, however. The direction of that interest is perhaps best illustrated by an anecdote.

An American mother who went to stay in Paris was very proud of her two robust sons. A French neighbor was very helpful and friendly, but one day confided to the American mother that it was a pity her two sons looked so much like peasants. After a term in French schools the American boys were so pale and tired from nightly homework that their mother was anxious. Just at this time the Frenchwoman congratulated her neighbor on the boys' development, saying, "They look more like scholars now." One medical survey after another says that French children's health suffers from overwork at school; educators often agree; so do parents when they are off their guard. Every now and then you hear complaints of *bourrage* ("stuffing"), and proposals to abolish the public examination system in its present form. Yet very little is done. Why? Because French public life, including most of the better jobs, is arranged on the basis of selection examinations. You either qualify or you don't. The examinations are the same for everybody [1]—in Paris, in Brittany, on the Riviera, in faraway tropical territories of the French Community. If you pass them, and go on passing despite the ferocious competition, you will come to the top. France herself gets a remarkable development of her brightest children's intellectual powers. The brilliant are given every chance and encouragement. Absolutely no favor is shown to money or to family connections, though in fact a majority of the children in academic secondary classes are from "white collar" homes. This does,

---

[1] That is to say, they are officially set and regulated under centralized control; but an already noticeable variation in marking standards (as between different types of school) seems likely to be accentuated by 1962–1963 changes which may make the *baccalauréat* more of an "internal" examination like the German *Abitur*, or a partly "internal" examination like the Italian *maturità*. In any case, more weight is given to school records as an alternative to examination criteria.

of course, raise questions of equal access and equal starting conditions in the great academic steeplechase. In times of rapid technological change it also introduces doubts about undiscovered aptitudes and uncultivated reserves of skill; but now let us concentrate on the matter of equality. Intellectualism is a French tradition; equality has been a war cry of French republicanism. The present school system is an attempt to combine both. But does it?

Before we look into the question of equal opportunities in the strictest sense, we should examine the most outstanding feature of French education and French government, namely, centralization. Paris is the hub round which France rotates. Just as in the ancient world all roads led to Rome, so in France today all roads lead to Paris, literally and figuratively. France has a unitary system of government. The 94 *départements* (like counties in some ways) have local administrations, and so do the cities and townships; but each nucleus of French life is directly manipulated by the control of the central government, and subjected to meticulous regulation. In education the same is even more specifically true. There are major educational regions called *académies* (21 since 1964), each with its university and its *recteur* who is in charge of all education from the university down to the level at which the "prefect" of the *département* takes over responsibility for elementary education; but even there the prefect is responsible back through the *recteur* to the Minister of Education in Paris. You can imagine the system as a sort of wheel whose spokes are based on Paris; each spoke at its outer end terminates in another little wheel, again with a central hub and radiating spokes. So it goes on down to the level of the individual school, the individual teacher, and the individual child. If you look for a particular item in any part of the system, it is possible to find identical items in the corresponding position in the whole of France. Only technical education (a small proportion) shows any noticeable local variation.

On the other hand, though structural identity prevails in a remarkably uniform way, there may be many hidden differences in quality. There is certainly a variation in degrees of initiative. It has long been felt that a progressive denudation of provincial resources—in manpower, investment, and in opportunity—is a serious social disease in France. During recent years administrative decisions have been taken to correct this cityward gravitation, some of them affecting education. Among them have been the increase of the number of *académies* (and therefore universities) from 16 to 20, and the progressive fostering of cultural and technological responsibility in such cities as Grenoble, Lyon, and Amiens, with "university colleges" for the *propédeutique* year.

Centralization took place in the name of equality, at least in modern France. In the past, the centralizing tendency was already manifest in the Roman Empire before Christ, and in the Roman Catholic Church which has shaped so much of Christendom. France has many living legacies from both. French cardinals and French kings were extremely powerful before the Revolution (1789), and gathered political and ecclesiastical control tightly into their hands. Both Church and State were authoritarian. The gravest social and economic inequalities were prevalent in all aspects of life. Outlying provincial areas were neglected, despised, and exploited. But before the Revolution was anything more than a distant cloud, the *philosophes* of the eighteenth century had expanded British claims for individual independence into political manifestoes for the world. Among these were claims for education that should be available to all men. All men were equal in essence; they should be made so in opportunity. If this were done, mankind could be infinitely perfectible. Men could go on from strength to strength through the pursuit of reason, strengthened by useful knowledge. The privilege of ruling, of acting as champions for the less luckily endowed, would be entrusted to those who showed themselves the fittest. Fitness should of course be judged by reason—for reason, not faith or tradition or family power, gave the key to human progress.

During and after the Revolution every attempt was made to bring these fine notions (though they reveal manifest pitfalls to us) into reality. Eventually, French education took on the essentials of its present form under Napoleon in 1808. Napoleon was no democrat, no liberal humanitarian; but he was a man of the people who had had to struggle upward to eminence. As emperor he made it his main concern to strengthen France as a military power by drawing out the finest qualities of leadership. He wanted officers in military and civil life. He therefore reorganized the university and secondary school system. Though he paid no attention to elementary education, being willing to leave it for the time being to what he called the "Ignorantine Friars" (namely, the teaching orders of the Church), he gave the state a monopoly of university and secondary school teaching, and also a monopoly of examinations. Recruitment for military, civil service, and professional eminence was to be by way of these examinations. All Frenchmen, whatever their social or geographic origin, were to be given an equal chance of serving

France by uniform methods of selection and a disciplined training in hard work. The first modern *lycées* were founded for this purpose. Their strict regime can be fairly compared to that of the old-time barracks.

This egalitarian approach of Napoleon's led after his collapse to the development of plans for universal elementary education. A society was founded for this purpose in 1810. Despite the many political upheavals that have taken place since Napoleon's downfall (two kingships, one emperor, five separate republics, three near-dictatorships, and so on), the Napoleonic system is in full force today in the schools of the fifth republic. It is highly centralized; it is secular (i.e., allows religion no place in the public system of schools [2]); it is uniform throughout France; it is compulsory in the sense that all children must go to a public or private school between 6 and 14 (16 after 1968); and public primary and secondary education is free. The state still maintains a monopoly of approved examinations, which are centrally supervised. Even those children who go to private schools (mainly Catholic) are compelled to prepare for public examinations which effectively determine the choice of curriculum and also indirectly affect the teaching methods strongly.

In actual practice, however, even here we note some tempering of uniformity. The examinations are the same; but the criteria used are not always the same. The final decision about who passes and who does not rests with a local *jury* selected by the authorities of the *académie*. A loophole for human frailty can be discerned here. Sometimes it is utilized for humane purposes. For example, a *jury* will frequently permit itself a slight lowering of standards when deciding whether or not to pass *baccalauréat* candidates from *lycées* known to be of lower caliber— or even when deciding the fate of candidates who have entered a good *lycée* belatedly from a less favored *lycée* or *collège*. Frenchmen are are aware of this problem and not infrequently stretch the law to cope with it. This adaptive device seems likely to be called upon more and more during the difficult period of equalizing secondary education which began in 1959.

After 1951 it became possible for private schools to receive indirect subsidies. Every parent of a primary school child is now entitled to a sum of 13 new francs (about $3) every quarter. This sum is turned over

---

[2] Priests, rabbis, and ministers of other faiths are allowed access to school premises after school hours to give unpaid religious instruction to children in boarding schools whose parents specially ask for it. Facilities are also provided for such children to take part in appropriate religious ceremonies elsewhere, if they wish. The state preserves a detached impartiality.

either to the public committees or to parents' associations for private schools, for general scholastic purposes. In the case of private schools, it is expressly intended for the raising of Catholic teachers' salaries, which are unsatisfactory. A total of 10 percent of the local educational budget may also be allotted to school needs designated by either public school parents (through public committees) or by private school parents (through parents' associations).

In a bill introduced in 1959 (as a result of the Lapie Commission) three new relationships between private schools and the State were envisaged. On request such schools could be entirely adopted by the State; alternatively, certain teachers or activities could be entirely financed by the State; or thirdly, varying degrees of cooperation between private schools and the State authorities could be negotiated, with proportional aid in return.[3] It took the near-dictatorship of General de Gaulle to achieve this solution, and it still remains to be seen how far these recommendations can be implemented.

It will be noted that under the pre-1959 arrangements and after the Lapie proposals the aid to private schools is permissive and not obligatory. It will also be seen that parents with children in private schools do not receive anything that parents of public school children do not also receive. In addition, of course, public schools are built by the local community (with varying amounts of aid from the central government), and public school teachers are civil servants with satisfactory wages. Private school parents must somehow find the necessary money themselves.

Teachers in the publicly maintained schools have to be well educated and efficient by strict official standards. Many in private schools are also efficient, of course; but some are not. Salaries for private school teachers are unattractive as a rule, except in the very few "prestige" secondary schools which correspond to English "public schools" and American "ivy

---

[3] Under previous arrangements Catholic schools, and other nonpublic schools, could receive not more than 10 percent of their running costs in money or kind from the state, the *département*, or the local community; but the express permission of the Minister's Central Advisory Council was necessary in each individual case. This reluctant support probably recognized two factual situations that go against the general principles of French education: first, such help was given more freely under the Pétain regime, and still survives in part; second, financial difficulties prevent the public authorities from establishing all the (secular) secondary schools they would like, so that it seems preferable to make use of existing Catholic institutions. Moreover, the presence of tax-supported scholarship-holders in Catholic schools is a source of revenue from public funds.

league schools." Prospects of promotion for private school teachers are also rather dim. For these reasons ambitious teachers and parents tend to look elsewhere if possible, though the exceptions to this rule (as we shall soon discover) continue to grow, and cause the secular government some embarrassment.

The importance of private schools is shown by a few figures. The approximate total of children in state schools in 1959 was 6,976,500; in Catholic schools there were about 1,535,900 below the university level. These figures may be broken down as follows: in public primary schools there were 6,013,100; in Catholic primary schools about 1,091,-400; in public secondary schools of all types there were 684,000, while Catholic secondary schools enrolled 444,500. In addition, the public universities and technical or professional institutions catered to about 200,000 students on a basis of very strict competition. There are about 8000 students in denominational private "faculties" (who will sit for state examinations), and about 5500 in theological colleges. It will be seen that although fewer than 20 percent of French children go to a private elementary school, the secondary school population shows above 40 percent of its total in private schools, mainly Catholic. Many of these are, of course, girls whose mothers want them to have a convent education anyway; but many are said to go to Catholic secondary schools because admission is easier. Those who fail to be selected for public *lycées* may nevertheless be allowed to attend Catholic schools, especially if they can pay the fees charged there. Moreover, the academic regime in the public secondary schools is stricter; if children cannot keep up with the pace of work and fail the various examinations they may have to leave, whereas in Catholic schools they are very often allowed to repeat the grade and have a second chance. This seems more humane to outsiders; but it causes many French parents and students to criticize the Catholic schools for unfairness and respect for money.

This is not, however, the main reason for criticism, which is bitter and almost an obsession with the anticlericals. (Many of these are Catholics in faith, or even in practice; a few are Protestants; the majority are agnostic.) They passionately resent clerical control of any schools and fear its spread. The dread of many republicans is that there will be a reversion to the *ancien régime* of king or emperor or aristocratic privilege, with the Church dignitaries in powerful alliance. It is a matter of history that during the past century's ups and downs each French antirepublican government has allowed the clergy more control of education and more financial and political strength. Each such government has also cut down the amount of science or other "modern" teaching in favor of more traditional subjects, and has also tended to slow down the extension of educational opportunities to other categories of children and other careers. This does not necessarily say anything about Catholicism generally; but it explains why so many Frenchmen fear, despise, or even loathe the clergy in France. In fact, the French words for "the school question" simply mean the question whether more aid should be given to Catholic schools or not. It is by far the hottest question in French politics. A similar controversy splits Belgium from top to bottom, and another form of it arouses bitter animosity in Holland and other European countries. Extreme anti-Catholics, who in other countries might be just republicans or Protestants or freethinkers, tend in such circumstances to look with a friendlier eye on Moscow. Thus the two factions drift farther and farther from understanding, and farther from a combined effort to save their country and its schools. It is peculiarly difficult for the Frenchman, therefore, to keep a cool head and concentrate solely on the extension of education or its modernization. It is really surprising that so much has been achieved.

France is one of the larger countries of Europe. It has two-and-a-half times the area of the United Kingdom, or four-fifths of the area of Texas. Its population is over 48,000,000. Though there are important heavy industries in densely populated towns and cities, and also rich mineral industries, almost one-third of the whole population is directly employed on small mixed farms. These are cultivated with the greatest care (one might almost say affection). A vivid memory of any part of France recalls weed-free fields of vegetables and salads, as well as bountiful cereal crops. Wine production and fruit-growing are very important, and there are extensive fishing enterprises. The secondary industries supported by agriculture, and the many service occupations, keep a large part of the nonagrarian workers in small towns and villages. These generally have a strong individuality and deeply rooted traditions. In the intellectual professions success may be literally measured by nearness to Paris; but by most French people Paris is loved better at a distance. Though centralization is so strong—not just in governmental matters but in all the nationalized industries and their subsidiaries, such as railways and banks—France is made up of very localized industries, shops, and other enterprises of the greatest independence. "A Frenchman—an individual!" they say, and they mean it.

In these circumstances, to say nothing of France's turbulent politics, it cannot have been easy to secure equality of educational opportunity.

Perhaps that is one reason why the revolutionaries were so eager to maintain the traditional centralization of France. Otherwise there might have been educational backwaters, and there would certainly have been local fortresses of reaction. Therefore it seemed advisable to insist that education would belong to the state, and that teachers should be free from the contemporary equivalent of "un-French activities." Republicans have always pushed ahead with educational expansion. As an opposition senator said in 1880: "A demand for compulsory schooling is to be expected from a secularist, just as tyranny is to be expected from a usurper." (His point of view illustrates the bitterness of opposition.) The champions of education had their way; but Jules Ferry in 1881 estimated that one-sixth of the state's entire revenues would have to be allotted to the public education of children. Local resources in cities and towns are expected to provide the cost of buildings, but these can be helped out by central funds. No industrialized country spends anything like one-sixth of its income on education today. This is a measure of French eagerness. Now every village has its school. Every child's standardized schooling is made uniform in the interests of equality of opportunity in all parts of the land.

There are real drawbacks, however. Judged by modern standards in more experimental countries like the United States and Britain, the system in France is excessively formal and bookish. It bears little relation to the everyday life of the average French community, and even after reform still takes fatally small account of France's urgent need for greater industrialization and modern workaday "know-how." This the outsider can see. The French peasant, still wearing the traditional blue garb of his calling, sees even more to complain about. At home they may all speak patois, a local variant of French; they have local songs, traditional dances; the whole of life rotates for them round the farm, the store, and the café. For all it means to them, the school's strictly correct French and standardized offerings might be far away in Paris. It is true that the local school is still every child's avenue to professional success. Through it opportunity lingers in every village. But the teacher in the small village school is seldom as good or as experienced as those who have found promotion in the larger towns. Not every parent wants his boy to have a "remote" education anyway. Absenteeism is therefore a real problem, and is only combated by discontinuing state family allowances if it happens too much.

Not surprisingly, the proportion of country children who are successful in competitive selection examinations is lower than that of town children. Parents with modest incomes, especially at a distance from large towns, may not even think of the *lycée* for their children. If a youngster is selected at 15, or before, for a *lycée*, it may be necessary for him to live away from home in a boarding establishment. Costs here are low, and financial assistance is always available where necessary from public funds; but the upheaval and the sacrifice are something for rural parents to reckon with. Many parents do not want their daughters, especially, to be away from home. It should be realized how thinly spread over the land much of the French population is. Transportation on anything like the British scale (to say nothing of the American) is unthinkable. On the other hand, school equality does come evenly into the countryside, and disparity of opportunity on the American scale would be entirely unacceptable in France. It certainly helps to improve the rural provision of schooling when all teachers get the same pay according to their qualifications and experience, and when even the most able primary school teachers fresh from college are directed to wherever their services are needed. But no one can pretend that identical competitions are quite fair for rural children.

A greater criticism of the system for anyone brought up on Anglo-Saxon methods is that the vast majority of French children, undergoing a "general education" of standardized type, encounter little or nothing of homely, topical interest to bring their schooling to life. Reform movements have not impinged very markedly on the system in the remoter areas. Such criticisms do not worry the French parent or teacher as much as we might expect. Old-style rationalist notions are strong among Catholics no less than among their opponents. "General education" (*culture générale*) is believed to result from formal intellectual exercises, and from acquaintance with the great ideas, great books, and supporting facts. Vocational and prevocational orientation have traditionally come after school life and still substantially do despite all the postwar proposals and reforms. In the most technical or professional training, thoroughly practical though many of its ingredients are, the sense of training the intellect is still paramount; and this emphasis continues through all schooling. Reason is seen as a sort of searchlight on life, illuminating whatever it turns on. There is little of the British or American feeling that by grappling with practical problems or by organizing experiences the child can build up a pattern of understanding that is none the worse for being tentative or only partially completed. The Frenchman wants a short cut to the "principles."

There is another factor that supports this educational interpretation.

Catholicism has always been conscious of "original sin." Natural curios-
ity and natural inclinations are said to be "prone to evil," and to "need
correcting by discipline and self-denial." Play-ways and the experimental
approach are not therefore supposed to have the magical potency attributed to them by many of our own countrymen. These activities are
known to be pleasant; but they are not thought to be automatically
enlightening. "The world" and "the flesh" are well understood in
France; but there they are so often distinguished from the mind and the
soul which are supposed to triumph over them that a little mistrust (or
at least impatience) of them is carried over into educational attitudes.

That is not all. Even the anti-Catholic faction (who share many of
the above-mentioned suspicions) have their own reason for supporting
the mind as distinct from physical involvement in one's daily context.
The influence of Plato and of Descartes is very strong. In fact, Frenchmen are proud to boast that their educational system is "Cartesian."
Descartes stressed that the intellect is paramount; for him it was the
rational process (not the near-animal propensities of the body) that gave
man his essence. Instead of encouraging educators to think of personality as a harmony of complementary activities, such a view emphasizes the ascetic cultivation of "the mind." "We are priests of the intellect," says the representative French teacher.

So the French 6-year-old on his first day at school sets his foot on a
sternly intellectual road. The battles continue to rage around him, and
new notions of how to bring up children seek rather timidly for admission. Parents and teachers, priests and politicians are all agreed that
school is for "the mind," and the child had better pay attention to it.
The human reason gave the "open sesame" to the philosophers and
revolutionaries. The power of the mind will prevail over all imperfec-
tions according to both the priestly and the secular dispensation, provided that the mind is well disciplined and enlightened with the great
traditions. As Plato would have approved, the program is strictly co-
ordinated to this end. "The good" that the child pursues is well-nigh
unchangeable. It is a marvel that there have been so many concessions
to the times.

All the boys and girls in the elementary school wear a standard pinafore or overall. Sometimes it may be a reasonable color of blue; but
usually it is dark steel-gray. Some new schools are of exemplary cheer-
fulness; most are gloomy and oppressive. The books nowadays include
some attractive publications; but the majority are cautious and dull.
They are all official. Americans will not find the head teacher's role as a

sort of regulation-observing official quite so astonishing as British observers will. In small towns and villages there may be only one teacher or two. The senior one will also be official secretary to the mayor, and will help to issue such things as fishing and shooting licences. The elementary school teacher (even if he takes extended classes up to the age of 16 or 17) is called an "instructor" (*instituteur*), a name that sets him in an inferior category to that of the secondary school teacher (*professeur*).

The *instituteur* has not had the same education and training as a secondary school teacher. The older members of this group passed from a special course in the top part of an elementary school to a teachers' college (*école normale*) when 16 or 17, and successfully competed in a difficult examination to do so. The typical *instituteur* of prewar days (still the vast majority) had probably never been outside the scope of the primary (elementary) system of schooling. It is true that his studies included a teachers' college course of four years, and that this in more recent years took him up to and beyond the highest flight of the secondary school examination (*baccalauréat*). It might also be said that this experience exercises a student academically quite as much as most American teachers' colleges, or as some British teachers' training colleges. The fact remains though that the elementary school teacher in France is still in most cases a life-long product of the elementary school system itself. Especially in former times he had no experience of *lycée* or *collège*, and he was even further from the university. As late as the end of 1957, a small majority of the students in *écoles normales* turning out France's primary school teachers (though recruited by a stiff entrance examination) had been not to a proper secondary school but to the *cours complémentaires*, or supplementary courses, about which we shall read later. There all the courses of study and all the teachers, though undoubtedly of good quality, had been under the exclusive control of the primary administration of the Ministry of National Education. Such a future teacher was never called "student"; the word for him was always *élève* (pupil), the same as for the 6-year-old beginner.

The traditional European divorce between elementary education for the masses and a superior opportunity for the elite is gradually breaking down; but in France change is slow. Both by choice of words and by carefully nourished attitudes French public opinion hangs on to the old estimation. At the same time, it should not escape our notice that these "inferior" teachers now get the *baccalauréat* that automatically entitles them to begin a university course when they so choose. More than that, the best students every year in an *école normale* can now win their way by difficult scholarship examinations to an *école normale supérieure* (higher teachers' college), and thus become very much members of the elite among university students. The *école normale supérieure* is one of the *grandes écoles* or higher professional colleges described later; it is open only to those who enter by a harshly competitive examination, usually at the end of a particularly brilliant career in a *lycée*. It is primarily intended to provide the specialist subject teachers for the most advanced and academically formidable flights of the secondary school; but a measure of its distinction is given by the fact that a majority of university teachers in the faculties of Arts and Science are among its alumni too. So the great gulf between the primary school and the most elevated plane of the university can be bridged, though the bridge is flimsy and precarious, while the chasm is profound.

It should be noted that in actual practice the possessor of the *baccalauréat* or school-leaving examination not only may succeed in obtaining a post in primary school teaching in the many places where there is a shortage, but may actually succeed in being registered as a qualified teacher (*titularisé*) after five years' teaching experience if he attends summer courses in "pedagogy." This very fact indicates the gulf between the most esteemed secondary school teachers and their colleagues under the primary school administration.

French austerity in these differentiations must not be judged too severely. Though we must emphasize that the education for all children under the age of 11, and for the majority destined for vocationally biassed courses afterwards, is always considered to be inferior to the more academic kind, foreigners should not feel too smug. Popular education is usually treated rather shabbily in the most sympathetic of communities. If we make due allowance for the French preoccupation with intellectual eminence rather than breadth of experience in life, French teachers' colleges do as complete a job as their British or American equivalents, to say the least. Moreover, the future teachers have competed very strenuously in difficult examinations both to get into the colleges and to pass the qualifying standard at the end of their professional course. They are academically advanced by our standards. The proper point of comparison is that they are of inferior quality and training to the teachers in secondary schools by French standards; their pay is lower; their prospects of promotion, geographic and social mobility, and of social acceptability are also much less.

All this discrimination must clearly have its effect on the children in those schools. It still perpetuates in France a class distinction whereby some children are given a socially superior education after age 11 or 15, and others carry on with what our grandfathers were honest enough to regard as an education for the lower orders. Selection for higher prospects in France is ensured by the same intellectual criteria for all. In Britain the method is partly similar, partly very different; it depends to some extent on parental status or on where you live. In the United States disparity is prevalent, though the mechanism of discrimination is dissimilar, and the ages are different. (This is a warning of storms to come.) The French are supremely logical, and will not stand for humbug. Though they would very much like to offer equality of educational opportunity, with widespread differentiation of equally acceptable types to suit different children and different careers, they have not progressed so far just yet; therefore they do not pretend that progress is achieved by altering a name or two.

Until 1959, French schools were in a position not very different from those in England and Wales before the 1944 Education Act, or from those in Germany before World War II. It is a much shorter time than most Americans like to believe since a similar state of affairs prevailed in the United States, especially in the rural areas. No country has yet rid itself of the "lower orders" pattern of thought about children and schools. If we pretend the opposite, we are only delaying the cure. As we have recognized, the French elite is an intellectual one, and is recruited as fairly as centralization and uniformity can make it. The system's inequalities derive from regional or rural difficulties, the unequal status of parts of the teaching profession, and from the assumption that the "mind" and old-style intellectual callings must be given unchallenged pre-eminence. It must be admitted that this last named assumption is particularly associated still with distinct types of schools.

It seems certain (not only from the objective evidence but also from the considered opinion of leading French educators) that despite the spectacular mandates which from time to time have transformed the rules in recent years, the pre-1959 pattern and the new are destined to coexist for some time, if only because existing premises compel it.

Before 1959 three types of secondary schools had already grown up in addition to the continuation of the elementary school beyond the age of eleven. These secondary schools included the *lycées*, the *collèges*, of which there were several types, and the *cours complémentaires*. The *lycée* was undoubtedly the prestige school, as it still is; but then in particular the term applied only to the definitely preuniversity school concentrating on the Classics or on a particular group of bookish subjects. More recently the term *lycée* has come to be applied to several kinds of schools which before 1959 were called *collège*.

During the period since World War II there has been a gradual process of promoting formerly inferior kinds of secondary education to a more highly esteemed plane. *Collèges modernes* for example used to be called "higher elementary schools." They gradually included more academic subjects and extended their provision beyond the age of about 15 or 16, until many of them were indistinguishable in the subjects offered from traditional *lycées*, though their standards of attainment and their teachers were usually inferior. (A well informed French spokesman described them as "a sort of *Mittelschule*.") Though the past tense is used here, the present must continue to be understood too.

Since 1959 all the former *collèges* have been called *lycées*, while the term *collèges* is now applied to such institutions as the former *cours complémentaires*. The latter were senior classes parallel to the upper grades of the elementary school, offering a more "secondary" curriculum, but taught by elementary school teachers. Children passed from the *cours complémentaires* at the age of about 15 or 16 to employment, or sometimes to other forms of training.

In particular the city of Paris provided some very advanced *cours complémentaires industriels* with a commercial or industrial emphasis. These recruited children of real promise through a competitive examination after the completion of the ordinary *cours complémentaires*. They offered advanced courses of technical theory and practice combined with an all-round education. Identical courses still continue, but are recognized as being integral parts of a more extended technical education. They are very arduous, demanding forty hours a week or more of attendance, and some homework too. When youngsters graduate from a *cours complémentaire industriel* or its latter-day equivalent at the age of 18 or later, they are skilled craftsmen with a preliminary trade certificate (*Certificat d'Aptitude Professionnelle*). This they can exchange for the full-fledged status of a craftsman after a satisfactory practical experience and a further test. The standard of these boys and girls is very high.

The new law of 1959 introduced compulsory school attendance until the age of 16 for those children *beginning* their schooling in that year. Thus the scheme would come into full effect ten years later. There had already been a tendency for many children (almost half of them in cities and large towns) to extend their schooling voluntarily beyond the compulsory age of 14. The old law theoretically required all children between the ages of 14 and 17 to attend apprenticeship training or part-time education. They were thus able to prepare themselves for a wide range of industrial and commercial careers. Apprenticeship centers financed by a tax on all industries not providing their own properly recognized training had been set up during the inter-war period. But of the two million children between the ages of 14 and 18 in France only about one quarter received training of more than a few weeks' duration, if that. Of these, about 88,000 were in short publicly provided courses, and about 100,000 were in private short courses of training. It was in its technical and vocational preparation that the French educational system showed its most grievous omissions. France must industrialize radically and rapidly if she is to maintain her world status and raise her standard of living at home. The provision of technical training is increasing, but not quickly enough or on a wide enough front.

Perhaps with this shortcoming in view the former apprenticeship training centers are now named "secondary technical schools" (*collèges d'enseignement technique*), discharging roughly the same function but also endeavoring to extend a general education at the same time. The new *collège d'enseignement technique* can also lead to further opportunities in technical education. Teachers for children undergoing this training are educated very thoroughly at the *École Normale Nationale d'Apprentissage* (ENNA). Similarly, the former *cours complémentaires* are now called "general education secondary schools" (*collèges d'enseignement général*).

This upgrading is of great potential importance; but the overwhelming prestige given to intellectual attainments and the "liberal" vocations acts as a serious brake on any alternative system of schooling. The hierarchic structure of all public life perpetuates a vested interest in the older interpretation. Parents know "what's what." Teachers, especially of the higher ranks, are often unwilling or even unable to change their notions. For example, a *professeur* (note the word) in a *lycée* or *collège* has a high social status, is well paid (comparatively speaking), and teaches as little as 15 or 18 hours a week, with no extracurricular duties whatsoever, and no marking to do. As is usually the case with teachers of this rank in continental countries (for example, in Germany, Austria, or Italy), he may give a few courses in a university, or undertake seminars with teachers doing in-service training. For this work he is handsomely paid. In any case the prestige value is great. Continental university teachers are frequently recruited in this way. Therefore, the *professeur* in a school tends to be constantly looking over his shoulder at the university where he would much prefer to be. In these circumstances, the solidarity of the teaching profession is a remote chimera.

So the child securing admission to an academic type of *lycée* is very much a chosen child. He may be only 11; nevertheless, he and his parents are conscious of a real distinction. Financial and other difficulties will not be allowed to stand in his way. His tuition is free; if he has to reside away from home, he can get a scholarship. If he is successful not only in the yearly examinations but in the impressive vista of competitive examinations looming in front of him, he can win his way to the highest positions—beyond school, beyond the university, beyond the research studies of a graduate school. There glows in front of him the vision of a modern French equivalent of Napoleon's baton. But the cost is heavy, none the less. A very large number of children are unable to keep up the strenuous ordeal, and are weeded out either in the disappointments of the annual examination or at the end of the school's "first cycle" (we might almost say "first round") when they are 15 or 16. In fact, most secondary schools do not take children beyond that phase. But if the pupil still holds his own, he can undergo the more arduous training for the *baccalauréat*.

The *baccalauréat* is an examination taken in two sessions (a year apart) at about the ages of 17 and 18. Some idea of its difficulty can be obtained from the fact that although all competitors have been selected and reselected, a large proportion of those taking the examination may fail. In 1957 61 percent of those taking the *baccalauréat* failed. A similar proportion failed in 1958. In 1959 there was an improvement. Some 45 percent failed the first part of the *baccalauréat* and some 37 percent failed the second part. The proportion of failures in 1960 and 1961 was further reduced to 30 percent in the first part and a similar percentage in the second part. The competitors in every case includes a large number who have failed previously and are making a second or third attempt.

From 1960 onwards the examination has been simplified in some ways, in other ways made more demanding. It is now easier for those with scientific (and presumably less verbal) abilities, or with technical experience, to succeed. The once paramount oral tests have been abolished, except for marginal cases. Physical education (including swimming) is now a compulsory subject!

The *baccalauréat* is, as the French say, the "sanction" of the school career; but it is not really a high-school-leaving certificate or school graduation—it is the first examination of the university. There is nothing quite corresponding to the school-leaving certificate of some other countries. It almost looks as though the *lycée* derives its significance only from its function as an avenue to the university and the still more elevated professional colleges (*grandes écoles*). Those who do not secure admission to such institutions of higher learning might be said to have wasted their efforts, or at least to have picked up an incidental kind of secondary education rather like crumbs from the Biblical rich man's table.

Parents and teachers in prosperous and progressive countries think of each stage of education as being worthwhile on its own account— a formative experience that will be valuable irrespective of what happens to children afterward. It is always recognized, of course, that any stage of education is more valuable if it is linked with an opportunity for further development afterward; but many of us are shocked if we are confronted with the plain statement that schooling is also a sort of filter, a device for keeping coarse elements back while only the finer material passes through. Yet that is what it is in many countries, and to some extent it is so in all countries even where such an intention is repudiated. Most democrats like to banish such unpleasant truths from their comfortable daydreams. The importance of schools as instruments of discrimination is more clearly recognized if we concentrate not so much on the negative picture of children being kept behind as on the positive notion of an increasing gap between them as the bright and diligent outstrip those who cannot keep up with them. The gap is greater when children are kept in separate institutions. We have already seen the selective process at work in French secondary education. We should note that it is continued even more effectively in France's higher education. Though higher education will be considered in detail shortly, it is valuable to stress this matter of selectivity here.

The small proportion of French children who gain their *baccalauréat* are entitled to enroll in universities. Since the end of 1957 alternative means of entry to higher education have been provided, in the shape of special examinations. Undoubtedly this will help those who are particularly suited to advanced study in one particular group of interests without possessing the wide knowledge or verbal skills appropriate to the *baccalauréat*; but we must not forget that, like the *baccalauréat*, new entrance examinations are intended to select quality quite as much as to entitle French boys and girls to higher education. Particularly since

1959, admission has been made easier for very able pupils short of some requisite qualification, and "university colleges" are more widely available for first-year work.

The fees in higher education are so small that they are nominal. Thus few people of the right quality can ever be debarred on financial grounds. Moreover, there are scholarships in suitable cases to enable students to bear the additional costs of living away from home. Inexpensive meals and lodgings are available, and students can benefit by reduced admission charges to establishments of an educational kind. However, admission to a *faculté* in a university gives no firm assurance of a royal road to success. Lectures are given to disconsolate and lost-looking students who sit in huge numbers while the professor drones on in the most impersonal way. Counseling and tutorial advice are unknown. Every student must fend for himself. It is no uncommon thing for even the children of professors to feel disoriented in their strange surroundings. Buildings and libraries are such as to deter all but the most resolute student. Furthermore, since the war French universities have started most students with a preparatory year of study (*l'année propédeutique*) which looks at first sight like a sort of "liberal arts" year intended to establish a general foundation for the more specialized courses to come; but it is really a further process of weeding out. The examination at the end of the preparatory year fails a high proportion of those who have proceeded so far and have surmounted all the hurdles of the secondary school.

In any case, the students at the university can already be described as second-best even before there is any immediate threat of failure in the *propédeutique* examination. Though the universities do prepare people for professional careers in the sense that their courses are indispensable for success in the degree examinations (which are *state* examinations, by the way, and not devised by the universities as such), the quicker and surer way to professional distinction is through the *grandes écoles* which have already been mentioned. These schools of advanced professional training recruit their students by the most difficult competitive examinations, success in which is almost impossible without two or more years of concentrated preparation in special classes after the passing of the *baccalauréat*. Such preparation is given at only a few centers (notably Paris, where there is superb accommodation for young women undergoing it). It is therefore a handicap for the provincial, especially if relatively poor and eager to help out at home. However, we are now simply concerned with examining French proc-

esses of selection, and we must postpone our view of the *grandes écoles*
and their students. We can easily see that French educators are intent
on getting excellent students; but we might not easily believe that the
selfsame process can be one of keeping down the numbers. Yet this
is true, and intentionally so.

Here we face one of the dilemmas of Europe—one which will appear again and again. In the old days social privilege and access to
governmental positions were regulated exclusively by family position
and wealth. A reinforcing instrument in the process of exclusion was
the criterion of education; it was necessary to have schooling of a
particular kind. At one time this schooling was recognizably vocational
(including the necessary Latin, and so forth). More recently, as in
France, access to education has slowly become more nearly universal;
but the result has been exceedingly heavy pressure at the entrance to
positions of wealth and privilege. Competition is ferocious, and must
perhaps become more so because of an overproduction of some kinds
of trained or learned personnel. In some countries (notably Italy and
Austria) there is more unemployment and frustration among well-
schooled people than there is in France. In France administration and
top-level executive posts cannot absorb all the available people. Moreover, manual occupations of every kind lack prestige, and as such are
no more likely to be sought by Frenchmen than jobs with poor pay
are likely to be sought by Americans.

Without industrial expansion (which in itself will bring unfore-
seen changes, especially with automation), France's economic position
is such that the country just cannot afford to employ her present well-
trained personnel in suitable positions. Intentionally or not, the present
selection procedure does serve to prevent one serious social embarrassment while it aggravates another. The disappointment and frustration
in French education cannot be considered apart from the basic problems of economic change and a possible revision of the hierarchy of
social esteem. When we examine the French school system in non-
French terms, which make us fasten on to its ruthless efficiency as an
instrument of selection, to such an extent that we think of much
secondary schooling as "unrealistic" or "purposeless," we are failing
to apply fairly the criteria which the French themselves use.

The position in France, though disturbing, does not seem quite so
objectionable to the French themselves, for a reason already given.
Even though the bookish and academic studies of the majority do not
reach a successful conclusion in the university, it is widely believed

that the "general education" of the mind which they have received will equip them as much as possible for any job or interest they then undertake. The searchlight, so to speak, is as high-powered and as carefully beamed as could be expected in their case.

In truth, the sheer amount of knowledge which a French child has amassed when ready to leave the *lycée* is enormous by any standard. Specialization has been rather limited; eight or nine subjects selected from a wide range have been thoroughly tackled by every child. They comprise philosophy, French, Latin, Greek, civic and moral education, two modern languages, history, geography, mathematics (including very advanced work indeed), chemistry, physics, biology, and physical education. Though subjects are grouped according to five different types of *baccalauréat*, with nine possible combinations of subjects finally selected, all (including the "technical" and "commercial" *baccalauréat*) require candidates to be examined in a very wide academic field. At the same time, each subject is intensively studied. By way of comparison it may be said that the French candidate offering English (as a foreign language, of course) has to cover as many authors and to answer questions just as difficult as an English child must when presenting himself for the "advanced level" of the General Certificate of Education at 18 or 19 in *his own* language. In fact, the French *baccalauréat* looks slightly more difficult.

It is impossible to make a comparison with the United States system, because there is nothing comparable. But R. M. Hutchins, former president of the University of Chicago, said that the child who passed the *baccalauréat* or the corresponding examinations in Italy or Germany at the beginning of the century knew as much as three American college graduates put together, and in addition had a mastery of his mother tongue. The European would be 18, and the Americans 22 years of age.

This is an example of a comparison which is no comparison, really, because the European systems and the American are not intended to do the same thing; but it should cause some misgiving when Americans ask themselves questions about the standards of technical knowledge and academic equipment they maintain. The American proportion of college graduates is much higher than the proportion of French youth passing the *baccalauréat*; but the proportion of French children could be greatly increased by broadening the basis of the subjects examined, and still more by lowering the standard slightly. But this brings us to considerations of resources and volume, and not of quality. The criterion Dr. Hutchins uses is that of quality or thoroughness. It might well be possible to modernize and democratize the system in France without sacrificing the integrity of learning or a liberal understanding of mankind's recurring problems in their modern context, and that is just what many alert French educators would very much like to do. American and British examples influence them strongly, but progress is very slow in changing the schools. It is peculiarly difficult for Frenchmen to throw off their shackles of excessive intellectualism.

The approach of reform can best be seen in the field of technical education. Some of this (especially in the *lycées techniques*) is still not very different from the ordinary programs of the academic *lycée* but with a scientific, rather than a technical, bias. Nevertheless, at least as many French children are now in technical or professional education above the age of 15 as we can find in old-style academic schools, and the number is growing. For many reasons, technical education in France is more free to develop in size and scope than formal secondary education, even where it suffers from handicaps of money, inferior status, and prejudice among parents and teachers.

Most Frenchmen believe that France already does excel in technical education because those who successfully pass through an academic school career and triumphantly graduate from the *grandes écoles* (or higher professional colleges) will stand favorable comparison with the products of higher technical education anywhere when it comes to research and the knowledge of pure science. But the proportion of French children with any chance of such ultimate excellence is minute. Engineers and technologists generally (as those categories are understood in the United States or Britain) are not produced in anything like the required numbers. Still worse is the shortage of trained technicians, maintenance staff for elaborate plant, production and distribution personnel, and so on. Therefore the present growth of technical education in the face of discouraging difficulties is to be welcomed by anyone who considers French progress as a whole. It might even be said that only development of this bread-and-butter side of French enterprise is likely to pay for the comparative luxuries of literary and philosophical brilliance. This is an inescapable consideration, no matter how much defenders of "general culture" shut their eyes to it. But to bring matters down to the level of the child's personal education or of those social and political arguments that tear French cohesion to shreds, technical or vocational education may offer France a possibility of evolution blocked elsewhere.

For one thing, it can absorb many who would be declared (or who would feel themselves to be) failures in a strictly academic system. They can make good, and contribute real good to France. They can matter. Secondly, working-class solidarity in France needs to be experienced to be believed. Many town and country workers do not think of sending their children to academic schools even if they could; they are suspicious of the local *bourgeoisie*, and they loathe or despise central administrators selected by the *lycée* system. An education that seems real rather than "otherworldly" is more welcome, especially when children bring home evidences of manual and creative skill. In this connection we should heed the French tendency for children to follow their fathers' occupations, a tendency which is hard to break unless children get a chance in school or in after-school training to manifest unsuspected skills that will bring in hard cash, or at least be practically helpful. Children can thus get on in the world without being suspected of a rather "unnatural" betrayal of their home circle. Thirdly, the Church does not take much practical part in the development of technical education in France (though it does in Belgium); therefore this is one sector of education in which all French boys and girls can get together educationally without being proverbial sheep and goats. Education can get on with its job without unhelpful distractions from outside. Fourthly, it is only in technical education that private enterprise (being secular) is both recognized and aided by the state; some private diplomas have public recognition, firms with private apprenticeship training are exempt from the apprenticeship tax, and there is mutual support in other ways. Good relations are enjoyed not just with employers but with the trade unions as well. Technical trainees in public schools or centers have opportunities for working according to trade standards under trade conditions; the technical teachers of practical subjects are recognized journeymen. Finally, it is only in vocational education that the prevailing centralization of French education is really modified for varied development. This may seem a small matter to those who normally experience decentralized responsibility; but a change in this direction might be a great chance for France.

Most apprenticeship centers for children aged 15 to 18 (now *collèges techniques*) have fewer than 150 trainees, and are controlled by local committees to secure close adaptation to local needs. The boys and girls, like those in the more advanced industrial *lycées techniques d'Etat* in Paris and other large cities, do not learn only "how to do it." Half of their forty-hour week is spent on general education; this includes physical education (not too well developed in conventional schools), and such subjects as home economics for girls. Every effort is made to train the children to think, and to be independent and self-reliant. The usually less popular subjects such as history and geography are closely related to the main trade subject studied. For example, history can be presented in a lively and attractive way through a central interest in fashion or in building construction, or even in glass technology. I have seen history taught in just this way to the three trades I mention; but this method is usual for all. Qualities of accuracy, honesty, and so on are developed in intimate association with the vocational training. Careful attention is given to the home background of the average child and also to the special needs of problem children. "Student government" and self-discipline prevailed in some of the former Parisian industrial *cours complémentaires* in a way unparalleled in most European countries. Some of these features may continue in new-style *collèges techniques*. In other words, character and "the mind" are developed simultaneously with vocational skills, as Condorcet argued. Paradoxically, the leaders of this practical education are often at pains to convince their fellow Frenchmen that they too are "Cartesian."

All the same, those who pioneer the most progressive forms of teaching in the vocational field are those whose pay and professional esteem are the lowest. Many, in the former industrial *cours complémentaires* of Paris, for example, until recently were under the supervision of the primary (elementary) administration. Their salaries were accordingly depressed. Each phase of French education, primary, secondary, higher, and technical, is as a rule entirely separate in its administration from the top to the bottom. (Only for a few special cases, e.g., some types of *collèges techniques*, is an exception made.) Each watertight compartment behaves as though there were no other section to think about. This makes coordination almost impossible. From the human point of view it aggravates the existing caste system; it makes parity of esteem, or the transference of students or courses, so difficult as to be impossible.

We have already seen that the elementary school teacher (*instituteur*) is regarded as a socially inferior being, even in his own profes-

sion. Those who teach in secondary schools are similarly stratified.
The lowest are those who just have their university degree. They are
seldom considered to be real teachers, even though they actually teach.
Their main responsibility may be to help out the regularly established
professeurs by supplementary teaching, or by supervising periods of
homework preparation and marking the work done, or by such extracurricular activities as supervising boarding arrangements and meals.
Established *professeurs* do none of this. Either they have completed
their professional training as young *professeurs agrégés* ("registered"
specialist teachers), or they have subsequently attained this dignity
by intense study and profound scholarship in their own academic
subject (for example, classics or chemistry or philosophy, *not* in "Edu-
tion") after having first gotten a university degree, an additional advanced diploma, and grueling experience as a subordinate teacher. In
either case, to be admitted as *agrégés* they have to crown all their studies
with what may be the most exacting examination in the world. Very
few indeed get as far as even competing for it; but out of those
seasoned and intrepid competitors only a small percentage pass. The
number varies from 6 percent in philosophy to 30 percent in some of
the science subjects.

Those who fail to secure acceptance as *agrégés* can compete for
the next best thing—the Certificate of Aptitude for Secondary Teaching, usually known by its French initials *CAPES*. This certificate for
graduates was instituted in 1950 to follow a year's course in the theory
and practice of education. Practice-teaching facilities are provided at an
educational center in each university town under the tutelage of proved
teachers called "educational advisers." There may be as many as 6,
or even 10 or 12, of these on the staff of a chosen *lycée* where the practical part of the course is spent.

At the end of the course there are written papers and a practical
examination before a national *jury* in Paris. It is estimated that 4
percent of the candidates will fail each year; but before starting the
course it is necessary to pass a competitive test which eliminates the
majority of applicants. Since 1959, mainly because of the shortage of
well-qualified teachers, the entrance examination has made a special
appeal to students who have just completed their first university course,
or are in "preparatory classes" for the *grandes écoles*. If they succeed
in the competition, they are now housed in special Institutes at the
university and receive a probationary salary while pursuing further
courses. This certificate is now nominally required of new teachers in

all kinds of *lycées*, in professional schools, and in teachers' colleges. Of course, it is necessary to obtain a *licence* (degree) before obtaining the *CAPES* itself. As usual, in French examinations more attention is paid to the subject matter taught than to methods of teaching. The teacher's interest is more in his subject than in the pupils, and many have their eye on university teaching posts. Below the *agrégés* and those with the *CAPES* (teaching 15 and 18 hours a week respectively) are those overworked and subordinate teachers in secondary schools who hope one day to emulate them and to be rid of all the routine work that teachers everywhere find tedious.

Highly competitive examinations rather like those just described are not confined to the teaching profession. In France they are essential for almost all public employment, and that covers a far wider range of occupations than an outsider would dream of. Success is won by wide and detailed knowledge of the special field, by substantial general knowledge of other things, and by great nimbleness of wit. The number of places available is always small so the proportion of successful candidates is usually about 10 or 20 percent. It is no wonder that these competitions are the constant preoccupation of teachers and parents.

If a child has been successful throughout a *lycée* career and has won his *baccalauréat* at the age of about 18, it is possible to go straight to the university. Since the end of 1957 it has been possible also for very able students without the *baccalauréat* to secure admission to higher technological education faculties by means of the special entrance examinations already referred to, or comparable exemptions. There is a university at the center of each academic region in France, making a total of 21 (five of them new since 1961). As we have already noted, tuition fees are exceedingly small, and it is often possible to live very inexpensively in lodgings in the "university city" or dormitory units. It is generally impossible for students to "earn their way" unless they are already qualified elementary school teachers, because they do not possess salable qualifications and also because there is so much studying to do. Universities have little or no social life.

On the other hand, it is often possible to pick out among the threadbare band of university students a few with finer clothes, a well-fed appearance, and a confident expression. These are probably not the children of wealthier homes, as might be the case in another country. They are those who have been successful in the bitter competitions entitling them to admission to the *grandes écoles* (advanced professional colleges). Before even entering these competitions it is usually necessary to stay on in the *lycée* for at least two years of advanced "preparatory" classes after the ordeal of the *baccalauréat*, and undergo incessant intellectual stuffing. Those who cannot contain all they are expected to must leave. In Paris they may be housed in a magnificent dormitory quite as elaborate as any to be seen in the United States. They are already given a taste of what it is like to be chosen; but the tantalizing thing is that most of the pampered competitors will be unsuccessful in the end. How galling it must be for them to search around for some inferior occupation after having come so close to triumph! Although there are scholarships, it is obvious that children from wealthier homes are much more likely to be allowed to gamble these precious two or three years; but certainly they must be brainy too.

If, however, a candidate is admitted to a *grande école* his worries are dispelled for a time. He is well fed and housed; he receives the pay of a probationary civil servant—more than enough to cover living costs; he knows that if he is successful in the college's final examinations he will be guaranteed a well-paid job in a public career that promises affluence and honor. Moreover, most of the *grandes écoles* are residential colleges with abundant opportunities not merely for attending lectures at the university but also for tutorial contact with the professional cream of France. Social life is usually lively; but that is not allowed to hinder study either in the ordinary university manner or with the special facilities available to the *grandes écoles*. Distinguished foreign visitors as well as France's own leading scholars may add to the local opportunities. In such surroundings it is usual for the students to complete the usual university degree course quickly, and pass on to higher diplomas. Then there is the special diploma or certification to be competed for at the termination of the course (usually 3 or 4 years). Most candidates, already preselected, will pass.

It should be remembered that these are all state institutions, and that the state has a monopoly of examinations. There is no alternative way of attaining the distinctions thus held out. Wealth or favor has as little influence as human ingenuity can contrive. All are specialists but have previously triumphed in "general education." The importance of these arrangements for France generally is shown by the field covered. Rigorous professional preparation is offered by *grandes écoles* (all specialist institutions at or above the ordinary university level, which is already very high) in each of the following interests: public administration, teaching, cartography, engineering, manufacturing and various technologies, fine arts, drama, physical education, agriculture, forestry, veterinary science, economics, statistics, war, aeronautics, naval studies, radio communications, roads, railways, physics, chemistry, and so on. Many of the *grandes écoles* are supervised by ministries other than the Ministry of National Education. Still, even with this impressive array, the nonscientific and nontechnological interests have predominated. Of all those who held French university degrees in 1950, nearly 30 percent had degrees in law (for administration), about 25 percent had degrees in literary subjects, 26 percent were graduates in medicine or pharmacy; only 19 percent had degrees in science, either pure or applied. However, changes are afoot. Ten years later, the number of students (not graduates) in law or administration were 18 percent of the total; those in the literary field numbered 28 percent; in science and technology, 34 percent; in medicine and pharmacy, 20 percent. It is anticipated that in 1970 the proportion for science and technology will be 43 percent; and that will be out of a greatly increased total student body, for the total 1970–1971 enrollments are expected to exceed 505,900—more than two-and-a-half times as many as in 1960.

A most important feature of French university life dates from the end of 1958, namely the "third cycle." It was instituted then for higher literary studies, and some two years later was enlarged to include the scientific field. Open to students with a *licence* or first degree, it can lead those who furnish proof of special aptitude in research to a *doctorat* diploma in two more years. The term "third cycle" refers to its being the third phase after the *propédeutique* and the ordinary *licence* courses. The program is so exacting that by far the most of those embarked on it devote the whole of their time to it; but of those also with jobs the majority are teachers. However, though higher standards in a field previously chosen are aimed at in the "third cycle," its intention is not only intensification; new needs, new skills, and new adaptability are (it is hoped) likely to be made manifest. Thus those who pass through the ordinary university courses—as distinct from the special opportunities of the *grandes écoles*—are likely to be recruited for the newer researches and evolving careers of their country's expanding interests.

So France is struggling hard, but in perplexity, to become a modern nation technologically secure and with a firm prospect of prosperity and civilization for her hard-working population. Though public life in France is in so many ways so highly centralized, the educational provision is split into parallel divisions which are still not united in a sympathetic or flexible system. Too many people have a vested interest in maintaining the cleavages, and many more have been trained to see no good outside their own specialty. Many of the pursuits and callings prepared for by public education in other countries are either considered to be the concern of noneducational ministries in France, or are allowed to fall down the clefts in the school system. Then the attempt to secure fairness by centralization results in the neglect of local needs and possible local "growing points." Religious and political quarrels breed intolerance; cooperation and compromise are little known in France. The pursuit of rationalism makes everyone certain he knows best; those who do not preach rationalism tend to preach authoritarianism with divine or political sanction. Recruitment by competition causes frustration and disaffection. France is divided by intellects—brilliant and lively, but often implacable.

Let us gather up our observations. The school system is even now a source of disappointment and frustration to the majority. For instance, half of the adult population is self-employed in small-scale private enterprises, many of them as peasant farmers. What realistic offering does the school set before them? In the larger towns and cities a very high proportion of industrial workers look to the gospel of Marx and his disciples. In recent general elections Communists totaled a quarter or more of the votes cast. They were sometimes the largest single political group. In a political and educational system where the devolution of responsibility on a decentralized basis is unfamiliar, such figures are understandable. People have no feeling of partnership.

Moreover, in 1943 it was estimated that in France there were 8 million "pagans" (or near-atheists) to whom the Church meant nothing but an abomination. So the Church could not supplement for them the educational work of other institutions. Hence the attempt to train worker-priests who would conduct missionary work while employed in ordinary labor. At one time there were 350 of these in the large cities; but in 1954 their ecclesiastic superiors closed down their activities. They were too outspoken and fractious, and their championship of the inferior and despised necessarily sounded left-wing to the luckier ones. Though some connections (like family ties) are stronger in France than in other countries, and though local patriotism is also strong, there is a general absence of personal contact in schools and a corresponding absence of it in public life. Once more, "A Frenchman is an individual." But in the complicated modern world an individual with frustrations is simply uprooted. He is ripe for violence or at least cynicism.

To do them justice, the French themselves are fully conscious of these problems. They try to make schools less formal. "New methods" are officially encouraged and demonstrated by the Ministry of National Education; "pilot classes" are found in all regional centers, and "experimental *lycées*" are maintained at six points. In Paris, the Ministry also has an International Center for Educational Study, where educators from all over the world meet their French counterparts in delightful surroundings to exchange ideas. There are contrasts of opinion, of course; but progressive ideas are usually acceptable to the French. The problem is that of embodying them in practical programs. The concept of an education that is self-experienced or self-organized through everyday relationships has not really grown in France. The rootstock is so far incompatible with the grafted *scion*. It is not all theory either; physical education and country holidays are now provided for overworked and space-hungry children, and special attention (though intellectual) is given to those denied an ordinary chance because of sickness or social misfortunes. But the religious faction call practical education "godless," and the prosperous call it "communistic." In all countries similar charges are leveled at educational change.

Especially in a country like France it is likely that educational and social reformers lay themselves open to such charges. The formal and informal power of centralized State and Church is so deeply entrenched that only radical measures seem potent enough. Many spokesmen of reform are occasionally too outspoken. It is notable that some of the prime movers behind the recommendations of the Algiers Commission of 1944 and of the Langevin-Wallon reforms of 1946 were well to the left in politics. As we often have occasion to note, people who in open or fluid democratic societies would merely be mild protestants may be driven by frustration to become iconoclasts in rigid societies. Moreover, quite apart from the historical and personal background, words like "democratizing" education are highly suspect in a country which habitually prides itself on the excellence of its elite, on quality rather than quantity. Therefore sound proposals come up before parliament again and again, only to be rejected or to become dead letters if they are passed as law. The 1959 reforms were passed by decree under the direction of General de Gaulle.

But every day's delay complicates the dangers in France, which is temperamentally (if not practically) a most progressive country. The legend of past glories and revolutionary principles lives on. Yet the millennium does not come. Jaded with overwork and disappointment, but irrepressibly vivacious, French youth plays hard. The world-wide "youth problem" is especially acute in France. Alcoholism is a national problem affecting even children. Sexual promiscuity is common among students. It looks almost as though the consequences of demanding too much of youth in school are the same as those of demanding too little.

It should be obvious by this time why it is important for anyone thinking of education in any country to pay close attention to the problems of France. We are not simply looking at an erring neighbor. We are looking at some of our own problems in an intensified form. Moreover, those who live in the United States and in Britain should note that when a hitherto underdeveloped country wants an educational model, it does not often go to them; it goes to France. The French system is not only very like those of Mediterranean Europe and Latin America; it has been copied extensively even in those Moslem countries which charge France with colonial oppression. This is not because of historical imperialism. It is because the French system is radical, intended eventually to be a universal provider of freedom, equality, and brotherhood, and also suitable for the quick preparation of a professional elite under close government control. Countries like Afghanistan and Iran, that have no historical connection with French imperialism, need to modernize quickly and perhaps ruthlessly; they have none of the deeply rooted institutions that are a prerequisite of the Anglo-Saxon systems. Therefore it is to the "universal mission" of France that they look for their interpretations of education. Desperately depressed countries cannot afford the luxury of waiting for experiments; moreover, even if they felt so inclined, they have simply not enough financial and material resources. They look for something streamlined and efficient for their purpose. They see it in France. The centralization of the Soviet Union owes much to France.

Moreover, even countries with a highly centrifugal and locally empirical tradition derived from Britain or copied from the United States (such as are Canada, Australia, and New Zealand) often tend towards centralization on the French pattern when faced with geographical difficulties or social and financial inequalities. This tendency is growing on a world-wide scale. It is often an unconscious or unrecognized consequence of industrialization, or a concomitant of great commercial organizations. The centralizing or standardizing assumptions of these can have immense cultural power even where the governmental or scholastic tradition is decentralized, as in the United States.

Therefore those in countries like ours who are concerned about the maintenance of what they believe to be the most democratic standards—equality of consideration that develops the *complementary* partnerships of differing and responsible individuals—may look with anxiety on the world-wide spread of competing alternative ideas. Three-quarters of the world's population (probably more) have no idea what democracy is. If they have heard of it, they think it incompetent. They may even think it is wicked, for they know that competition is not absent from Western democracies, and they often think that our competition is conducted on the least satisfactory basis. The French system, by contrast, seems to such observers to be both efficient and egalitarian. Still more, it is believed to pick the winners in the international race. The countries longest industrialized can afford (especially if they are rich in the supply of raw materials) to play their way through education. They can perhaps delude the masses with a semblance of universal education, while secretly "creaming off" the elite either by a lengthier schooling or by a more expensive education outside the regular public system. The result, the antidemocratic observer thinks, is the same: the brainy and the skillful are put in charge of development. In fact, it may be alleged, the retention of wealth by successful families blocks the adoption of a more efficient system like the French. Underdeveloped countries want food, not frills.

Without in any way accepting these ideas, we can see that others may welcome them. They challenge us on our own assumptions about technological superiority and its maintenance; they should make us ask if our own systems are as fair as we suppose. They certainly remind us that if we want our cherished notions to survive we must do some re-thinking about the new neighbors we have got to understand, and that we must certainly justify ourselves to them after some radical examination of our consciences.

For these reasons the turbulent story of France seems particularly helpful. Centralization, uniformity, and intellectualism are her disadvantages. They were intended to promote a rational and equal approach to the perfect state that would solve all our problems. Now her assumptions and methods are outmoded. We too should beware lest our assumptions and our confidence outlive the world changes which inevitably envelop us. Even on the home front we should beware of being sure we know the right answer.

What does it really mean if we claim to know the "right" answer? The French for "to be right" is literally "to have *reason*." The same turn of phrase is used in many Latin countries. We of the Anglo-Saxon tradition believe very often that a thing is all right if it works; but when we come to deep moral and philosophical problems we are seldom able to rely exclusively on pragmatism or expediency. However, we are not too happy about relying on reason alone, especially in education and public life. Some men claim to "have reason" as others claim to "have religion." Their neighbors are not so sure. If they are poetic, or perhaps just muddled anyway, they counterclaim that "the heart has its reasons" too.

When we assess anyone else's way of bringing up children we need to use every criterion available—reason, pragmatic or instrumental considerations, thought about the separate human beings involved and about their relationship with their neighbors. We cannot just plump for one criterion and stick to that. So it is when we turn around and look at our own system. Fundamentally that is the main purpose of our exercise in looking elsewhere.

So we leave France, where life still goes on for many at the pace of the ox, where the prizes of the school system are still only a mockery or disappointment to most of the population, and where many of those who most passionately love their country quarrel over her as over a mistress. It is paradoxical that France, the land of historical stalemate, is the source of many of our most progressive ideas.

chapter **4**

GREAT BRITAIN

Revolution with Reluctance

About twenty miles of sea separate England from the continent at the nearest point. That narrow but often turbulent sea is part of British minds. In their island fastness the British peoples—the English, the Welsh, the Scots, and the Irish—know that whatever family disagreements they may have at home, they share something that makes them different from continental communities. It is not easy for a Briton to think of himself as a European, although most British ideas and institutions are part of the European tradition, and although British social philosophy and political experiment were rationalized by the French revolutionaries in European terms to become an influence throughout the world.

This exemplifies the paradox of British life. Throughout history the Channel and the North Sea have brought invasion after invasion, as well as many cultural influences. In more recent centuries, as increasing national unity brought strength, the English and their sturdy sister nations have relied on the Channel as a bastion on which they could mount their resolute defenses, while they have swept the world in one bold enterprise after another. It is not from insularity that the English-speaking peoples ring the globe in a Commonwealth such as history has never known, and that the main world language of today is that spoken in Elizabethan times by a rather isolated nation of about four million people.

In the very act of turning their backs on the continent (until the twentieth-century Common Market), the British looked out upon the strange but not unfriendly world across the seas. The English words

EDUCATIONAL SYSTEM IN ENGLAND & WALES

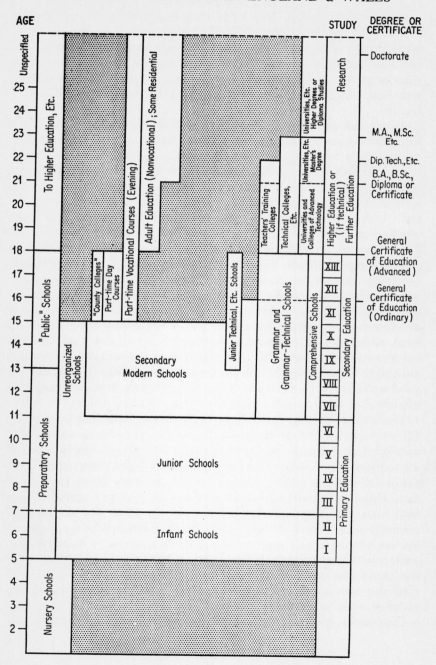

"overseas" and "abroad" have an inviting sound, unlike the corresponding words in the languages of landlocked peoples. The British, proud of their bold ventures, are not afraid of experimental uncertainty. They feel sure they can "go one better" than anyone else. To this extent their emphasis is on advance, even when lines of advance are tenuously stretched. Yet they are very reluctant revolutionaries and will not be hustled.

British self-assurance made victorious Napoleon balk at the Channel. The same incapacity for acknowledging defeat made Britons stand quietly firm under incessant aerial bombardment while Hitler's overwhelming might massed invasion forces everywhere. Stubborn habit rather than logic still makes Britons confident that their way is right even when others lay down the law. They will work things out their own way, and change only when a better method has been roughed out. The British themselves call this "muddling through," and laugh about it. Philosophers call it "empiricism," a school of thought characteristic of Britain for centuries. Educators call it "pragmatism."

This peculiarity of the British (shared in some measure by other nations who have copied their habits) claims special study by anyone interested in education, because it shows the virtues of an evolutionary approach and at the same time reveals the weaknesses of a patchwork policy in an increasingly streamlined world. After all, nobody believes that the medieval strip pattern of agriculture is a serious possibility today; nor does anyone care to tinker with an old car beyond a certain limit. Changed technology requires new methods, new models; it also brings other objectives in view, and provides the means to reach them. We recognize these truths in our daily life; but we forget sometimes that they apply equally not only to educational systems as a whole but also to our ideas about valuable or desirable types of man, about school subjects of lasting value, and about our own educational activities in relation to the human problems beyond our frontiers. Britain's external circumstances have undergone immense alteration in recent history. Every historic change alters the structure of civilization. However slightly, it modifies the formative pattern of human relationships; that is to say, it teaches people to behave differently toward one another. If people go on learning the old tricks while the world changes around them, they will soon be like educational dinosaurs armed cap-a-pie for the contingencies of yesteryear and just about as useful as dreadnoughts on dry land.

Historically speaking, the empiricism of the British has been a progressive movement. It has emphasized a changing response to changing challenges. It has encouraged a willingness to experiment, and a readiness to tolerate other people's experiments. So British political and educational ideas have not been proclaimed as manifestoes to be forcefully established by this revolution and to be forcefully torn down by counterrevolution. They have tended to be short-term, practical experiments awaiting a pragmatic justification or doomed to rejection if they do not work out. On the other hand the near-agnostic British feel a deep reverence for anything that has worked for a long time, whether materially or spiritually. Thus they have a monarchy, archaic trappings in government and law, and so on; but these things do no harm because their emotional claims do not hinder republican assumptions or modern citizenship.

Yet it can happen that a particular experiment (like the concept of the liberally educated "gentleman"—not at home in France or really native in America) survives its technological justification, at any rate in its ancient form. We tend to forget that a "gentleman" is an item of technology, a device for a certain social and economic purpose, whose usefulness is conditional upon its being present effectively and in the right number in appropriate circumstances. British domestic and imperial history has made the "gentleman" an effective instrument of government, public relations, and even of research; but the question is now being urgently asked if there has been overproduction of this commodity, at least on the mid-nineteenth-century model. Almost every Briton is fully in favor of having as many "ladies" and "gentlemen" as possible; but the whole context of "gentility" (though not necessarily its essence) has been changed by the specialist demands of the scientific and industrial revolution, and also by the fact that most children sooner or later realize they too can lay claim to it. Therefore, the "gentleman"-producing schools, methods, and subjects are now being re-examined, and in time they may reach a pragmatically justified relationship with the actual conditions of modern Britain.[1]

This sort of process goes on in all countries, of course; but there are not really many places where there is so little bitterness, or where such colossal changes have peacefully and permanently taken place. Parents and teachers everywhere want to combine the "best of the old" with the harsh realities of the new. In Britain they can see this tug

---

[1] See the appendix on "The Gentleman: The Evolution of an English Ideal" in my *World Perspectives in Education,* London: Methuen, and Indianapolis: Bobbs-Merrill, 1962.

of war going on under the rules of fair play. The solution is not yet clearly in sight; but the play is. Furthermore, in Britain it may be possible to foresee some compromise between the claims of centralization and those of decentralization. France's system was centralized and planned both by history and by revolutionary renovation; Britain's long-standing reliance on growth and local empiricism, her mistrust of planning and centralization, have perforce given way to national arrangements of a comprehensive kind. The chop and change of British educational development has left many serious anomalies which are still very far from being resolved; but it has also brought in some straightforward and exemplary solutions, and it shows some praiseworthy (perhaps temporary) compromises that others may envy. British religious and political history encourage tolerant experiment.

Thus, though the British are habitually protestant, they have evolved hybrid forms of Protestantism very different from those of Europe. British socialism too is unlike the continental varieties; it mistrusts theories and insists on evolutionary change. Radicalism is fairly polite, therefore, and cautious. The official Conservative and Liberal parties, instead of being more intransigent in their particular beliefs than their European counterparts, are less so; they are more socialistic, and are wholly committed (for example) to the social services program. To an outside observer, Great Britain is a land of paradox. There is an easy assumption that radical self-government is everyone's right; yet there is a monarchy and an hereditary peerage. The average working man has an earning power not much higher than the average American Negro's; but he and his family have complete social security in health, pension, and unemployment services; and a university or professional education need not cost him anything. There is also strict public control over the rich, their incomes, and their legacies. Class distinctions are strong, and subtly graded from the highest to the lowest; but external politeness should not hide from an overseas observer the fact that money and family prestige alone buy other people's respect and compliance less in Britain than in the United States, for example. Local self-determination is strong, not just in municipal and county government but also in the thousands of voluntary organizations that make British life such a nucleated system of attachments. These even impinge directly on many national activities like politics and education. Yet British central government is also strong. Though there are still many social and economic inequalities, more social changes took place during the first fifty years of this century than most bloody revolutions elsewhere were able to achieve; and since about 1944 an even more remarkable social revolution has been quietly engineered and consolidated.

Later in this chapter we shall see that recent changes in university and technological education seem likely to produce an unprecedented challenge to prevailing assumptions about the social order and to traditional prerogatives in the school system. Just here we should notice that such changes have involved urgent national planning, as distinct from locally based and empirical evolution. They have been particularly associated with postwar economic development; thus they have tended to escape notice as social and educational reforms too. It seems likely or possible that measures of this sort may bypass many traditional stumbling blocks in Britain, or make them gradually irrelevant. However that may be, planning is a growing and accepted feature of all public administration. Of socialistic origin, planning has been specially marked during the 1950s and 1960s under Conservative governments. It was under Conservative auspices, for example, that the National Economic Development Corporation was established, that higher technological education was put on a new footing, and that university expansion was accelerated. Yet these or comparable schemes have long formed part of their political opponents' plans; and the logic of their implementation is often resisted by Conservatives when we come down to the practicalities of local government or to the question of which pattern of schooling is likely to be fairest and most successful in developing and discovering talent.

These apparent inconsistencies can be understood in the light of what has been said before, that a fundamental assumption of British life is that every person or group is entitled to attempt a satisfactory way of living or doing things. Britons do not always live up to their principles, of course; but the "hands off" tradition is very powerful. Respect for disagreement has positive results in the response of minorities, which are very orderly because they do get a reasonable chance to develop. At a more trivial level the survival of ancient buildings, archaic roads, effete machinery, and so on, is due to unwillingness to destroy a thing that somehow works. Though British public administration is in some respects much more socialistic than that of the United States, for example, there is far greater reluctance to commandeer land for roads or to undertake big reconstruction schemes in the public interest. So many legal and customary safeguards protect the "small man." "An Englishman's home is his castle" is still a favorite saying.

It is difficult to find room for all the castles and prerogatives that this belief should justify. The United Kingdom (that is, all the British Isles excluding the autonomous Republic of Eire in the southern part of Ireland) has fifty-three million people in an area less than Oregon's. Of these, forty-five million live in England, which is slightly larger than North Carolina. The population density of England is over 823 to the square mile—a figure which is more astonishing when we take account of large moorland areas and of regions that are predominantly agricultural. In spite of the English moors, to any Englishman traveling abroad a predominant impression is that of space. The United States looks particularly empty, even in the industrial East.

Northern Ireland has its own parliament; but the rest of the United Kingdom is governed by Parliament in London, though certain powers (like Scots law and the control of Scottish education) are entrusted to the separate jurisdiction of the Scots. Education in England and Wales is subject to the supervision of Parliament in so far as it receives full or partial financial support from taxes. The very important private sector was not supervised before October 1, 1957. Although the 1944 Education Act which reorganized the system in England and Wales enabled the Minister of Education to inspect private schools, this inspection is only now beginning. The Ministry of Education does not own or operate any schools, employ any teachers, or draw up any syllabus. It is the Minister's responsibility to make sure that each educational district in England and Wales (called a Local Education Authority, or LEA) has a satisfactory provision for education at all stages within the framework of the law.

The LEAs (numbering 146 in 1963) can experiment as they like, within reasonable limits. They are guaranteed sufficient funds by means of equalization arrangements that assure a higher share of taxation proceeds to districts that need it most. Local education authorities employ teachers, and make recommendations about curriculum and methods; but the final determination of curriculum is left to a considerable degree to the head teachers of schools. Therefore there is nothing like the centralized direction found in American school districts, and there is no equivalent of the American school superintendent. Inspectors of the Ministry and the LEAs are, like American "supervisors," in theory, expediters and advisers. They cannot really order anyone to do anything, and they do not behave as though they wanted to.

There is not the same divorce between teaching and administration that is familiar in some countries (the inspectorate and administrative officers being recruited from successful teachers). Because inspectors by their very nature see a great deal of the most enterprising teaching in schools, they are able to pass on a lot of practical common sense and progressive thought in their visits to teachers. They also draw up advisory pamphlets which the Ministry publishes. The local authorities get the benefit of this service too, because the inspectorate advises them also, and sits in (by invitation, as well as by right) on a large number of advisory committees. Moreover, the LEAs have their own national organization in an Association of Education Committees, and their chief education officers are in close touch with one another. Of course, some are less progressive and generous than the best; but the moral pressure to modernize is very great. As a last resort, the central government (through the Ministry of Education) could withhold its contribution to local expenses. For a time, educational expenditure by local authorities was counted separately for reimbursement purposes; and during that period the Ministry of Education contributions averaged above 60 percent of local spending (sometimes more). Nevertheless, the use of these resources was the responsibility of a local authority.

Thus the British system of central control over minimum standards in education is powerful though gentlemanly. It permits widespread local variation and personal experiment; but it leaves no real loophole for slackers. This paradoxical tolerance (indeed encouragement) of local initiative combined with an insistence on the public interest has tended to cut down British reliance on direction from above and to increase both the amount of *permissive* legislation and the importance of rather polite advisory services. In favorable circumstances this state of affairs encourages a strong sense of personal as well as local responsibility; but its virtue, like many others, has an associated vice—that of inconsistency and hesitation. The organizational habits of centuries become a state of mind. There is little point in bossing a Briton. Before he will budge, you usually have to show him the logic of his move and produce some pragmatic sanction for it. This is not merely the constant message of his educational arrangements; it is the only justification for their present jumble.

It is characteristic that educational law does not compel parents to send their children to school; they are compelled to secure their children a proper education between the ages of 5 and 15. But it is also characteristic that children not merely go to school; they also are most faithful in attendance. The absentee problem familiar elsewhere is almost nonexistent. If, however, parents did persist in neglecting their children's education (which in practically every case would be by non-attendance at school), their children could be taken away from them temporarily as "in need of care and protection," and the parents could be fined or even sent to prison. Of course, the minimum insistence on education permits parents to employ tutors (if they are rich enough), to send their children to private establishments, or to avail themselves of the publicly provided schools. Private or partly private education flourishes to an extent very unfamiliar in most other countries (including the autonomous Dominions of the British Commonwealth). This is particularly true of England, and in England is especially true of the comparatively wealthy (for reasons which will be examined shortly). Some private schools are of exceptionally high quality; but some are, to say the least of it, no match for the publicly provided schools. There is increasing impatience with the present extensive range of different opportunities, still frequently leading to different social futures and different prospects in higher education. This range is wider, perhaps, than in any democratic country elsewhere. Sometimes it is a matter of superior schooling; but more often than not such social differentiation bears little or no relation to the intrinsic merits of the schooling given or of the children thus differentiated.

On the other hand, geographic or economic background is not allowed to affect a child's access to first-class education in the publicly provided schools. One important consideration is that teachers everywhere have the same basic rates of pay. Awards are made to them above the minimum for higher academic qualifications, for experience, for special responsibility, and so on; but these awards are nationally agreed between the representatives of the local education authorities and the teachers' unions, and they are enforced upon all local authorities. In London and some large cities with heavy urban expenses an agreed supplement is paid. Therefore it does not matter very much whether a school is in a village or a city; it has the same opportunity for teachers with good qualifications. In fact, some heavily industrialized and smoky cities are finding it increasingly difficult to get teachers.

At one time, different scales were paid according to the type of school in which teachers were employed. Now all the publicly provided schools pay the same for teachers with the same qualifications and the same proportion of responsibility. So it would be possible, for example, for a Ph.D. to be financially as well off in an infant school as in the top classes of a grammar school (academic high school). Of course, other considerations usually attract teachers to their appropriate level. The main advantage of present arrangements is that social distinctions between junior and secondary school work, and between work in the various kinds of secondary school, have been largely removed. Higher scales, of course, are paid in institutions of higher learning, such as teachers' training colleges, technical colleges, and universities; but here again the rates payable for the type of institution are normally paid throughout the country. It is an axiom of British educational thought that every child everywhere shall have equal access to the type of education for which he seems qualified by "age, ability, and aptitude," and that differences of origin and present circumstances shall be no handicap. As has been previously stated, educational opportunity is now open to all up to and beyond the university, and entrance to all professions is open.

This is a remarkable transformation from what can be well remembered by many people still living. Until 1902 the local school boards were not strictly entitled to offer any education beyond the elementary stage at the public expense, although many of them did. The meager higher opportunities thus afforded were in the higher classes of elementary school premises. Some school boards were not at all eager to spend money. They had been created only in 1870 to fill the gaps in elementary education as it had been provided until then by the religious denominations who received direct government grants for the building, improvement, and extension of schools. The first of these grants was paid in 1833; but their amounts had been gradually increased until in 1870 the Church of England had elementary schools in all towns and most villages, and the nonconformist and Roman Catholic churches also had numerous schools.

At that period public opinion could not consider any education worthwhile if it had not a firmly doctrinal basis and was not offered by convinced, practicing Christians. However, the Church of England's firm grip on public education (amounting to a monopoly in many small townships) caused so much dissatisfaction among other Christians that they eventually supported a campaign for nonsectarian public schooling financed by taxation. The resulting 1870 Act was a compromise, however. It let the churches retain any schools they had before that law was passed; yet it established "school boards" to supplement Church education, and not to supersede it. Thus the country was covered with a patchwork provision. Voluntary (church) activity had provided as much as it could, or thought fit; the deficiencies were made good by local school boards. Board schools were fully financed out of local taxes ("rates"). Church schools at first got no such help, though after 1891 they had support from central taxation.

Elementary education was not made free everywhere at first, because to forbid fees would have put church congregations in bankruptcy, especially where there were many children. Partly for this reason, and partly also because of misguided tenderness toward "parental rights," compulsion was not universally applied until 1880, though most local school boards had bylaws requiring attendance. Even then, compulsion was at first for five years' schooling only, from ages 5 to 10, though here again some local boards were more progressive. By 1891 elementary education was nearly always free, and the token fees (about twopence a week) formerly charged had nearly all been discontinued. This jumble of hesitant reforms exemplifies British "muddling through" in education. The people who suffered were the children.

Only in 1902 was a coordinated national school system secured. In that year, newly constituted local education authorities were required to make sure that elementary, secondary, and further education was completely offered in their areas. It could be provided by themselves or others; but they must make sure it was available. To make sure it was also accessible, they were empowered to pay fees and grant scholarships.

Thus public secondary schools linking the elementary provision with the professions and the universities were established in England for the first time. There had already been similar schools in Wales for 13 years, and for a much longer period in Scotland. France had had them for almost a century. Other European countries had left England far behind. In fact it has been said that the 1870 Act's provision of elementary education on a wider scale was demanded as much by the requirements of modern industry as by any humane considerations, and that the 1902 Act's extension of a higher provision with tax support was similarly called for by fear of European and American competition. Undoubtedly, skilled workmen and clerks were being imported from abroad. British economy had been cushioned against competitors by the very fact that industrialization was mainly a British invention in the early stages. Overseas markets were captured, and foreign investments on a vast scale gave the manufacturers and merchants an easy living which prevented them from seeing future needs clearly. Education on a much more thoroughgoing scale was one of the investments necessary. The many private or partly private secondary schools were not sufficiently numerous or available.

It would be unfair to leave the impression that only bread-and-butter considerations brought about an improvement in British education. From the very beginning of the nineteenth century the churches had been actively extending elementary education as a work of charity, keeping the children off the noisome streets of the terrible factory towns, and still more, keeping small children from day-long labor in factories and mines. But what they offered did not fully serve worldly ambitions. Self-help organizations of many types among the working people themselves had pressed for education—not merely elementary, but up to and including the university level itself. This voluntary provision, however, was severely limited by the difficulty of getting it after an arduous day's work, and by the lack of systematic preparation for university and professional examinations. All British universities and skilled professions are extremely exacting in their admission requirements.

Therefore the 1902 Act was revolutionary, even though some of its proposals had been set before Parliament as long ago as 1833. The revolution it has brought about is seen more clearly when we look at its results about half a century later. British society is transformed. Voluntary effort (nowadays called "private enterprise" in economic circles) is no longer trusted alone to provide the nation's requirements. There is still very much more private initiative in British tax-aided education than in American, for instance; but it is brought under public supervision and regulation with increasing vigilance. Voluntary effort is not so much curbed as prodded. If it does not move nimbly or skillfully enough it is superseded. This is seldom done by suppression; the public provision is eventually raised in quality and extended in scope, wherever possible, so as to make other arrangements unnecessary. At the same time, vigilance is growing to prevent money spent privately on education from being a disguised way of buying privilege in later life. Of course, to remove this possibility altogether would be a superhuman task. A great deal of unfair advantage is still perpetuated by private schools; but the extent to which children now move toward maturity with equalized chances would have seemed impossible a generation ago. The term "elementary" is no longer used, because it was associated with a type of schooling kept deliberately inferior. Children have free primary education (to 11); free secondary education (11 to 15, as a minimum, or to 18 if they wish and show ability); free university education if they satisfy university entrance requirements and do not come from very prosperous homes; and either free or very cheap admission to all kinds of technical and commercial careers. At any rate no financial barrier stands in the way of an able child. Admission to higher education in a university, college of advanced technology, and most technical and art colleges, almost invariably secures the student a scholarship giving free tuition and substantial or complete maintenance costs during the period of study. Where wealthier parents pay a contribution, this is usually only a payment of what it would cost to keep the student at home. This aspect of financial support inevitably makes the over-all expansion of higher education a more burdensome public liability than in any other noncommunist country; and it in part explains British preoccupation with university admission standards.

Inseparable from the school provision is that offered by the social services. The national health service assures the child complete medical attention (including hospitalization, surgical, dental, ophthalmic, and psychological services when required) from the beginning to the end of his life. This service is very like the school provision in that everyone pays taxes for it, but no one (physician or patient) needs to take part in it; 95 percent of all doctors and over 80 percent of the population do participate, however. Patients choose their own doctor. No one is denied full health opportunities by his own or his parents' poverty. Children get vitamin foods and school meals at subsidized prices, or free if necessary. In real hardship they can even get free clothing. All these advantages, though dreamed of, must have seemed remote at the beginning of this century. There is no genuine, ascertainable need not catered to in the attempt to provide every child with everything needed for full development—at home, in school, or in special services for the handicapped. A generation ago it was still possible to see children whose education suffered severely because they were undernourished or diseased. Now schools are full of healthy youngsters well cared for there, and also very well cared for by their parents. Homes are much more (not less) responsible places than they were in 1902.

The grudging nature of most early provision for popular education and health has made all parties in Britain determined to secure comprehensive facilities now. Differences arise only over the questions of how much, by whom, and in what circumstances the social services can be best provided. Voluntary efforts in the past prepared the way for national schemes; but they were unequally distributed, spasmodic, and incapable of securing fair opportunities for all. That is why everyone now is so eager to make comprehensive arrangements. Past inconsistencies also account for the survival of terrible difficulties in education.

Among the difficult problems that still defy solution is the future of the many kinds of private school and the denominational tax-supported schools. The vast majority of these latter are Church of England; but a large number are Roman Catholic, a few belong to other denominations, and a handful are Jewish. The teachers in almost all cases are lay persons; but Catholic schools are sometimes taught by nuns, brothers, or priests. Church schools were paramount before 1870. They were denied support from local taxes after 1870, though they could still sometimes get per capita grants from central funds. However, the Act of 1902 enabled them to draw all their running expenses (though not the cost of initial building or maintaining the premises) from local taxation ("rates"). All recognized Church schools catering to children of compulsory school age—those that were called "elementary schools" before 1944—benefit in this way. Their teachers get the same salaries as other local authority teachers; but they are usually appointed by the local clergy with or without advice. Naturally, they belong to the appropriate denomination in nearly every case.

Church secondary schools catering to children between the ages of 11 and 18, and offering a rather more advanced type of education, can also benefit in this way provided they apply for status as an "aided" school and are recognized as doing the same kind of job as a local authority secondary school of the same type—with the additional characteristic that they are religious schools. In many of them (especially Catholic schools, of course) the teaching and administrative staff are nuns, brothers, or priests. The religious authorities who engage them use the same academic and professional criteria as the local education authorities, who are satisfied on secular grounds that the teachers are competent, and therefore pay their salaries. Where such an arrangement is made, education, like education in the local authorities' own schools, is free. The Catholic community, and some (but not all) members of the Church of England, think this partial support is very unfair in view of the rising costs of building and reorganization. Yet over the years the proportion of denominational school costs paid by taxation must amount to not less than 90 percent, and may actually reach 95 percent.

Some other Church schools (nearly all primary, and nearly all Church of England) have preferred what is called "controlled" status. They get the local education authority to pay all their costs in return for handing over their buildings. The LEA will then appoint all teachers, except that, for the appointment of the head teacher and of "reserved" teachers whose job it is to offer denominational instruction, the LEA will consult the foundation managers of the school. Such denominational instruction is then given for two periods a week.

A much smaller group of Church schools are called "special agreement schools" because they were in an intermediate position, or in the midst of assisted reorganization, at the time of the 1944 Act.

In Scotland the arrangements for denominational schools are quite different from those in England. Since 1918 all Church schools have been transferred to the management of local education authorities, which maintain them and select and pay their teachers. Safeguards are given to protect their denominational character and the sectarian character of their staffs. Religious education is not inspected. In practice this means that most primary schools in Scotland have strong Church associations, being either Protestant (mainly Presbyterian) or Catholic. In Holland a similar arrangement prevails, except that there is a third group of schools—the secular. Dutch educators complain that their country is being increasingly divided into three camps—a complaint that is certainly justified.

A number of Church schools in England and Wales take advantage of other arrangements open to private secondary schools generally, whether religious or not. They are able to ask the Ministry of Education to recognize and aid them as "direct grant schools." Nonsectarian trust foundations are the usual recipients of this recognition, which is granted only if the schools are not conducted for profit, have a high standard of secondary education and premises, and give a proportion (at least a quarter) of their places to children who pay no fees. "Direct grant schools" may also be required to allow the local education authority to fill a further quarter of their places with children for whom it affords free places by paying their fees to the school. Even ordinary fee-payers must be of a high standard. In 1943 there were 232 such schools; in 1950 there were 164. In 1962 there were 179 direct grant grammar schools—the number having grown because of the inclusion of some previously independent schools.

The majority of schools in the category of "direct grant" were not primarily intended to be denominational schools. They were once exclusive secondary schools catering to wealthier children, though they now admit an increasing number of free-place children. However, it must be admitted that the "snob value" of these schools is noticeable. They are often able to take their pick of the bright children applying for admission. In addition, they are sometimes able to afford better facilities and smaller classes than the schools maintained by the local authorities. Finally, they sometimes attract better qualified or more enterprising teachers who have their eye on improved prospects of promotion. The majority of these schools are not associated with the Church of England any more, though at the time of their foundation it was probably assumed that most "respectable" citizens were.

In discussing this last category we passed from the strictly denominational classification to the partly supported independent or semi-independent schools which have attracted public support from taxes because they were once the only ones offering secondary education at a reasonable price. The Ministry of Education (or the Board of Education before it) thus indirectly made good the lack of publicly provided schools. The local education authorities can also assist schools for particular educational purposes. As a rule the acceptance of public money means coming under some public control; this is normally limited to agreeing to provide a certain proportion of free places to children who have attended public primary schools. Yet we must urgently question whether the existence of all these semi-independent and socially attractive alternatives can be financed in their present form alongside the public system if they "cream off" children (and teachers) for social or intellectual reasons from the publicly maintained grammar schools (i.e., academic high schools), and thus impair their development.

Outside the wide range of schools receiving partial tax support there are the completely independent schools financed entirely by fees or from ancient foundations. They number about 5000 and have 500,000 pupils, of whom 10 percent are over 15. A small minority of such schools enjoy international fame, and rightly. Examples are the great "Public Schools" such as Eton, Harrow, and Winchester, which are not public but very exclusive and expensive. Many independent schools are comparable only with the publicly maintained grammar school. Indeed, the majority perhaps are nothing like so good, being really genteel alternatives either to the grammar school or to the secondary modern school, accommodating children who for one reason or another have not been catered to by the tax-supported institutions. A very large number of them are in fact primary schools (though he would be a bold man who told them so!), which prepare boys and girls for the minor Public Schools. The majority of such schools are undistinguished, but on the whole they do a useful job. Independent schools receive no tax support (with rare exceptions of a merely token kind), and until 1957 they were not inspected by the Ministry of Education unless they cared to invite inspection so as to secure "recognition as efficient," which a number of them did for prestige reasons. Yet the independent schools are of really great importance in Britain's social system. In prosperous London suburbs and among the elite of the provincial towns they have a high popularity because they impart a socially desirable accent to their young charges, because they prepare children in the appropriate subjects for the examinations that admit them to Public Schools, and because they often have smaller classes than the publicly provided primary schools. The importance of the southern English accent and of examinations in British life will be dealt with shortly.

It is a matter of historic interest worth mentioning here that the Public Schools got their name because they were once what it implies, being monastic foundations intended for the education of the less wealthy. However, instead of being ladders for all, and leading poor boys to a career in the Church or the professions, they have in recent centuries been the preserve of the governing classes. As late as 1962, over 40 percent of the students at Oxford University and 60 percent of those at Cambridge University (thus enjoying a socially favorable start in public life) had been to boarding schools of this type. During the nineteenth century especially, the majority of present Public Schools were founded to cater to the rising manufacturers' and merchants' sons. As reformed by such crusaders as Arnold of Rugby and Thring of Uppingham they have given a very thorough though sometimes very formal preparation for all the more respectable professions. Perhaps more than any other instrument they account for the astonishing absorptive capacity of the privileged upper middle classes, especially in England. The ruling class will generally accept anyone who can "make the grade" and conform to the exacting requirements of the "approved type." Among these are the possession of the southern English accent (not native to any part of the country, but polished as a class index) and an habitual confident elegance. These are, at least in the intentions of Public School educators, only the external tokens of strength of character, of what psychologists (but not economists) call socialization, and of cultivated sensibility. It is important not to underestimate the high standards of teaching, study, sportsmanship, and service in these schools. Their academic requirements for admission are severe. Their regime is strict, often Spartan. Their fees are high, fairly close to an average man's yearly wage for a child's annual schooling and residence. Scholarships are few. Several proposals (like the Fleming scheme) have from time to time suggested that some should be made available to the poorest children. It is not surprising that the combination of these high academic and social standards, and a strong insistence on "character," with the careful home backgrounds of the pupils, have given the Public Schools immense prestige. Many people still assume that leadership and personal integrity can only be developed in them or according to their fashion. Though rather less than 3 percent of British children go to such schools, their access to positions of wealth and influence is conspicuously easier than for others.

In particular we must notice that the ordinary English "grammar" school (that is, the really public academic high school) has been shaped by the example of the Public Schools. Some day grammar schools are so ancient that they antedate most residential Public Schools, which grew up in their present form to attract the children of administrators and well-to-do people from all over the country; and there have always existed some day grammar schools for the children of the locally successful. Therefore when tax-supported secondary schools were introduced in 1902 it was not surprising that they were given an ancient name and some features of the Public Schools, which were themselves increasing greatly in number to serve the newly rich. The chief executor of the 1902 Act, Sir Robert Morant, was of Public School type to the marrow. During the last quarter of a century before publicly provided secondary schools actually arrived, however, many expected that they would be of a much more technical or directly prevocational kind. That was the direction of public demand and also what manufacturers envisaged. Yet the prestige of Public Schools and of the older grammar schools was such that the newer academic public secondary schools are not only officially called "grammar schools" but also copy their organization of "houses," prefects, school loyalty, team spirit, and so on. To an astonishing degree this has enabled the products of the public grammar school to compete academically with Public School products on their own ground in the struggle for university and professional places; but it has also resulted in much frustration and perhaps misdirection of effort.

It is of the greatest importance for an understanding of British educational problems to appreciate the long unchallenged sanctity of all that the Public Schools stand for. This is, after all, the characteristic British contribution to educational thought and to school organization. As always happens everywhere, those more recently emancipated aspire to the conscipuous tokens of success. It is difficult for newcomers to discern the differences of social context, of professional orientation, and indeed of historic and economic circumstance that make their own case different. Society has been and is still being revolutionized, but not its legends or its holy symbols. Therefore what sociologists call "social distance" is still measured in Britain largely by old-fashioned criteria very different from those of America. In the very top bracket one includes the titled nobility (who nowadays may be captains of industry, successful administrators, and former trade-union officials); but one must also include the learned professions such as university professors. Universities are exclusive, and their faculties highly esteemed. The big men of industry and commerce frequently come rather lower in public estimation. Prosperous local manufacturers and storekeepers may even now be socially equated with teachers in good schools though their incomes are much greater. Recent public opinion polls and broadcast discussions bear out what professional sociologists say. Indeed, to come down to brass tacks we may say that the way an Englishman talks and moves is much more likely to affect his immediate social mobility than the amount of money in his own or his father's account. Speech alone is a significant social ticket. The vital importance of socially "good" schools is thus enhanced.

Of course, there are subtleties, as there are with all class distinctions. Local speech in the British Isles shows strong differences of pronunciation, idiom, and intonation. Much of it would at first be unintelligible to a person who knew only "standard English," and the more vigorous local peculiarities would defy an outsider's understanding for months. (Nothing is said here about the different *languages* such as Welsh, Gaelic, and Irish; attention is being paid only to variants of English.) As a kind of compromise between the extremes of dialect and the central norm of standard English, most towns of any size have a distinctive speech of their own. Citizens highest in the local hierarchy have progressed furthest from local idiosyncrasies. In some occupations a cosmopolitan English accent is not called for so strictly as in others. A Church of England clergyman, a lawyer, and a doctor must generally "speak well"; their children certainly must. Secondary school teachers must also do very well, as a rule, though not necessarily if they teach science subjects. Factory owners need not. So it goes on. Some local speech survivals are less welcome than others. A Scottish accent of medium strength is something of a distinction, an Irish one is much less so. Ambitious Welshmen are careful to change their vowels, but some surviving Welsh intonation is not unattractive. A strong Lancashire, Yorkshire, or Midlands color is a downright social drawback for the ambitious, however, even in those very regions; in London and in high academic or administrative posts generally, it is even more so. These absurd but cherished talismans profoundly affect geographic and still more social mobility—very much more than in Germany, for instance. We cannot separate from them the very high prestige (and effective social importance) of the Public Schools and other schools that are semiprivate. At the moment, considerations of speech and social punctilio are perhaps the biggest hindrance to a wider acceptance of common schools for all children.

Having sketched in the background of influential forces still at work, we can proceed to a more formal examination of the school system in England and Wales. Scottish methods are different in certain important respects. In England and Wales compulsory free schooling begins at the commencement of the first term after a child reaches the age of 5. There are three terms a year, each of about thirteen weeks. Twelve weeks' holiday is the usual length, generally divided into six summer weeks and three weeks each at Christmas and Easter. (Winters in Britain are mild, spring is early, and the summer is cool. A favorite joke is that Britain has no climate, only weather.) Schools have a five-day week, usually from 9 A.M. to 3.30 or 4 P.M. with an hour's dinner break at midday and two shorter breaks in the morning and afternoon sessions. Local school authorities have complete discretion to arrange all these matters. It is also usual to have a short mid-term break of perhaps two days in each of the three terms. Physical education is an essential part of the curriculum, and in addition games afternoons may be one or two a week. In most schools, except those for very young children, much extracurricular activity is encouraged. In the "grammar" schools (academic high schools) this is specially vigorous, and highly prized as a formative influence. A British school is certanly not a place for instruction only.

All the same, the school means business. A child beginning school soon after his fifth birthday starts straight away to learn. There is no official program or method. The head and assistant teachers do what seems best, and adjust themselves to the children's needs as much as possible. Young children will be grouped according to ability and speed. By their sixth birthday they are usually well able to read simple books and do elementary sums. They write without hesitation, usually in script. In addition, they paint, sing, dance, and make a first acquaintance with each other and the world about them. The infant schools (5 to 7) and junior schools (7 to 11) are usually the most progressive parts of the British system; they are bright and cheerful places, and the most up-to-date methods are now usual. Unfortunately, the postwar increase in the birth rate, the heavy cost of reconstruction after bombing, the worsened international situation, and the shortage of teachers have all meant that classes are much too large. Forty (and sometimes even fifty) are found in one class. Schools also have a playground, a place to assemble, and a place for meals and exercise. Books, stationery, and other necessities are provided.

The work done in the first year is consolidated and improved on in subsequent years. By comparison with some other countries the pace is rapid; but it is certainly not forced. When a child is about 11 (i.e., in his sixth year) he is doing work comparable with that of perhaps the seventh grade (or higher) of the American school, and the average standard of proficiency in school subjects is high. By this time the pupil-teacher relationship has become more formal. This is partly because it is traditional, partly because people think it works out better, and partly also because of the anticipated selection for secondary education at about the age of 11. Local authorities can choose as they wish; but some form of examination is usual. It typically includes intelligence tests, attainment tests, critical compositions, and reference to the school record.

Nowadays every child in the publicly provided school system (except in a few special areas) is transferred at about the age of 11 to "secondary" school. At one time this term signified simply a more privileged school with a curriculum leading to the university or the professions—an old-style grammar school. Now it refers to the public provision of any type between the ages of 11 and 18 or 19. Three main types of secondary school are recognized: "grammar" or academic; technical; and "secondary modern." Some remarks have already been made about grammar schools. The grammar school offers systematic preparation for university, technical, and commercial occupations in a wide range; but it also sets a high standard of personal and civic responsibility before its pupils. Work is very earnest; but so are the numerous activities so diligently followed. In addition to plenty of games and athletics, we usually find numerous debates, concerts, and dramatic presentations of good quality. Art and singing are taken by everyone.

Competence in self-expression and public speaking are expected and trained for. There is usually an orchestra. Clubs such as scientific and naturalists' societies; stamp or chess clubs; camping, scouting, and similar organizations—all these are common. Nowadays some foreign travel is often organized on a voluntary basis, and pupils regularly have pen-friends abroad with whom they correspond in French or German. Life in a grammar school is very busy indeed.

The subjects taken, though not so exactingly pursued as in France (where they tend to exclude extracurricular possibilities of any kind) are numerous and serious. Nearly all pupils take the same subjects at first, though there is increasing specialization as they advance. In the first "form" of a typical grammar school (ages 11 to 12) they begin algebra and geometry; they also begin a foreign language, and start on either general science or elementary biology; they also take English (which includes "speech," drama, etc.), history, geography, music, physical education, and nondenominational but Christian religious knowledge. Children may elect not to attend this last subject if their parents object. A second foreign language is begun in the second year, as a rule; in the third year a third language may be added. The third year also sees a beginning of physics or chemistry or biology proper, or a combination of these; in mathematics, trigonometry may be added. Girls may also include domestic science and boys some workshop skill, usually woodwork.

But it is already obvious that if these subjects are to be maintained at a businesslike level, as they certainly are, something must be dropped. Early specialization distinguishes British schools from those of Germany and France. Specialization is adopted for the sake of higher standards, and also because of timetable difficulties. German may clash with Latin or Greek, for example; or it may be necessary to drop a language or a science where no proficiency is shown. But every pupil will retain the core subjects such as English, mathematics, and history; and the optional or elective subjects will usually have compensatory subjects accompanying them to prevent one-sidedness. It is important to realize that an elective subject is normally studied with real specialization from the moment it is taken up until the time a public examination is taken in it at the age of about 16 or 18, or both. It is usual for children in this type of school to stay until they are at least 16, and their parents promise they will secure this. But in some poorer sections of industrial towns there is a certain falling away at the age of 15, when compulsion ends.

The examinations referred to lead to the General Certificate of Education. Questions are set and marked externally by examining boards operated by the universities. At least half and often more of the examiners are teachers. They draw up syllabuses on which the examination will be based. Schools are profoundly influenced by these syllabuses, which in a language, for example, may prescribe certain authors for detailed study. It is true that head or even assistant teachers can get a paper set on any subject, or on any special aspect of a subject, particularly developed in their school; but few avail themselves of this facility even though the additional cost is negligible. As has been said before, the choice of a school's curriculum is left almost entirely to that school. The influence of external examinations keeps them all up to standard, and to some extent restricts modifications in the curriculum, though it need not do so. Despite many attempts in recent years to minimize concentration on examinations, there is no doubt that the results attained in them have an enormous influence on future careers—at least in the initial stages.

It will be of interest to suggest the standards attained, though that is rash. A 16-year-old boy or girl would offer English as a compulsory subject, and might add mathematics, physics, chemistry, biology, history (perhaps geography), and French. Another might choose history, geography, mathematics, French, Latin, and Greek in addition to English literature and language. Other combinations are possible in a wide range. It must be remembered that other subjects are followed in school but not for examination. The examination subjects, sometimes after five years' study, are not infrequently known and examined at the level of much American *college* work. By the time pupils take the Advanced Level of the General Certificate of Education at 18 they could usually stand comparison with the major subjects of the average American college's senior year (where students are 22). In recent years many teachers of classes at this level have innocently begun to use American college textbooks, which are often admirably produced and are in some ways specially useful for review or consolidation work because their material is arranged in a different way. The teachers in question assume that, as in the British idiom, "college" is a synonym for an academic high school (that is, a British grammar school). Unfortunately, these books are usually too expensive for the British pocket.

Not even this level of attainment will guarantee pupils the opportunity of entering a British university to *begin* a course, however. They need to be exceptionally good for this. British universities are highly specialized places, concerned with a restricted range of academic interests, and preparing only for the highest grades in a few professions. The manifold services offered by American universities, for example, are provided by other institutions in Britain.

It will be noted that nothing is implied in my remarks about the comparative personal worth of the education offered as between Britain and the United States. Talk about standards of attainment may touch a tender spot; but it does not say everything. A country like Britain, which has limited raw resources and must earn abroad by its skill at least half the food it eats, just cannot afford extravagances with time. "If you don't earn, you don't eat" is a lesson that is dinned into British heads incessantly in postwar years, though in various grades of politeness. Standards of skill and knowledge can hardly be abandoned without disaster. Industry, no less than the universities, demands ever higher and higher attainment. The critical problem inside the grammar school therefore is one of deciding largely between specialization and breadth. It is not beyond human ingenuity to foster increased understanding of world-wide problems and deep human issues even when specialized studies are followed within a restricted field; but there are manifest dangers. Particular attention needs to be given to them—and not just in the grammar school, where many attempts are already made to widen interests and develop human concern. The very important Crowther Report [2] dealt with these problems, and contained excellent information about the evolution of British schools for this age range. I do not, however, accept some of its more conservative conclusions.

The grammar school, which has become the pivotal point of most British skill and enterprise in the twentieth century, has its own special problems. It has not changed enough with the times, either regarding the range of subject interests covered or in relation to social attitudes. It certainly has its own special types of narrowness. For example, segregation is usual—not of people of different colors (for that would be both illegal and shocking in Britain), but of boys and girls. Only a few grammar schools are coeducational, though most primary schools and secondary modern schools are. The ancient Public Schools and grammar schools were for boys only, and girls' education was an afterthought. The ancient fashion still prevails in modern grammar schools, and plenty of reasons are thought of to justify it. Also, it is usual to expect boys (or girls) to wear clothing of a distinctive type. This cuts out vulgar ostentation and also sloppiness; but it may cramp individuality. One

[2] Crowther, et al., *Fifteen to Eighteen*. London: H. M. Stationery Office, 1959–1960, 2 vols.

advantage is that it helps parents' budgeting. However, the very fostering of *esprit de corps* by this method is also associated with the spirit of
the "old school tie." There is no doubt that people in grammar schools
feel themselves to be socially as well as intellectually superior, on the
whole. They represent between 20 percent and 25 percent of the
children selected at 11. Some local authorities select a much higher
proportion of children for grammar school places, and this fact indicates
once more the uncertainties of selection at the age of 11. Attention to
manners and speech, as well as the very real difference made to professional prospects, make almost all parents eager that their children should
be selected for grammar schools. Although parents can express a
preference, only a few of them can be satisfied. Several noteworthy
results must be mentioned. Parents of children of about 11 become
very anxious about the selection examination (and so do the children
themselves). Some parents have their children specially coached, and
others try to make sure by sending their children to "preparatory
schools" (private junior schools) instead of to the public junior schools,
though they seldom do much better. Finally, a number of those dis-
appointed at the selection send their children to fee-charging independent grammar schools, whose admission requirements may be lower.
This practice is growing. A number of this last group of schools are run
by religious organizations.

The Public Schools such as Eton, Winchester, and a very large
number less well known, have their own kind of selection examination,
taken at the age of 13. The tests include papers in Latin and French,
and in fairly advanced mathematics. Therefore it would be normally
very difficult for a child from an ordinary tax-supported school to compete, even if his parents could afford the fees. To serve these requirements, a large number of "preparatory schools," not tax-supported, are
found in prosperous suburbs. Since the usual pattern of selection followed since 1944 has virtually made the free grammar school the main
preserve of juvenile intelligence (at least, as indicated by tests), many
preparatory schools also make a point of preparing children energetically
for the "eleven plus" examinations as well as for the Public Schools'
"common entrance."

All these considerations, in a more or less articulate form, have been
brought home to parents whose little boy or girl is faced with selection
procedures at 11. There has been a crescendo of protests—against the
ordeal, against its restrictive influence on the junior school, against the

reliability of the selection, against its finality (despite marginal adjustment up to the age of 13 or even 15). The protesters have become more influential as their number has included many who, before the war, could have paid fees to get their children at a lower intellectual or attainment standard into grammar schools that are now free. University professors, heads of schools, and professional men find their children excluded. Influence and money count for nothing, except in so far as children from wealthier and professional homes are more likely to do well in an impartial examination.

The sort of anxiety felt by parents and many teachers (to say nothing of the poor children themselves) is indicated by the fact that they, and sometimes the local education authorities as well, are often aware of a "pecking order" of prospects not only in the junior schools which may lead to grammar schools but as between the grammar schools themselves. This latter "merit grading" is based upon university prospects afterwards. The selection procedures at about 11 are now known to be fallible, or restricted in their purview of scholastic potential; yet the mere placing of children in an alleged order of merit, combined with the slight latitude for parental preference allowed under the 1944 Education Act, results sometimes in children being enrolled in grammar schools at some distance from their own districts or towns, though of course within the same local authority area. Meanwhile, other children with brighter (or duller) prognosis at 11 are brought in from other towns or districts. School buses are unusual in Britain; but those who have to travel far will have free passes for ordinary public transportation. Thus, between 8 and 9 A.M. on school days, it is a regular thing to see great numbers of children in different colors of uniform crisscrossing each other's paths or "commuting" in opposite directions— all because of school selection. The whole, immensely valuable concept of a "neighborhood school," with its educative links of all kinds that transcend academic or career considerations, is in urban Britain a dwindling prospect at present. What is said here about a "pecking order" of grammar schools applies more rigidly than ever to other kinds of secondary schools in relation to them. These remarkable peculiarities (almost entirely absent from other civilized countries) are, to be fair, accentuated by the post-1944 determination to eliminate favoritism derived from parental position and to substitute instead an assessment of the child's supposed merits. However, the fallibility of tests, the narrowness of the field of personality under review, the ignoring of contextual

factors in education, and the whole emotional insensibility involved
have come under severe criticism as the process gathers strength because
of the pressure of claims to privileged education.

It is rightly assumed that protests would not be so energetic if the
alternatives to the grammar school enjoyed that "parity of esteem" so
cheerfully anticipated by legislators at the time of the 1944 Act. This
happy state has not been reached, though remarkable progress has been
made. There are several reasons for social and educational distinctions.
At one time the old elementary school carried the stigma of lower status,
being intended for the laboring poor. It often used wretched buildings,
some of which are still in use as junior schools or secondary modern
schools. It was "creamed off" by scholarship awards. Its teachers were
worse trained and worse paid than those in grammar schools. As the
effective life of a teacher is some forty years, it is obvious that many of
those now in service in secondary modern schools date from the pre-1944
period. Although many are exemplary in their social attitudes, in their
teaching ability, and in their good will, it would be rash to state this of
all. It cannot be claimed that the older teachers on the average are as
well-informed as the younger ones who have come into the schools from
the universities since the equalization of pay made such service more
attractive. The best of the secondary modern schools combine some of
the general educational advantages (though not the academic standards) of the grammar school with greater resourcefulness. A greater
proportion of money is, however, still spent on grammar schools for the
number of pupils involved, regarding both capital equipment, like laboratories, and books and teachers. And in any case careful analysis shows
that the best jobs not already taken by the people from the great Public
Schools continue to go to grammar school pupils, though these are now
more democratically recruited.

It would not be too much to say that the secondary modern school
still suffers from an unofficial downgrading. Teachers and administrators
protest against such a statement; but parents and politicians make no
secret of the common opinion. The Ministry of Education has a long-
term study in progress to help the secondary modern school to realize
its potentialities. Its status is rising very slowly, partly again because of
examinations. Sometimes pupils take the very same examinations for the
General Certificate of Education as grammar school pupils; usually more
commercial examinations are taken, and a most important innovation is
a new Certificate of Secondary Education. Yet it seems likely that the
secondary modern school (if it continues in its present form) must

justify itself and win public esteem simply by its performance—not an easy matter with its disadvantages. Perhaps the incentive value of the Certificate of Secondary Education's many electives will help, because these are intended to provide the secondary modern school and the average child with examination success below the level of the General Certificate of Education and more in keeping with "all-round" training rather than purely academic futures; but a removal of the sense of underprivileged isolation will help much more.

In some ways, though not in the excellence of its buildings or in the money available, a progressive secondary modern school can be compared with the ordinary small American high school. The standards are generally very similar in academic matters, though not yet in pupils' activities; there is an attempt at the same orientation toward a happy and responsible life at work and in society. It is not yet the "people's school" in popular affection, even though more than two-thirds of the population pass through it. It may have a better chance of becoming that when the projected raising of the school-leaving age to 16 takes place. The secondary modern school suffers from a historic hangover, and from unfavorable comparisons. Some of these had their origin partly in factual differences of standard and partly in somewhat fictitious differences (such as those of speech and mannerism). The social stratification which is exemplified by the grammar-secondary modern distinction is the most hotly debated issue in British education today. Scotland has its own historic way out of this difficulty; but England and Wales are not quite ready with their solution. Certainly more money must be invested in schools than the 4½ percent of the national income spent in 1961—itself a 50 percent increase in six years.

A third kind of public secondary school may be of increasing importance, though it is not found everywhere. It is the secondary technical school, arising out of the junior technical schools that have existed since 1905. These recruit children (usually boys) by examination about the age of 13, sometimes at 11. They take in the abler children from secondary modern schools but sometimes also recruit from grammar schools. Schools of Art also take in gifted children at the same age. In neither of these schools is education narrowly vocational; but it is given both backbone and insight by being related to skills that obviously have a practical value. Suitable examinations act as incentives, leading either to craftsman status or toward the research or managerial studies of higher institutions.

This tripartite division of schools into types really had its origin in historic accidents and in social and economic stratification; yet it actually has resulted in a widespread belief that there are really three "types of mind"—bookish, practical, and technical. References to this are made in legislation and supporting memoranda. Fortunately, this oddly schizo-phrenic psychology is now discredited. An increasing number of experi-mental schools comprise curricula of more than one type.

The earliest of these combined schools were called "multilateral." They kept up the cleavage in the classroom; but they gathered together the children of the three quite distinct teaching departments on one campus, with common assembly halls, playing fields, and corporate activities. Not many such *schools* exist, mainly because the whole idea of real secondary education for all is new, and also because of financial stringency. Britain's housekeeping is very straitened indeed; yet so-called multilateral *programs* are increasing rapidly. This means that in many secondary schools (usually after the "creaming-off" of the grammar school complement) a growing variety of distinctly grouped courses may be offered. They are seldom so markedly separate as to deserve the name of "departments"; but it is noticeable that over the age of about 13 an increase of specialization and prevocational realism lends not only distinctness but a greater sense of purpose. This in turn leads many more children to stay on after the end of compulsory schooling; and of these a growing proportion enter the "sixth form" of grammar schools or some kind of further education (for example, a technical college or a college of commerce). In all, about 35 percent of all boys and 7 percent of girls enter skilled apprenticeships, in addition to those taking courses. Such courses and apprenticeships in Britain (as in most European countries) follow the secondary school phase and are not counted as part of it. Indeed, they normally take their pupils far beyond what may be called secondary education.

"Bilateral" schools are similar to the multiple types just described, except that in some cases a selective and a nonselective school may operate on the same campus sharing a number of activities or studies. Alternatively, a grammar and a technical school may so share their premises, or a technical school and a secondary modern school. Within the elastic framework of permissive legislation in Britain, any number of organizational patterns can be found. For example, some counties allow successive transfer of children according to proven interests or ability up to the age of 15, and many do transfer the brighter pupils to grammar schools or further education then.

One of the best known experiments is that of Leicestershire. In 1957 this county divided its secondary phase into two parts. Children from neighboring primary schools are transferred at the usual age of 11 to the nearest secondary school, which retains them to the age of 14 or 15. Such schools are called "high schools." A number of specially gifted children (as revealed by optional examinations) may be admitted at 10, and so complete their programs one year earlier. Though these 11–15 schools are called "high schools," they correspond roughly to the American junior high schools or to the various "middle schools" now being experimented with in a number of continental countries. At the age of 14, a more advanced school (usually a former grammar school) receives *all* those children whose parents wish them to complete the grammar-school type studies offered there; but the parents must promise that they will stay to their completion. Incidentally, these studies are available in a wider range than usual. The Leicestershire plan eliminates premature selection almost completely; it is already proved practicable and successful; and it combines both enrichment and expansion for a wider range of young aptitudes. Its effect as an example is considerable.

A more recent and infinitely more controversial proposal is that the comprehensive type of school common in America should be adopted. More bitter words have been spoken about this than any other educational problem, except about denominational schools. Public opinion in Britain is not ready for such a manifestly "socialistic" solution as America's. Half the electorate votes Labor in a general election; but educationally the British remain conservative. It is widely known that a common school for all the children of a neighborhood is a characteristic shared by the United States and the Union of Soviet Socialist Republics, though suspect in the liberal democracies of Western Europe. It is also recognized that the common school (*école unique, Einheitsschule, scuola unica,* for example) has been a plank in every proper socialist platform for at least a century and a quarter. Everyone knows too that the widely publicized but the relatively few comprehensive schools in London were the work of a Labor-dominated London County Council; they were established for the most part against local opposition and the outspoken misgivings of the Minister of Education. The opponents of these schools do not hesitate to call them socialist devices, or worse.

But such names would not in Britain be a sufficient condemnation, and they would not be accurate either. Many staunch Labor supporters declare themselves to be in favor of "leveling up, not leveling down." Some mistrust these schools even in their English form, where children do not follow a uniform course (that would be still worse!) but are "streamed" into groups of homogeneous ability within the school. They say comprehensive schools must inevitably hold the bright children back at least a year, or perhaps two, though nobody has shown exactly why. This sort of criticism-in-advance is being belied by the excellent results already manifested by comprehensive schools; but criticism is still strong on all sides. Unflattering reference is often made to the schools in the United States by people ignorant of the fact that slower progress there is probably linked with lack of "streaming," and is also almost certainly due to the quite different concepts underlying American education. This defense, however, is taken with a pinch of salt. Britain as a whole cannot afford the luxury of lowered educational levels. A higher standard of living depends on more skill and knowledge, not less. Besides, working people know only too well that their children in the grammar schools are now able to compete for the universities and professions with the products of the great independent schools, and they wonder about the results of any alternative arrangement. Sincere educators know too that the first English comprehensive schools in the larger cities were established for political and not strictly educational reasons; they feel that a birthright of culture and of social opportunity may be gambled away.

After the first passionate outcry, however, the credit side is being examined. The old tripartite (and false) psychology would be avoided. The dubious "eleven plus" tests would fade out. Social handicaps would no longer mean so much in secondary school selection; and social futures would not be made or marred so early. There would be more flexibility in school arrangements, both to suit children's widely scattered interests and to prepare for Britain's rapidly altering future. The practicability as well as the justice and economic desirability of this proposal have been abundantly shown by all kinds of pioneer experiments. Different new courses of many varied types now seem likely to keep 75 percent or more in school until the age of 16 by 1970, no matter whether that is made the statutory school-leaving age or not. In addition, as we have seen, a growing number are taking on further training afterwards. Whatever the merits or demerits of comprehensive schools as such, self-differentiation in formative and evocative situations is proving more reliable and popular than "eleven-plus" could ever be. Distinguished public figures deploring the wastage of known ability (to say nothing of unobserved talent), simply because it does not fit the Procrustean bed of old scholasticism, accelerate the trend toward "comprehensiveness" —not always in so called "comprehensive schools."

A few rural areas in England and Wales have had near-comprehensive common schools for a long time, usually for reasons of economy. In Scotland the common school for all children has been the traditional arrangement, though not in a way that gave all children an equal degree of consideration. Scottish schools have always tended to be formal, and to push academic children and academic subjects forward even if this has snubbed other interests and children with other possibilities. The teachers have urged promising scholars toward the university, which has always been the lot of a larger proportion than in England; but the slower and less bookish pupils have been somewhat neglected. Englishmen know the very high regard Scots have for education, and their conspicuous success in getting top jobs in England; but Scottish experience has not been called in support of English comprehensive schools because Scottish practice in the smaller towns was not "comprehensive" in the European or American sense. Indeed, large Scottish towns have English-style selective grammar schools or "academies."

It seems probable that home experiments, and the example of the Scandinavian countries and other communities with high educational standards, will lead eventually to an extension of the comprehensive pattern. But British conditions do not favor a clean sweep of the board. There are too many alternative private enterprises that might spoil prospects. Centuries of experiment have also sanctified certain values in school life that will not lightly be abandoned. Besides, it is altogether unrealistic in British circumstances to ignore the incalculable influence the Public Schools have far beyond their own proper domain. The comparative egalitarianism of modern Britain has been achieved by the expansion of privilege through competitive opportunity. When Britons talk about equality of opportunity they usually mean an impartial competition. With their specially favorable staffing ratio, their manifest scholastic advantages of many kinds, and still more, the less definable intangibles that secure their possessors' success in all the "interview situations" with which British life abounds—with all these, the Public Schools are still in a paramount competitive position. This is a factor no champion of the people can ignore when he is thinking of how to reconstruct what Americans and Canadians call public schools, that is, those supported out of taxation. It is, therefore, not surprising that any development of comprehensive schools (which many are committed to) will be hedged about with all kinds of safeguards for the many excellent qualities that the publicly maintained grammar schools have already displayed.

Approximately half the pupils in grammar-type schools now attend until they are 18. The vast majority of all children leaving school at 15 or 16 go to work. A small proportion enter professional or commercial schools for such things as typing and shorthand, which often are still omitted from ordinary schools. All young people under the age of 18, if not already in full-time attendance, are expected to attend part-time education during the day. Very many do, though postwar difficulties have delayed the establishment of County Colleges for this purpose as foreseen in the 1944 Act. (Only a very small number of experimental ones have been established.) In addition, about one-tenth of those who have left school sooner or later attend either vocational or general-interest courses. A rich and varied provision for adult education of all kinds is typical of Britain. Much is of high quality, though relatively little is directed toward university degrees or diplomas. Local authorities are bound by law to ensure that a complete range of liberal and/or professional education is available in their areas. Some of it they provide; some of it is started independently but earns support from taxation. Aid is generously given.

British universities, as we have noticed, are highly specialized places; they accept already specialized students at the level where most American colleges leave off. Many professional subjects found in American universities are not featured in British universities, but are trained for in other kinds of college which award or prepare for professional diplomas. Despite an almost doubled postwar population, British universities are far from satisfying the demand for places.[3] The 1962 figure of about are far from satisfying the demand for places.[3]

---

[3] The Robbins Report on *Higher Education* (1963), adopted by the government, proposed: six new universities immediately in addition to those already projected; the establishment of 5 "special institutions for scientific and technological education and research"; the upgrading of the colleges of advanced technology to be degree-granting technological universities; the upgrading to university status of 10 regional colleges, Colleges of Education, and other central institutions (with more later, as their provision matured); opportunities for absorption of some college departments into universities. Institutions of "further education" below university status should continue to provide university-level courses, but a Council for National Academic Awards could award degrees to those of their students not migrating to university departments before graduation. A constant upward flow and continuing evolution were envisaged.

These alterations could be largely based upon existing institutions, if rapidly expanded. Because of the supply of well qualified students from schools, there need be no loss of standards. Numbers would expand to 506,000 by 1980, of which 350,000 would be in universities. Corresponding figures for 1973 would be: total, 392,000; universities, 219,000; Colleges of Education, 122,000; and 51,000 in further education. (In 1963 there were 130,000 in universities; 55,000 in Colleges of Education; and 31,000 in "further education"). All the above figures refer to full-time students.

Not only in numbers and size, however, but also in character, higher education in Britain is in a process of rapid evolution. There were 25 British universities in 1962, several of them with distinct colleges in different places. Four additional universities were designated in regions of the country which hitherto had not been too well served. Though British universities are very much public institutions, in the strict sense of the words there are no state universities. All are privately endowed; all are autonomous; but all receive Treasury grants apportioned by the University Grants Committee. This is a body drawn from the universities themselves and enjoying the greatest respect on all sides. No government or local authority control is exercised over universities, which, however, discharge their public responsibilities quite as well as any public scrutineer could demand, albeit conservatively. The salaries for the various ranks of university teachers are practically uniform throughout the country, there being a small addition for London.

Courses leading to university degrees normally last for three years, occasionally four. Medical degrees take much longer. All universities are coeducational, and all provide for postgraduate research. A very high standard of serious, independent, and critical study is prerequisite to a degree, with a great deal of wide and deep reading. Critical independence is indeed fostered much earlier by the essay-type written work always expected in a grammar school. ("True-false" answers are extremely rare in British education except for diagnostic tests at an elementary stage.) Students' final performance in degree examinations is categorized into classes. A "first class" demands a magnificent performance and an outstanding intellect. It stands its possessor in good stead for many years, if not throughout life. Reference has already been made to the fact that nearly all university students can now obtain grants covering the whole of their tuition fees, and the whole or most of the cost of residence away from home. There is, however, a means test, which is not severe. British students are discouraged from trying to "earn their way through college," which would be almost impossible because of the required study (to say nothing of lower wages than in North America). Higher degrees in British universities are usually difficult to get, demanding long periods of independent work. For example, a Ph.D. in Education from the University of London takes 6 years of full-time study after the first degree, or 10 years of part-time research. Hence a doctorate is still a mark of real distinction even among the members of a university teaching staff. A D.Lit. or D.Sc. is a still higher award, based upon research and substantial publications.

Next to the universities proper came the colleges of advanced technology (until recognized as technological universities "after Robbins"), then major technical colleges teaching at university degree level as well as in preparation for the Diploma in Technology, the National Diploma in Business Studies, and certificates awarded by professional associations in recognition of full professional education. In Britain these take the place of the majority of degrees awarded in American professional colleges. A British university degree is usually a more advanced award, based on a larger body of fundamental knowledge; it does not always (even in the more technological subjects) indicate that very much attention has been paid to the application of research to the daily problems of life and industry, whereas the professional diplomas do. Bankers, accountants, surveyors, architects, and journalists are not usually graduates. The possessor of a university degree was traditionally expected to look toward continuing inquiry and research, or administration, rather than to be preoccupied with the many practical on-the-job adjustments that are increasingly becoming his lot after graduation. The old assumptions are changing, however, especially in "sandwich" courses or in relation to them.

Though colleges of advanced technology were not, strictly speaking, technological universities, they had many features of such institutions. They enjoyed, for example, a wide measure of autonomy, receiving direct grants from the Ministry of Education instead of being dependent upon local resources. Their students were of university caliber, and after taking the Diploma in Technology (which is the award made on the satisfactory conclusion of one of more than a hundred different courses) they can now proceed to postgraduate studies in a university, or to a more "applied" kind of research under guidance for three years which may lead to Membership of the College of Technologists. At this level interchange of university and CAT students and teaching staff was common. Though the Diploma in Technology was not instituted until 1955, it has already had a marked influence on ordinary university courses in science and technology, in which fields some two-thirds of university degrees were already awarded. Moreover, for such *postgraduate* diploma courses as that in Management Studies (established in 1960), university and CAT graduates or diploma holders are combined. It will be seen, therefore, that the most senior of technological colleges prepared their students for university degrees (awarded after an "external" examination by the University of London), for one of the equivalent variants of the Diploma in Technology, for various minor diplomas (not all of graduate equivalence), and for some postgraduate diplomas. During the transition period, many such courses continue.

Some of these courses are followed on a full-time basis; but a large and perhaps increasing number are "sandwich" courses, that is, there is either an alternation of periods spent in college and in industry, or else a preparatory year in industry followed by a college or university full-time course and rounded off by another year in industry. A majority of courses following the first pattern last for four years, though a substantial minority extend for $4\frac{1}{2}$ or 5 years. A few similar courses can be concluded in 3 full-time years in college which must, however, be followed by a further year's full-time industrial training, so that the overall time spent is about the same.

"Before Robbins," there were 10 colleges of advanced technology. A condition of their status was that they should develop all work at the university level exclusively, at which they have been operating. Not quite at that level, but overlapping it, came the 7 "national colleges" specializing in particular technologies. These also enjoyed considerable independence under their own boards of management. At a somewhat lower level come 27 "regional colleges of technology," whose number may increase to 40, and then over 340 technical colleges offering full-time study with a further 220 for part-time work. These colleges do not enjoy university status in any way (in British terminology); yet more than 175 of them give instruction in one or more technologies at the level of the Higher National Certificate or for one of the newer Higher National Diplomas. The latter, according to a definition of the Ministry of Education, are of a standard which "approaches that of a university pass degree" (i.e., not quite of the honors standard now usually insisted on for a university degree).

So it is obvious that a heavy volume of work comparable with that done in *Technische Hochschulen* in Germany or in colleges and graduate schools of universities in the United States is in Britain undertaken by institutions which for the most part are not recognized as having university equivalence. They offer a kind of pyramid of technological education facilitating the upward progress of able students outside the universities—usually in relation to topical and practical need. Indeed, this manifestly utilitarian outlook may be open to criticism. However, it is a requirement of colleges of advanced technology in Britain (as in their equivalents in the USA) that all students shall take counterbalancing or liberalizing courses in the humanities. The gradual development of this and comparable university-like features is one of the cares of the

Further Education Staff College set up in 1961 to help teachers and administrators of the top-level technical institutions in the development of the most progressive and experimental aspects of their work.

Important though these features are in their own right, they take on an added importance in Britain because of the increasing pressure on all the universities. These are restricted in part by their insistence of very high academic standards within a particular range of scholastic idioms; but this is not the only restrictive factor. Postwar financial difficulties and the great expansion of the sixth forms of schools supplying candidates for admission have caused entrance requirements to be pushed ever higher. An important proportion of seemingly well-qualified students fail to get in. Many of these take up courses in technical colleges. However, dissatisfaction at the method of selection is revealed by the setting up of centralized arrangements for university admissions from 1963–1964 onwards. A pilot scheme had already been tried. Some indication of the bottleneck (even if we allow for double applications or more) is shown by the fact that in 1961 there were 190,000 applications for university admission (by fully qualified candidates) other than at Oxford and Cambridge, while only some 25,000 could be admitted. It is often stated that all who really want to get in can eventually do so, if they have the right qualifications; but when so many are turned away it is obvious that many sound students must be rejected or disheartened by the ruthlessness of it all. Previous school experience and the accidents of home or social background must be influential in such marginal cases.

Technical colleges and colleges of commerce also act as a supplement to grammar schools and technical schools, in that students who have not been to such institutions, or who have not completely succeeded in the examinations taken there, can have an opportunity of doing so. In recent years this aspect too of technical college work has very rapidly increased, and has helped to mitigate the apparent finality of selection for secondary (and subsequent) education at the age of 11. In fact, the boundary between the upper end of many secondary schools of various types and the lower end of technical colleges has been rather hazy for some time, particularly in some districts. Above all, where schools are short of good science teachers or equipment (as may be the case even in some of those schools which enjoy high social prestige) a steady trickle of pupils passes into technical colleges for the two school years leading to the advanced level of the General Certificate of Education, and thus to university entrance. Technical college teachers are often paid more than secondary school teachers, and career prospects are broader and brighter. As the secondary school population grows in size and becomes more exacting in its academic requirements, the undefined territory between school and further education seems likely to become a region for many experiments.

The huge reconstruction of technical education at the higher levels which gathered pace from 1956 onwards has more recently taken under review such ill-defined areas as that between school and further education, either in colleges or in apprenticeships. Britain has no "junior colleges," though notable proposals for them have been made in recent years, entirely superseding such notions as those relating to "county colleges" expressed in the 1944 Education Act. Moreover, the link between school and vocational training, mostly in part-time courses, is unsatisfactory and wasteful. Nearly half a million students (mostly part-time) are struggling through a bewildering labyrinth of courses, examinations and qualifications. Not only is there heavy wastage, itself a consequence of poor counselling; there is also imperfect account taken of the extension and variety of secondary education in many new forms which might lead straight on to further education. Those trained are still only a small proportion of those who, in the interests of industrial efficiency, ought to be. The link between schools and technical training is, accordingly, in full process of being tightened.

The professional education of teachers in Britain is different from what is usual in the older systems of Europe and also from the regular American pattern. It is undertaken in one of two ways. The majority of teachers are admitted to 3-year colleges of education ("training colleges") after a good performance in the General Certificate of Education at Advanced Level in a grammar school. These colleges teach "subjects" of ordinary academic type, also the pedagogical subjects such as psychology and history of education, and they pay much attention to sound teaching methods. A teacher's certificate (not a degree) is awarded on the results of the final examination. This is not conducted by the state but by a university with which the training college is associated for this purpose; but at the end of a probationary year the certificated teacher is "recognized" by the Ministry of Education. Colleges of Education, following the Robbins Report, will also provide for an expanding number of students, new 4-year courses combining with the professional training a degree (B. Ed.) of the university with whose School of Education they are associated. Some able students may transfer to ordinary university studies in mid-course. Many colleges have long wished to develop their "university" aspect; and, in the development of further and higher education at present under way in Britain, this ambition may come closer to fulfillment, though most teachers with certificates teach in junior or secondary schools of the less academic type.

Students who wish to become teachers in academic (that is, grammar) schools or technical schools must normally go to the university and get a degree of the usual Arts or Science type, and follow this with a year's professional course in the Education department of a university. Such a year consists of practical training and theoretical studies. It leads to a teacher's diploma or postgraduate certificate (not a Master's degree). For a Master's or higher degree in Education (as in any other subject) a longer and more arduous postgraduate study involving research is required. For permission to embark on it, a second postgraduate diploma is usually a prerequisite.

It will be noted that a distinction is made between the teachers in grammar schools, who have a longer and more difficult professional education, and the teachers in other schools. There is this further separation, that to teach in a grammar school it is not strictly necessary to have more than the ordinary academic degree without professional follow-up. On the other hand, as we have seen, all teachers have had a sound grammar school education before going on to college and university. This makes impossible the cleavage that is implicit in the older continental pattern of recruitment from different types of secondary school for the two sections of the teaching profession. Moreover, an increasing number of university graduates find their way into teaching in schools of the nongrammar types. This, with the equality of basic pay, helps to alter the internal social structure of the teaching profession in Britain. Moreover, the universities' "Institutes (or Schools) of Education" are in special relationship with the colleges of education in their areas, keeping up their standards with advisory boards, and undertaking the work of examination.

The other kind of segregation from which teachers can suffer— namely, isolation from those who have pursued "liberal arts" or graduate studies—does not apply to graduate teachers in Britain. They start out with just the same sort of university education as the other professions, and they have very often done equally well or better in the same university examinations. They are encouraged to pursue researches and attain postgraduate awards in their original academic fields as well as in "Education." Moreover, those who impart their professional education to them, and those who supervise or administer their work, can usually claim real academic distinction of the best university character as well as sound experience in schools and school problems.

In addition to initial training, teachers have a good deal of in-service training too. The Ministry of Education, the universities, and the local education authorities all provide courses. Numerous advisory pamphlets are published by the Ministry, and also by the teachers' own professional associations. Pamphlets and courses are very far from being only of the "how to do it" variety. Many encourage a critical and independent analysis of contemporary problems.

The British Broadcasting Corporation (BBC) is a national system. It is financed out of public funds collected in the form of a small license fee from each radio owner. There are no advertisements. The BBC's affairs are administered by a largely independent body of experts representing public affairs, entertainment, and the arts and sciences. Programs are generally of a high standard. An hour each morning on one channel is devoted to school broadcasts in sound, and an hour each afternoon. Teachers' and children's pamphlets are issued in connection with this service. Three main programs are provided, with regional variations. The "Third Program" regularly provides talks of a university standard for adults, as well as music and plays of the highest quality. There is also a BBC television service and an independent television system; but school television began only in 1957. Films and all kinds of audio-visual aids are common in schools.

Intellectual and civic life in Britain is also enriched by such officially sponsored but largely self-regulating bodies as the Arts Council (to promote music, the arts, and associated interests) and the National Foundation for Educational Research. A distinctive feature of Britain is the number and variety of tax-supported organizations operating in the public interest and under close public scrutiny, but with an effective measure of independence and self-determination. In addition to these, and on top of services connected directly with schools, there are also official organizations like the Youth Service (catering to the leisure of young people between the ages of 15 and 20), which is organized by the Ministry of Education in association with the LEAs, and the Youth Employment Service, which acknowledges young people's need for help in securing satisfactory and beneficial employment.

It will be recognized that although the United Kingdom is in many ways a near-socialist republic, committed to what its critics call the welfare state and what its supporters call the social services program, it is still custom-bound and strongly conservative. The "rights of man" are not talked about; they are acted upon. Life seems to most overseas visitors very orderly and polite and loyal. There are no flags in British schools, except in the cupboard for rare display, and there is no daily declaration of allegiance. Strangely enough, there is always a "corporate act of worship" and there is also religious instruction of an agreed non-denominational kind (except in Church schools). Pupils can withdraw from both of these on conscientious grounds. Yet surveys made in 1957 showed that only 14 percent of all denominations go to church on Sunday; 70 percent believed in God, but only 41 percent in a personal God; 85 percent believed that Christians need not go to church. Church attendance, Bible reading, and formal observance are taken less seriously each year. Crimes of violence, drunkenness, and the like have greatly increased again in recent years; but still they are proportionally little or no worse than they were fifty years ago. Policemen are not armed. Young people's sexual morals are much slacker than they were; but they are still more conventional than serious surveys indicate for many comparable countries.

What are the controls? Custom, and self-regulation through the many types of association and belonging that every Briton takes for granted. One of these is the school, with its strong emphasis on character-strengthening, though far less socialization goes on than in American schools, the emphasis being on responsible personality. "Student government" of the American type is also very rare indeed; but one way and another the prefect and "house" systems and all the numerous societies communicate a similar message in a more paternalistic way. Parents and teachers expect and get considerable respect. Education at school and home is not "child-centered"; but in the better homes and schools children are given "equal consideration in equal circumstances." There is still much loosening-up to do, however, and a need for more diversity with subtler reaction to a changing world. The old social structure (with its injustices) and the old international situation (with its imperial advantages) are changing faster than habits. The schools' increased opportunities are bringing about a social revolution; but many of their assumptions remain conservative.

Some time-honored criteria need to be changed. The premium on certain kinds of ability, on certain "gentlemanly" subjects and mannerisms, on certain professions—all this needs re-evaluation in a transformed social and international context. "Character training" of the old-fashioned defensive (or "stuffed shirt") type can well be replaced by an informed and active social responsibility. In some ways this change has begun; but it needs to be speeded up, systematized, and also communicated to that majority who previously had little dynamic character training in school. The old constraints that made conventional proprieties seem inevitable are now relaxed. It would be a pity if emancipation brought no positive opportunities for learning civic and personal responsibility.

Honesty demands the admission that, as an official document said before the 1944 Education Act, most British children still suffer (to use a photographic metaphor) from being underexposed, underdeveloped, and under-fixed educationally. British education is not popular in the strict sense of the word. Too many people slip through its meshes affected only didactically; too few find much relationship with their lives; too many think of it as restrictive or childish. By contrast with other English-speaking countries, British schools (and still more their social consequences) often seem complacent and unevocative.

If ever the old school patterns had a real and persistent virtue in themselves (as distinct from the homes where they were cherished) they cannot automatically diffuse virtue to a wider population now in a world that has altered so much. For educational no less than hard economic reasons, much more understanding and responsibility will have to be rehearsed in workaday situations—in relation to jobs, on the job, and through the job. Jobs are still considered altogether too much in terms of knowledge, proficiency, and examination-type excellence—whether we are thinking of plumbers or professors of Greek and Latin. Therefore personality, citizenship, and broader humanity tend to be either taken for granted or developed in a purely hortative way (as in old-style adult education classes). This is a danger particularly acute in Britain, for at least two reasons. British society is so rich in manifold types of "belonging," in venerable public and private associations—each with its own system of rehearsal in public or private virtues—that decency and human dignity seem to happen naturally without cultivation. But the old-fashioned matrices of social decency need to be replaced or modernized. The second reason is that even now it is often assumed that the more admirable characteristics of man belong to a special class of society, and can probably not be associated with "common" people engaged in "common" pursuits at work or play. Only a few diehards dare to put such thoughts in words; but the schools often exemplify them in stratification, isolationism, or other-worldliness.

Now that a vast proportion of Britons, previously underprivileged, are not only "in the money" but determined to show themselves as good as their neighbors, it is urgently necessary to repudiate the old suspicion that they are essentially inferior or uncultivable because they do not display certain kinds of intellectual nimbleness. It is equally necessary to call for and reward more fully a really responsible copartnership in industry and public affairs. Millions of Britons and hundreds of their towns still show deep scars of former contemptuous treatment and near-servitude. It is difficult for them not to feel hostility and a "two nations" attitude toward the privileged, especially as "parity of esteem" and "equality of access" are still so far from being achieved in the nation's schools. If the schools could really become the people's institutions, linked effectively with the learning of a job or other daily preoccupations, and leading to a fairer range of the professions, more would be done to combine "cultural" considerations, "gentlemanly" attitudes, and civic responsibility with the interests of what are still sometimes called "working class" children.

External history and internal social change have brought about a revolution in Britain more radical than some countries have achieved with bloody cataclysms. Some have been swept into totalitarianism for less. Others have been driven to reactionary conservatism. British habits of "muddling through" have made it possible to retain what seems to be the "best of the old" amidst a desperate struggle to come up to date. Britain's attempt to establish social justice is orderly and likely to succeed, though for efficiency no less than social justice some downright alteration of the school system is long overdue. The schools of Britain are the chief instruments of social change—more so than in most countries; but only a radical alteration of the school's orientation as well as of their practices can help a formerly imperial and hierarchical country to live effectively in its present circumstances. Britain needs an alert and coordinated adjustment (itself flexible and changing) to the world which she has done so much to transform— economically, socially, scientifically, and politically.

chapter 5

THE UNITED STATES OF AMERICA

A Nation on Wheels

The United States has been aptly described as "the great experiment." It is a nation very largely made by conscious human contrivance. The building of it during the past century and a half has been in accordance with plans originally devised for universal human betterment—though, of course, Nature and chance and human vagaries have all helped to baffle the calculator. Nevertheless, as things stand, the United States is a nation second to none in international power, superior to all in its material standards of living, and probably fourth in the size of its population (180 million in 1961). Only China, India, and the Soviet Union are more populous.

If it were not that its educational devices and its history have welded a passionate nationhood, the United States might be a loose federation. Its territories are vast. The area of the continental United States is over 3½ million square miles, little short of that of the whole of Europe. If the moon could be imagined as a disk laid flat on the map of the United States, the Atlantic and the Pacific coastal states would be well exposed at the sides. The Northern states have severe winters, during which the farmers gaze for months on a lonely white landscape dotted at rare intervals with clustered farm buildings; while in the South at the very same time the roses are in bloom on New Year's Day, and the streets are lined with date palms. Between the near-tropical splendors of the Gulf coast and the Northern silences there is almost every imaginable type of terrain—gentle green lands like England, huge mountain areas where great forests are smoky with mist,

plains of vast extent, the Rocky Mountains bare and wild enough
for the moon itself, extensive and fantastic deserts, mangrove swamps
that are the homes of ibis and alligator, and the Pacific pines and
orange groves. It is not surprising that even without conscious encouragement the settlers who struggled out into this remarkably diverse country developed strong regional characteristics. The mere winning of a livelihood must so often have been a fight for self-vindication. In such circumstances men are bound to work out their own
way, and if they were refugees from other people's dictation (as so
many of these settlers were) autonomy and self-sufficiency were doubly
valued.

As though the lessons of sheer survival were not enough, the men
and women who made North America their home very often brought
with them systems of religious or secular government that were schools
of self-sufficiency also. Except in the oldest colonies settled by Englishmen, congregational types of parish regulation and of civil jurisdiction were transplanted from England to a freedom for development
that they had never fully known at home. Self-determination became
not merely customary but a right and a virtue. Indeed, even the
oldest colonies with their hierarchical and regal administrations championed universal claims for unrestricted self-government and self-development when the time came for a breakaway. To this very day
this is the core of America's message for the future, her central legend.
And the legend is supported by facts. There are not merely fifty sovereign states; there is a most thoroughgoing decentralization of authority even in towns and villages. These are called cities in the American idiom when they are incorporated, though by British standards the
majority of these self-governing communities are very small. Certain
powers are reserved to counties, as in Britain; but the over-all tendency
is to encourage decentralization wherever possible.

Among modern and fully developed nations, the United States is
the supreme example of a decentralized system. This characteristic
applies particularly to school arrangements. Each state is sovereign in
regard to education. It determines the length of compulsory schooling,
makes its own school laws, sets standards for teacher training and
recruitment, and so on. Yet these definitions may be considered the
outside boundaries which, though strictly enforced, permit local initiative to enjoy a great deal of latitude. A city usually has its own
school system, which it pays for substantially out of its own revenues;
it can go far beyond the minimum requirements of state legislation

EDUCATIONAL SYSTEM IN THE UNITED STATES

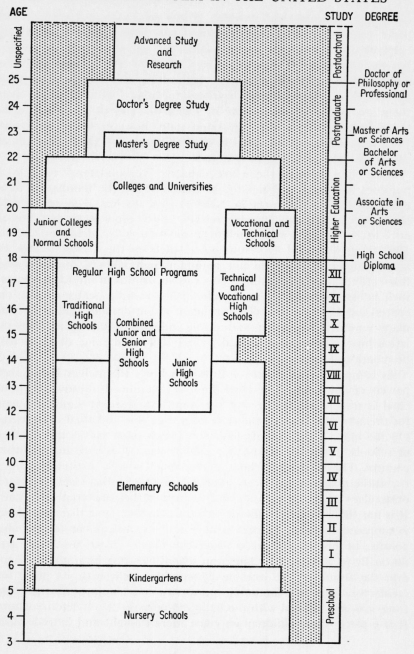

in what it demands and provides; it can set its own curriculum and make ordinances of a very detailed and independent kind. Unincorporated communities are regulated by school district or county boards. One state (Delaware) has a unitary state system. The size and resources of these education authorities vary greatly. The City of New York, for example, legislates for many more children than there are in the whole country of Denmark, and in an equally centralized way. Within the very same state, however, there were also 7912 responsible school districts in 1937, some of them very much poorer in ideas as well as in resources.

Since then, as over the whole country, "consolidation" for school purposes has proceeded rapidly, so that by 1960 the number of fully responsible school districts in New York State was reduced to 596. Discrepancies are still amazing within nearly every state, but this is only to be expected where self-determination is so highly prized. In 1960 there were still 47,594 school districts in the United States. A large number of these do not maintain high schools, however, and fewer still have college facilities. For various reasons of interdependence, such as basic financial help and scholarship awards, greater reliance on centralized direction has been growing in recent decades. There are also many unofficial sources of centralizing influence—quite apart from relationships with state or federal government—and some of these will be mentioned later.

As compared with those of Britain, schools themselves have small powers of autonomy. The curriculum is determined already; the principal is responsible to the city (or county or district) superintendent for the administration of the state education law and local ordinances. On the other hand, parents have very much more say in the running of schools and policy-making for schools than they have in any other country. The American school is very much a folk institution. From the earliest days it has been intended to respect the ideas (religious or secular) of its community and to further their material ambitions. It is not the channel of officially correct enlightenment that the school is supposed to be in France; neither is it an instrument for the dispensing of norms and graces from the upper classes, as it was traditionally in Britain. The American school has long been an extension into the future of the working community itself, with its plans for satisfactory jobs and for public prosperity and comfort. At the same time, it is also imbued with the hallowed purpose of self-determination. It is a place where children are given more thought and latitude than

they enjoy in any other school system. The somewhat contradictory influences of the community and of the individual's own growth requirements are discernible in any American school to a very marked degree.

The typical American school (though it is dangerous to talk in such
terms of a land so diverse) is a bright and cheerful place. With their
generous supply of impressive pictures, the American information
services have familiarized the world with how the schools look in
any go-ahead city (and that is what each American community considers itself). There is certainly an American flag; in fact, one may
be displayed in each classroom. Well-fed children in a gay variety of
clothes—all the more informal because the interior is very warm—
evidently feel that the school is their very own place. Mobile desks
and chairs facilitate rearrangements for group work and other types
of "sharing" (a hallowed word). Books are very well illustrated and
expensively produced; their contents are directly related to problems
within the child's daily interests. They are usually weighty in the
literal sense only. There is practically no suggestion anywhere that
they represent authority. Nor does the typical teacher, if it comes to
that. The school is a place where a community of children is housed,
with suitable personnel to help them realize themselves in their world,
and with suitable aids of other sorts. In their material aspect the classrooms are often lavish, including not merely pictures and wall charts
(many devised by the children themselves) but radio, films, and television in the bigger schools. Considering the generosity with which these
audio-visual aids are provided, a European is sometimes surprised at the
relative lack of apparatus for children to use in a search for knowledge
(that is, microscopes or lenses or simple scientific apparatus). However,
there is abundant provision of wood and metal and automobile work-
shops in schools of any size for older children, and "home economics"
for girls is efficiently and gracefully taught.

In this very point of contrast with many European schools we find
something distinctively American. A twofold emphasis prevails in the
United States: practice in skills directed toward visible and practical
ends; and a suggestion that manipulations enjoyed (as in a construc-
tional workshop) have a near-absolute merit in themselves irrespective
of whether they contribute to human knowledge and happiness or not.
Europeans are struck by these assumptions in schools and teachers of
all types. Under American conditions they are more to be expected
quite apart from the prevalence of Dewey-sponsored philosophy and
methods. Indeed one may say that Dewey was a spokesman and

philosophical planner for the basic assumptions of the typical American school. Regard for knowledge is often limited to its instrumental value —not a bad notion if we take a farsighted and comprehensive view of human problems. The criterion for its usefulness must be conceived in children's terms; and the children must find their own pace and their own way into the future. These have been the clarion calls of the great European educators from Rabelais through Comenius onwards; but they have received their fullest (though sometimes travestied) realization in the American school. Paradoxically it might be maintained that the Americans are the only true Europeans—the only people who have so far carried out the great traditions of the West with the richness and universality that industrialization has made possible. It certainly seems that these aims, socially speaking, if not always scholastically, come nearest to realization in the best of American schools. Why should this be?

It is impossible to give simple reasons. It is certainly not because Americans care more for education than others. In some ways they do; but foreign visitors usually believe the opposite when they see what American schools do. Nor is it because Americans spend more money on education than others; in proportion to their incomes they do not. Do they love their children more? It would be rash to claim so. It is certainly true that most Americans, living in a rich and still imperfectly exploited country, still feel they can well afford to spare the time and resources necessary for their type of education in a way that no other nation could, just as they can throw away longer cigarette butts and waste more food and use up automobiles faster than other nations. But why should they wish to? There is no need to hazard a complete answer that would be false anyway; but some suggestions are contributed by a glance at American history and America's industrial prospects.

The American settler's eye has always been away from the past, and turned toward the future. The prevailing inclination has always been away from absolute authority and toward some pragmatically justified solution for today and perhaps for tomorrow. "Universals" and "absolutes" often got lost in the rigors of forest and frontier life. We should remember that these hard conditions have not altogether disappeared now, and that they are actual memories of thousands if not millions of grandparents. They still live in the anti-intellectualism of most small provincial cities. Moreover, the conditions of westward expansion—achieved by generations of spasmodic migration at walking pace, from scarcely established settlements out into an unknown challenge—created and recreated opportunities for women and children no less than for men to show themselves equal in practical use as well as in personal value. Accuracy of shooting, skill with the ax and plough, toughness in the face of acute physical distress—all these things superseded old-style parental and governmental authority. They left no room for a leisured class making "culture" its playground or badge of office. They also made more tenuous the old interpretations of churches, and made new dispensations seem not merely inevitable but right. Criteria of immediate expediency must often have been the only law in many pioneer settlements. It would not have been surprising if cynical ruthlessness had become the characteristic of American society, which after all is a very new and relatively untried thing outside the older Atlantic settlements. Instead, the traditional British experience that self-government is responsible government, and the often consciously religious sense of a "manifest destiny" that was missionary, added a leaven of self-righteousness to practical considerations. This has from time to time resulted in wild extravagances, of course. The long-term results have included both a keen concern that children should be brought up to be useful and civilized, and a feeling that the children's frontiers should not necessarily be the same as that facing the parents at present.

Moreover, the inclusion of many non-American and non-British immigrants in the pioneer settlements dotted at immense intervals over this vast land strengthened the conviction that the future belonged especially to the children now brought up to be Americans in a country strange to the parents. Conditions for growing up were at least unfamiliar. On the whole they were more evocative and richer in rewards than the parents had known in their day, though they were sometimes very much worse, as is seen in the conspicuous degeneration of some mountain communities derived principally from the purest English stock. Even now, the sense of an ever-moving frontier and of an horizon of limitless possibilities is a most infectious experience for the visitor welcomed to an American community. Indeed, the very richness and reality of that welcome has a bearing on Americans' attitude to education. There is room for you, even with your odd speech and odder ways. If you can "make out" you will be all right too. This sounds as though there is no need to conform, and in some ways there is great freedom from such a requirement; but it is necessary to stress in advance the reverse or compensatory side of American life, which is one of the most highly socialized patterns on earth. However, in so far as we are considering the effect on children's relationships with their elders, we have to note the extraordinary degree of self-determination or self-justification permitted to the children and indeed expected of them.

This theme could be pursued at length; but we have to pass on to the influence of monumental mechanization in a land already abundant in natural resources—so rich, in fact, that the production of food is widely restricted by government subsidies. Each hour worked in the United States produces more goods than anywhere else on earth. This is not individually true of all Americans in all their occupations, of course; but it is true on the average. The amount of mechanization, and its intricacy, have become a byword throughout the world. American pure science has a glorious record of its own in recent years; but Americans are much more successful in the application of scientific discoveries to practical problems. Britain pioneered the world of industrialization; Germany and other European nations have been in the forefront of pure scientific research; until recently only a few of the great leaders in this field have been Americans; but no country has been so overwhelmingly successful in turning its own and other people's discoveries to the production of material abundance. This is partly due to the blessings of geography and the quirks of history; but credit must also be given to the restless ingenuity of Americans, native born and immigrant, in making more things mechanically—and therefore more cheaply in the long run.

Unlike India and similar nations where excessive manpower combined with land shortage and lack of capital make mechanization a prospect full of problems, the United States is constantly concerned with underconsumption of its brimming production. Sales campaigns daily and by every conceivable means urge Americans to use more or at any rate to buy more of everything. So they do. American economists truly tell us that their whole economy is geared to reckless consumption, if not to waste. In an almost closed economy that is nearly independent of imports and exports, no immediate harm is felt at home; but there are many and varied social results which directly or indirectly affect the educational pattern. Some of these must be postponed for later consideration; but one aspect at least is of present importance.

In the present state of American "know-how," a very extensive adoption of automation would offer no serious mechanical or managerial problems. Yet it is very unlikely to take place in the immediate

future. Why? Because even now there is little need for young people
to go to work at an early age or to earn their way in the world. It is
increasingly anticipated that young men and women need not be professionally qualified before the age of 25 or thereabouts. Even now
the chances of their holding down a really skilled job in a post of
responsibility are postponed year by year. That is not to say that
Americans do not work hard—they do indeed; but their final involvement in occupations at normal adult American status is perceptibly
later as time goes on. Excellent wages can be earned anyway in
unskilled or semiskilled positions if necessary. If automation were
allowed to reach its full logic, it is difficult to forecast the outcome
in the United States. As things are now, the schools are unmistakably
faced with a custodial (rather than a training) problem that is unfamiliar in other countries. The difficulty is not that of getting boys
and girls ready professionally in the shortest possible time, so that
they can help with the national housekeeping; it might until recently
have been somewhat unkindly described as that of keeping young
Americans happily and rather profitably occupied as long as possible
before getting them ready. American abundance, it was long thought,
could well afford this kind of paternal indulgence. Parents were proud
that it was so. Criticisms of American education based upon its slow
progress (at any rate in the typical school) miss a very important educational assumption, and also underestimate the interplay of economic
and scholastic considerations which are vital to a fair interpretation
of any educational system.

In the years since 1957, however, Americans themselves have accelerated and broadened the critical enquiries with which a minority
among them had seemed to support criticism from outside. Evidence of
Soviet technical progress stung discerning Americans like a challenge;
reliance to anything like the previous extent on foreign-born or foreign-
educated researchers and instructors might be a security risk; and
such home-based criticism as that contained in the writings of Dr.
J. B. Conant raised many questions about equality of opportunity and
the quality of much publicly supported schooling. The National Defense Education Act of 1958 by its very title and orientation aroused
the country to the implementation of its domestic and international
responsibilities. The magnificent achievements of the space research
programs have in recent years enthused the youth of America as well
as educational leaders—all the more tellingly because of initial anxieties.
From inside the United States it seems as though the great ferment

going on—with evidences of increasing competition, "higher horizons," and national merit scholarship awards—is rapidly transforming the educational system.

This may indeed be the consequence over an extended period of time; but short of a national disaster any radical and overall revision of a such diverse agglomeration of localized experiments seems unlikely in the extreme. At any rate for the youngest Americans, the schools seem to retain their national characteristics. As late as July 29, 1962, *The New York Times* reported a survey of elementary school textbooks under the significant title "Baby Talk," and complained of the proven deterioration of English in college students.

School is still a sort of oasis, a happy land shielded from the stresses and competitions of adult life—a children's garden in more senses than Froebel's *Kindergarten* was ever expected to be. Latter-day prosperity combined with the love and promise for children that are traditional in America have made the modern American school a wonderful place in every material way. Observers from other countries will find much to profit by; but they will also find every school a playground of paradox such as they have not encountered elsewhere, for the simple reason that no other country's schools are either as experimental or as favored as those in the United States. Some detailed instances of paradox will be examined later. It is important to emphasize here that although the American school is very "realistic" in terms of child-centered education as a rule, it postpones the child's realization that the world is not child-centered or even (with all respect) America-centered. Gone are the frightening bugbears of other countries (examinations, corporal punishment, child labor, and so on); but perplexities of a different kind may be detected, as we shall see.

In the United States the effects of school life are more marked than elsewhere, for several reasons. The building of the American nation into an independent federation was a pre-scholastic task; but the assimilation of millions of immigrants' children (a problem just as difficult today as previously) and the establishment of a technologically advanced society were the responsibility of American schools and colleges. American education has had more to do than most other public systems, not least because of the remarkable mobility of the American scene.

Another reason is that even at the college or university level it is usual to speak of "school." If an Englishman asks which school you went to, he is quizzing you about whether Eton or Winchester or some other Public School can claim the credit for you. By the same question an American is asking you which university you enjoyed. Moreover, in the United States that is a friendly and not a snobbish question (as it would tend to be in Britain) because it is assumed that you went to college anyway. Soon after World War II one-third of the then adult population had finished high school (that is, they had stayed on until 18 years old); nowadays about 95 percent of the children are in school from ages 6 to 17 or 18. In towns of any size perhaps a third of these will sooner or later get to college. Perhaps a higher proportion will have a little experience of it. The terms "college" and "university" are regularly used as synonyms in the United States, and both are included under the comprehensive term "school." This significant extension of use for "school" indicates a continuation of juvenile guardianship not found in other countries' universities. Therefore "school" in America covers a much larger proportion of the population for a much longer period than elsewhere.

Moreover, for the reasons already outlined, school is from the very beginning a place where children find their own way of life in their own community, and where the psychological compulsion is away from elders' authority and leadership. Socialization (in the psychologists' sense) is extremely marked, not only because it is inevitable in the circumstances but also because parents wish it to happen too. Some schools have observation rooms with a one-way screen behind which parents and other observers can watch progress. Needless to say, mothers have many questions to ask; but the first one in nearly every case concerns junior's sociability. It would be absurd to make much of this inquiry if it were not followed up to the very end of school life by similar anxieties. Without exactly setting out deliberately to do so, the American school pays enormous attention to "community mobilization" at the junior level. In certain spheres of socialization the American school is bound to take priority. We have already remarked on the need felt by many immigrants' children for emancipation into the new world of which they will be citizens. Long-settled countries with innumerable normative mannerisms and manifold rehearsal systems in public life do not need to have overt standardization programs like the Americanization which extends down from the level of adult immigrants to every newcomer in the American school. Every school day begins with a salute to the American flag and a declaration of loyalty. This little ceremonial, at first embarrassing to a visitor who takes loyalty for granted, is not attended to perfunctorily but with some solemnity.

Seen dispassionately it shows once again the community emphasis of American schooling, which is brought out again daily if not hourly by many activities involving corporate work, in elective pupil bodies organizing particular aspects of school work and play, and in a remarkable concern lest any child be unusual. Until Sputnik, many parents worried lest any child appeared intellectually outstanding, though there were no inhibitions about being especially good on the sports field. However, inadequacy in the more glamorous sports is not by any means total failure in the bid for popularity, because all kinds of opportunities are provided for each child to be at least in something the king of the hour. The pace and scope of school life are skillfully regulated to minimize any appearance of competition, at any rate on anything like a non-American scale. Despite what Americans believe to be a great increase in competition recently, their system has still to be described (in comparison with other countries) as one generally lacking serious competition inside schools or as between schools. This is true despite wide differences in standards, for differences may be ignored or unappreciated. However, some diminution of competition may be a needed corrective in a society that is economically so competitive and sets its social sights so high; but it makes a school's pace seem laggard by any European standard, and it often makes children's behavior seem lackadaisical. Many Americans do not use such a critical word. They see what the foreigner sees but they approve. However, growing numbers are increasingly worried by what they feel to be a lowering of intellectual levels, a devitalizing of initiative, and the risk of uniformity. These are charges that ring strangely in the land of independence and enterprise, and we shall have to examine them more closely in due course.

The American school has innumerable successes to attribute to this very process of assimilation. Children of all types of orientation and from very unequal social backgrounds are taken in to receive a new and promising status. The hardships and perhaps coarseness of the older America are being effaced by an easy-going gentleness in personal relations. To this is added the very real chance of social mobility through access to an unlimited range of jobs. Children whose forebears less than a hundred years ago were red-necked frontiersmen in a one-street wooden town (or perhaps even in this century thought a thirty-mile journey an occasion for a three-day visit) are now cosmopolitan Americans with a world of opportunity open to their confidence. Ethnic, religious, and social backgrounds are little handicap to those of European stock. That is more than could be said in most countries of Europe. Moreover, Americans as a rule are tolerant and generous. They are characterized by a real if not always very logical reverence for the great human principles of the Renaissance and the Enlightenment. In some ways they are the only true Europeans. The American common school can claim the credit for that.

That is why "the little red schoolhouse" has a place of real affection in American legend. This is no mere nostalgia for childhood; it is also a record of appreciation for an institution that, like the trundling covered wagons and the railroad, has made modern America possible. Those who observe the United States from outside, or even from the big cities, should not imagine that the schools of today are all huge and glossy. The average size of American schools is probably around four or five hundred children, though in all large towns and cities schools with two thousand children and more are now common. An uncountable number of American schools are still literally of the "red schoolhouse" type, and in most of the states it is easy to find schools that have only one teacher for all the children. The impressively empty countryside that surprises any European is thinly populated with little settlements whose children mainly attend small schools. The automobile and the school bus are slowly transforming school-going; but even in a populous and rich state like California a recent report revealed as many schools of what Europeans would consider a "village one-room" type as of any other. Of course, their total population was small compared with that attending consolidated country schools or city institutions. Consolidation is a growing practice. The yard of most country schools now shows a row of old-style yellow buses waiting throughout the day to take home the children they rounded up that morning. It is characteristic of American assumptions that in some areas these buses are driven by senior schoolboys. The traffic in the vicinity of schools (even in busy towns) is also normally regulated by the children themselves; they wear distinctive white helmets and other insignia.

The consolidation of schools is more economical, in teachers' salaries, in heating, and in other expenses; but above all it gives the children in remoter areas a much better chance of effective and lengthy education than they would otherwise have. School attendance is sometimes very difficult to enforce in the poorer rural areas. Some school-district authorities are far from being as diligent as the rest in attending to this matter. Moreover, even if children are brought to school the educational opportunity set before them varies considerably in extent and quality. Local committees decide fairly freely how much money they are able (or willing) to spend on education. States usually make some gesture toward equalization by subsidizing the poorer areas; yet great inequality prevails not only within any state but between the states themselves. This is one of the major problems in American education.

Cities acting as manufacturing or trading centers and thus serving a rural territory as a local metropolis very often have much better education facilities than their supporting hinterland. Indeed, within any urban area living off a single economic complex we may find several "cities" that are educationally independent and are endowed with schools of different quality because local tax resources and policy vary. Sometimes this variation depends on the social class or ethnic composition of the population, though not always. In no modern nation is it possible to find greater inequality of access to education from different localities. This is one of the penalties to be paid for such complete decentralization.

It is always a source of astonishment to people outside the United States that public school systems in the favored residential districts outside Chicago, Detroit, Boston, or Cleveland (for example) manifest most of the characteristics of private schools elsewhere. It is true that they are public in the sense of being maintained by that section of "the people" who are privileged enough to live locally, and that the schools are open to all local residents (as a rule). But effective zoning of one sort or another in a land of commuters often enables a community to boast that it has "the best school system in the United States," or in its own state. Preferential salary rates, experimental and career opportunities, or even ephemeral fame make the educational provision extremely disparate. Indeed, the mischances of residential fashion may make a district's school level fluctuate violently within a single decade. In 1959, F. M. Hechinger said: "The American school as we know it today does not offer anything resembling fair and equal opportunities." [1] Since that time discrepancies have grown, not diminished, though this fact is usually overlooked or disguised from "the people."

---

[1] F. M. Hechinger, *The Big Red Schoolhouse*. New York: Doubleday & Company, Inc., 1959.

Responsible officials and legislators in every state do their best to "level up"; but there are limits beyond which it is nearly impossible to drive American local sentiment, especially as it is institutionalized in local politics. Education is a political matter not only in the sense that it is a matter of universal public demand, but also because American devotion to "Jacksonian" or "grass roots" democracy causes many offices (such as school superintendent) to be elective in many districts, even though most foreigners think this notion as crazy as the idea of having elected engineers or elected physicians. In Britain, for example, educational officials are professional, though they are closely supervised by the "watchdog" lay committees who finally determine policy. But then county districts in the United States may also have elected judges, elected tax assessors, and so on. It all goes to show how firm is the belief that schools must be not only under electoral supervision but directly under electoral (i.e., parental) manipulation.

In practice it does not appear that children altogether gain from this Jacksonian approach, at any rate in poor communities. Many schools certainly lack the enviable facilities of better placed neighbors. Teachers' salaries vary enormously, not only between states but sometimes inside a single state. In 1959–1960 the average school salary in California was $6525 per annum; in New York State it was $6400; in Arkansas $3245; in Mississippi $3175. In 1960 extreme ranges were about $2000 for beginners in some rural states to over $10,000 for fully qualified men in some Eastern high schools. There are different requirements for recognition as trained teachers, different pension and promotion prospects. The absence of uniform arrangements in these relatively uncontroversial matters means that the standards of professional skill and academic knowledge vary too, even from district to neighboring district.

However, American parents are normally free from the sort of anxieties that plague British parents, for example. The typical family, enjoying middle-class standards of affluence, lives in a town well-served by schools. In fact, before any neighborhood is built, sites are set aside for publicly provided and maintained schools. They can be seen marked on ordinary local maps by those wondering about the location of their new house. Every child, it is assumed, will go to the school in his neighborhood. It will probably be as good as the next one in the same district or town. At least, that is the traditional expectation, though we shall soon see that this may need to be modified. At any rate, little question arises of additional private expense in search of a "superior" accent or other desirable social badges. Of course, some snobbery exists as in all human institutions; but it is trivial by other countries' standards as a rule, being mainly confined to differences in clothes and in family automobiles. However, fine houses are the latest status symbol in the United States, and if present tendencies continue they will certainly affect the choice of residence (and therefore, in many cases, school district) greatly. They will accentuate a discernible trend to differentiate the quality of tax-supported schooling according to the parents' income and social position, inextricably bound up as these are with questions of housing. Indeed, growing post-Sputnik anxieties are making the best-informed parents directly relate their choice of residence to the proved existence of "good" (that is, more demandingly academic) schools in the neighborhood. The ever-growing "commuting" distance traveled from home to workplace makes it just as easy to colonize a good school area as to colonize the perimeter of a country club or golf course, which cynics often say amounts to one and the same area.

However, not many parents are wealthy enough to satisfy such ambitions, and in any case the overwhelming majority do not have the information or criteria by which to judge scholastic merits or demerits; for, after all, the same names and mannerisms and the same amount of time for various activities may equally characterize quite distinct kinds of school provision. Therefore the typical American school is, and will doubtless continue to be, the neighborhood school. The sort of open or hidden enquiry about "which school?" that is usual in England would be either incomprehensible or disgraceful. The number of private schools in America (that is, excluding the parochial schools which in most respects resemble public schools) is small, though growing significantly. The public schools afford as high a standard of intellectual life as most Americans want; otherwise they would do far more about them. Under American conditions of school management they have every opportunity to do so. As it is, the schools offer a higher standard of social apprenticeship than any other country can boast. That is not to say that many things—personal, social, and academic—could not be improved without doing violence to American susceptibilities; it is simply meant to indicate that the American child on the whole benefits greatly by attending his local school rather than any other. The outstanding American child, over a wide range of talents, can usually win through to any desired distinction with the additional gain of a real understanding of what other people's qualities and problems are.

Though Americans are great churchgoers (about 80 percent of them being regular attenders at church) the public schools are all secular. In some states a minimal amount of Bible reading is permitted; but this is unusual. The private schools (including the denominational or parochial schools, a high proportion of which are Catholic) enroll only about 15 percent of the children. It should be noted that the number in private schools has risen sharply from 10 to 15 percent in about a decade, perhaps on social and academic grounds as much as religious. This is a reflection of dissatisfaction, therefore, and of willingness to pay for something better; for private schools receive no support from taxes for their programs, buildings, or equipment. Religion is considered to be a matter for the home. In fact, in some states the constitutional separation of church and state is extended to a refusal to provide public transportation to parochial schools—a ruling which has become a delicate political issue, especially as federal law permits this and also makes food for school meals available to all children.

At the same time, all kinds of inquiries are made in casual conversation about a visitor's religion, as the assumption is that he will have religious beliefs or at any rate observances which he will not mind discussing as in other countries one discusses hats or favorite sports. It is perhaps an indication of American community pressure that this conformity-of-belonging is so keenly sought, though no one seems to mind what you belong to. In other countries with mixed religious communities, questions about one's personal position in regard to them are often felt to be in the same category as questions about family relationships—suited only to the circle of closest intimacy, and therefore avoided. Advertisements in American papers and in subway trains assume that you will link all kinds of ambitions and commodities with church membership. The critical and most indicative words are perhaps "membership" and "corporate life." A great deal of life goes on round the churches. In comparison with other countries less is said and perhaps less is felt about *being* and believing. As far as the average American child's school is concerned, however, religion is an entirely private matter. There is not, as in France, an attempt to instruct the young in the principles of morality on a secular basis as part of the curriculum; but the stress of community example is powerful. This can have its negative as well as its constructive side, and will be worth examining again when we consider adolescence.

The usual age for beginning school in the United States is 6, though kindergartens exist in many places for children under this age. Seven

of the fifty states require children to attend for 8 years; thirty-three
for 9 years; five for 10 years; three for 11 years; and one for 12 years.
These are the legal minimums. As we have seen, most children attend for about 12 years, and many longer. On the other hand, in many
areas the attendance of rural children, white as well as colored, is
still not really satisfactory though it has greatly improved with the
provision of good consolidated schools to which they are conveyed
without charge by bus. The number of days in the year on which
attendance is required varies a good deal, sometimes for climatic
reasons. For example, in the Deep South temperatures in May (when
school finishes) and October (when it recommences) are stifling.
Again, a lot depends on the energy and concern of the local officials.
The average number of days attended has grown in the past 50 years
from 99 to 156 each year. In Britain the figure is nearer 200; but the
climate there is unusually temperate (if cool), and in a crowded island
there are no real problems of distance.

Boys and girls attend the same school not just in the lowest classes
but throughout. Americans are always surprised to learn that segregation of the sexes is usual in Britain, and are puzzled to know why.
No real problems of any sort—either social or educational—can be
fairly attributed to common schooling, and there are many gains. In
most Northern areas and an increasing number of Southern districts
no formal or systematic attempt is made to keep colored children out
of any particular public school. Until recently 17 of the then 48 states
legally required the separation of whites and Negroes not only in
schools but in public transport and many other places. Several of these
states, all in the South, and not usually distinguished by a high
standard of education, have expressed their determination to resist
United States Supreme Court orders which declare this segregation to
be unconstitutional even if a semblance is maintained of granting
Negroes "separate but equal" opportunity. The most important of
these orders was published on May 17, 1954. Long before that time
the process of allowing Negroes to enroll in hitherto white schools instead of in inevitably inferior Negro schools had gathered momentum.
Since 1954 many school districts even in the South have announced
their intention of complying, and integration has in most such cases
been achieved with little disturbance. The Negro cannot yet be said
to have genuinely equal access to education even in the North; but
during the hundred years since slavery, and especially during the past
generation, the position of Negro children has been transformed with

surprising speed. In 1940 Negroes were undoubtedly the majority of the two million American children between 6 and 15 who were outside any school. Most Americans are now eager that Negro children should have an equal chance, though subtle social distinctions are still maintained in many places by human frailty and selfishness. Equalization has undoubtedly made great progress, but it still has far to go. Not surprisingly, many Americans in socially advantageous positions would greatly prefer the equalizing of opportunity to begin in schools where their own children do not go.

Colored people are predominantly poorer than whites. Some are quite wealthy, and there is a small but expanding Negro middle class; yet the total of those who do not live in very poor districts is still small. It follows that even without formal segregation many colored children will be in schools that are almost entirely Negro. Dwellers in slums and ghettoes throughout the world find that their children suffer during school life from lack of contact with a better or more promising social world. It must be admitted that the standards of attainment, of reading, of interest, and sometimes of civic responsibility prevailing among children from poorer homes compare unfavorably with those expected elsewhere. Although that is no good reason for punishing them further, and no justification for piling up social evils for the future, people do this sort of thing everywhere. In the United States it is particularly tempting to do so, because it is so easy. The recognizable badges of discrimination are distinctive: pigmentation, features, and accent are used to discriminate against Negroes, Japanese, Poles, Jews, Puerto Ricans and other members of the community—even though American born. Moreover, the district system of schooling makes it easy for well-to-do parents to send their children to school in communities where the unwelcome ones are "priced out" or even illegally kept out by the "gentleman's agreements" of house agents.

It is no service to American education or to American civic ideals to pretend that these things do not happen on an extensive scale. It is fairer to record that even so they are neither representative nor in keeping with what Americans officially and unofficially recognize as the ideals of their way of life. In fact, discrimination of all sorts is a diminishing factor in the United States even in respect to the Negro, as anyone can see by comparing present practice with the customs of a generation ago. In connection with this tendency we should stress the assimilative force of the schools' formal and informal socialization processes. It is obviously very important for the children of Poles, Germans, Swedes, Italians, and so on to be undistinguishable Americans. The same is true for the children of any less favored economic group. The common school is a remarkable instrument of social mobility for them. For the United States as a whole it is the indispensable instrument of "the great experiment" of nation building. Those who feel misgivings about some of its intellectual standards ignore the multiple emphases of the school (which is not the single-purpose instrument of some other nations), and they also forget that American intellectual standards have not merely advanced considerably during the past century but have done so on a very wide front. Well over 70 percent of all American children between 17 and 18 are still at school.

While it is important to bear in mind that there is no federal Ministry of Education, and that the national administration has no control over education (which is a state and local matter), there is nevertheless a strongly national character about most schools in the United States. We must not underestimate either official or unofficial all-American influences in education. A crescendo of federal legislation started with veterans' affairs during the World War II. It gathered strength in the National Defense Education Act of 1958 by rewarding local initiative, encouraging science and foreign language study, and by research contracts and scholarships. By specific grants (such as the $10,000,000 a year dedicated to the study and treatment of delinquency) it has advanced particular projects. Indeed, if we care to look back beyond the post-1917 legislation and even the land grants which followed the Civil War, we can always find some healthy encouragement to education by the administration in Washington. The United States Department of Health, Education, and Welfare has no directive powers whatever as far as the general school systems of the country are concerned; but, in addition to sponsoring such important projects as cardio-vascular research, it supplies a vast quantity of world-oriented educational advice which may or not be utilized by those directly responsible for teaching or school administration. More information about the United States, not to mention other countries, is something that many "grass roots" administrators and teachers really need.

Moreover, the National Education Association, the teachers' colleges and interested departments of universities, and the extremely influential educational publishers of the United States combine with the above statutory bodies to perform many (or most) of the advisory functions of a Ministry of Education—at any rate in such a permissive country as the United Kingdom. Responsibility for advice and guidance in relation to educational practice and policy is hard to pin down in the United States; but there is no doubt that that guidance is given. The city and district superintendents in a progressive state were shown by Dr. Henry Brickell [2] in 1961 to have been quietly responsible for much more educational advance than the university departments of education. Some of the most thoroughgoing recommendations for reform in recent years are the result of government research grants for individual enquiries or team investigations. Some are already inducing great changes.

Most of the 26 million children in about 95,500 public elementary schools would still find a familiar atmosphere wherever they went throughout the United States. That is not to say that the organization and curriculum are uniform—far from it. In fact, the division of school life into phases varies widely. The older style was to have 8 years (or "grades") of elementary (or "grade" or "grammar") school between the ages of 6 and 14. This was increasingly extended by high school to an average age of 18. In very many school districts this 8–4 pattern, or a variant of it, is in vogue; but an increasing tendency is to have 6 years of elementary school followed by 3 years of junior high school and 3 of senior high school. Sometimes the same district will have variations on these themes within its single system.

Children move around from school to school, and from district to district, without disadvantage. Americans are surely the most mobile people. The overwhelming majority of the world's automobiles are on the roads of the United States. It is said that if every car in America were filled by the inhabitants, there would still be an empty space in each one. What was, within living memory, a full day's trip by cart or wagon may be less than an hour's journey by automobile today. It is nothing for "commuters" to travel by car up to a hundred miles in a daily round trip from home to their place of work. I myself have taught university classes starting at 8 A.M. which included students who had traveled over 120 miles that morning, and several others who came more than fifty miles. "Commuting" is a daily experience for millions of Americans. It is also a common practice to change homes at frequent intervals. During the period following World War II, the average length of time spent in one house by the typical American family was

---

[2] H. M. Brickell: *Organizing New York State for Educational Change*, Albany, 1961.

two years. Though this is still generally true, a yearly or even more frequent house change is about the average in southern California.

It is not unusual for the opening gambit in a conversation to be
an inquiry about where you are from. This is notoriously true of Texans
and Westerners; but it would be quite appropriate in many other parts
of the United States. The growth of California is exceptional; the 1950
census showed a 53.3 percent rise in population over that of 1940.
The 1950 figure was an 86.5 percent increase over the 1930 census return. Since 1950 the rapid rate of development has been further accelerated. But, though the rate of migration to California is exceptional,
it is only a latter-day example of a tendency for westward movement
that has been characteristic of America. The covered wagon, the railroad, and the automobile represent a crescendo of traffic whose bulk
is as portentous as its rapid movement. Nowadays air travel is commonplace and cheap. For example, in 1962 it was possible to travel the
2800 mile air journey San Francisco–Dallas–New York for less than
$174. In these circumstances, Americans and their children move around
with astonishing facility. This has a direct bearing on their expectation of school life and urban living generally.

Parents, children, and teachers expect to find close similarity between the nth grade in any two cities. Though they do not always
strike it lucky (or unlucky), they usually find what they expect.
Standardization is of course more marked in the towns than in the
rural areas; but divergence is perhaps more often a mark of backwardness than of advance, except in those rich and progressive cities
which pay their teachers high salaries. The teachers themselves are
perhaps unwittingly responsible for much of this standardization, because the majority of them have been trained in 4-year teachers' colleges, or in specialist "colleges of Education" on a university campus.
The teachers' colleges are usually recognized as of university rank and
give university-style degrees, but they are seldom truly accorded that
recognition by the more reputable universities or even accepted as
equals by the other "colleges" or departments which go to make up the
same university. The characteristic feature of most teachers' colleges
(though not of the best) is the tremendous time allotted to courses on
how to teach this or that subject, how to administer this or that
activity, how to cope with this or that problem. "Education" is broken
down into a multiplicity of separate, stylized courses. Books in huge
and often profitable abundance are produced to suit them. Consequently degrees in which the candidate has "majored" in "Education"

are seldom as highly thought of as other degrees, and there is a tendency not to say too much about them. It is not the undergraduates who are chiefly to blame for a somewhat uncritical attitude, though they must take their share of reproof. The staff of many Education colleges are chiefly responsible, and those who prepare and publish and prescribe *"the book for the course"*—a concept unimaginable in universities outside the New World. Fortunately some of the more radically reforming colleges and universities are at last heeding the crescendo of American criticism and good example; and a growing number invite foreign professors and advisers to assist them in the necessary reorientation.

Just as children move around with their parents, so it is customary for students to spend their four undergraduate years and any further years of graduate study in different colleges. It is undoubtedly educative in itself to move around, and to learn to adjust to different circumstances if that requires some responsible reaction to events and teaching or some control of circumstances. Adjustment-by-compliance is a frequent risk but too seldom recognized in American schools. Also, the sheer mass of students thronging every American institution requires some conveyor-belt handling. For example, examination answers are often machine-marked. There is a temptation for educational administrators (a different and somewhat superior profession to that of teaching) to streamline and equate until the whole thing ticks over like a well-conducted factory designed to turn out a standard product. Many Americans are extremely outspoken critics of this tendency. Some problems arising will be reviewed in detail later. Here we are more concerned with the standardizing effect on the elementary and high school, and on the intellectual and social prospects of the young Americans who experience their "life adjustment" there.

As we have seen, children in the United States enjoy in some ways a finer opportunity for self-differentiation than children in other countries, and that is one aspect of the American legend. On the other hand, Americanization, group work and adjustment, and the influence of administrators, teachers, and books bring about a socialization unparalleled outside the communist countries. I hope to show later how close are the assumptions of many responsible American educators to those acceptable in the Soviet Union. Readers will decide for themselves if this is good or bad. Some well known and highly patriotic American books, however, give the impression that only the American school is "democratic," that democracy can only be established by its means, and that democracy is also its inevitable result. It would be a great help to clear thinking on American virtues and achievements if a distinction were drawn more often between the central and humane inspiration of the American "myth," its actual embodiment in programs which have advanced the material lot of so many millions, and the merely accidental features introduced by mass production. Through such a distinction it should be possible to make a more critical appraisal of the many virtues and comparatively few weaknesses of American schooling. It is a wholesome thought to remember that Ortega y Gasset in *The Revolt of the Masses* declared that what Europeans called "Americanization" was simply the result of mechanization. It would be a pity if Americans themselves got the impression that their sole merit consisted of being a "nation on wheels." The wheels are meant to "take them places." The destination and the delights of the journey should be a matter of responsible choice and not of further automatism. Therefore it is no treachery to the American way of life to reserve praise for features that well deserve it. After all, American self-criticism is the most virulent of any.

Linked with the influence of the schools is the special character of American city life. The older cities of the East often retain features that reveal a European origin and preindustrial assumptions about living. But as you move farther westward the cities are obviously much newer creations that have served the direct purpose of exploiting and distributing America's resources in as straightforward a way as possible. They are nearly all built or rebuilt on a squared plan, with the streets at right angles. The majority of the towns and cities west of the Appalachians are less than a hundred years old in any effective urban sense, and a surprising number have mushroomed up since the advent of the automobile. Communications are streamlined, provided you are not a foreigner or too poor to have a car (and that applies to very few indeed). By contrast with Europe, there is a remarkable sameness about American cities, not so much in their geographic layout as in the stylized nature of their assumptions and their services. Most of these are now geared to the automobile and the problems of parking. In the older part of a city you will find stores, supermarkets, eating places, garages almost exactly like those anywhere else in the United States. There is the same standardized service or lack of it. In the newer neighborhoods you will find very large shopping centers in which most of the space is reserved for cars whose owners do a round of quick shopping at small branches of the big downtown stores or at chain stores. Either there or elsewhere there are drive-in movies, drive-in eating places, drive-in banks—even drive-in library facilities. Shops are very often to be found open until late in the evening. Eating places (not the convivial cafés or pubs of Europe) can be found open at any time. In big cities the traffic never seems to stop. People are always dashing around, "going places," and getting things. The simple foreigner will be forgiven for wondering if they ever have time to *be* anything, or even to do or have anything that is not engineered or "laid out."

If you want to relax you can go out to a movie, or go home to the television set, or read the paper. For more than 90 percent of Americans this last is a local paper (though almost certainly manipulated by a chain). On the average it will devote little more than a quarter of its abundant space to news that is not provincial or even downright local. For many small-town American newspapers the United States and its government hardly exist, except as sources of news about crimes or "love-life" or of unwelcome taxes and regulations. The world outside the United States is a place of un-American activities. It is much better to crowd it out with page upon page of lavish advertisement or even with "funnies." Whether printed or on the radio or televised, advertisements tell you what to buy, eat, and use; how to "have it now" on increasingly easy terms; what things you and your family must have to be modern or American; how to enjoy life; how to have your food and yet avoid the calories; even how to "enjoy your fun." Whatever it is you want you must have a lot of it, have it now, and have it typically. Also, everybody must have it.

The spread of urban and mechanized assumptions is not confined to cities as Europeans understand the term. Small villages with one street have their little replica of the big city, which is glamorized rather as tractors and engines were hymned in early Soviet days as the heralds of human advance. Indeed, it is no longer necessary to have a city to enjoy these urban delights. Old-style concentrated cities relied on the railroad, coal and iron power, heavy industries; new-style urbanization is a much more diffused thing, as we see when looking at the new industrial life of the South. There is a permeation of the countryside with small enterprises that rely on electricity, motor transport, and natural fuels piped in underground from as far away as Texas. When every home has or aspires to central heating, refrigeration, a car, telephone, radio and television, and the whole battery of marvelous kitchen gadgets and prepared foods, it is not surprising that in education too every American child comes to expect "the whole works." Everyone must have it, and have it now.

It is an everlasting credit to American determination and skill that so many children do have educational opportunity. The colossal task of supplying it at what looks like a uniform standard is even more gigantic when we consider the geographic difficulties, the very uneven resources, and the obstinate independence of so many local interests. Under the circumstances, a preoccupation with near-uniformity under the guise of "the American way of life" or "democracy" is easy to condone. Any foreigner who has experienced the freedom, generosity, and forward look of American education will fully appreciate its actual achievements to date and its dynamic promise for the future. Every other country has much to learn from it. But Americans as a whole are very self-critical in private, and their criticisms do not spare American education if they have some understanding of what goes on in other countries. Parents, businessmen, university professors (outside the colleges of Education) are increasingly unwilling to accept the easy assumptions of some teachers' colleges. That is why so many powerful programs are afoot for the reform of American teacher-training, and why progressive colleges take up the study of Comparative Education. This should, however, be a critical and not a self-congratulatory exercise. The time has come for the United States to reach toward greater perfection in education by a greater use of differentiation and qualitative criteria, which have markedly increased since 1959.

Indeed, since about 1955, questions of quality and wasted talent have received insistent attention in the United States—so much so that it is impossible here to refer representatively to the literature on this theme; but it is true to say that until the end of that decade effective action based upon such misgivings was neither widespread nor popular, though hundreds of thousands of students have since gained thereby. Such ventures as the Talented Youth Project (organized in 1953), the Advanced Placement Programs which had long admitted able students to shorter university courses, and the National Merit Scholarship scheme have been sharply criticized by some professional educators as "European" and "un-American"—by implication if not in those terms. Even the introduction of specialist teachers (e.g., for art or music) is hotly resisted by influential teachers' groups. Slowly, however, the general expectation from a high school course has been raised, the process being helped by various schemes of accreditation for university admission qualifications, and above all by the College Entrance Examination

Board in New York. A summary of relevant enquiries and experiments is contained in the Board's publication *The Search for Talent*.[3]

A typical elementary school curriculum in the United States gives children lessons in arithmetic and English (which will normally appear as several different subjects—reading and literature; language arts and listening; speaking; spelling; writing), in health, in physical education, in social studies, and in music. Children over the age of 12, if still in elementary school, usually take up additional subjects with a practical core of interest such as home economics or "industrial arts." Neither of these last two is purely manipulative, but links a good deal of general information to the practical activity. On the whole, by comparison with any other advanced country, actual competence in the school subjects is somewhat meager. Many parents have long been aware of this, as has been shown by the ready sales of books with such disturbing titles as *Why Johnny Can't Read* and *Quackery in the Public Schools*. The vast majority, however, were blissfully content until the first Sputnik set educators by the ears, and the challenge had to be met. Parents take an incessant and active interest in the public school, which enjoys the support of parental advice and gifts of apparatus or gadgets. Children's needs and even their preferences are individually discussed; the children themselves very often help to regulate progress, and will "share the difficulties" of their weaker brethren. Though work is frequently done in groups, there is little formal "streaming" or "homogeneous grouping" if it can be avoided. Promotion from grade to grade officially depends on satisfactory completion of a year's work; but in fact, the child's schoolwork must be unusually bad (perhaps through absence) to make him repeat a grade. There are practically no real examinations as other countries understand them, and the standard by which a child is usually graded is his own average expectation. Not only is there reluctance to let nimble wits run ahead, but in some places there has been unwillingness to recognize the special needs of backward children. However these "exceptional children," as they are called, now get careful attention from teachers who have specialized in their problems, and American remedial work in these areas is outstanding.

For the sake of contrast with other countries (which is not altogether satisfactory) American schools may still be described as comparatively indifferent to subjects, to academic accuracy, and to progress at any given speed so as to complete a curriculum (like those determined in other countries by economic considerations or pedagogic prescription).

[3] New York College Entrance Examination Board, *The Search for Talent*, 1960.

Even hard facts are given secondary importance by many teachers. They are much more eager to have cheerful children developing "wholesome social relationships," "evaluating" and discussing daily experiences, and understanding their role in society as they see it. In achieving these aims the schools are phenomenally successful, and most of the children are quite delightful to know; but astronomical delinquency figures make many wonder if enough is expected of children, and if they are sufficiently occupied and "committed" to develop a sense of purpose.

Nearly every American child goes on to high school from elementary school at an age between 12 and 14. Of the 30,000 high schools, 84 percent are free public schools. Many of these public high schools are in rural districts which have been handicapped by isolation and smallness, but increasing trends in consolidation and mobility are improving this situation. The children "graduate" at around 18. At one time this graduation entailed a very serious examination rightly supposed to be a challenge to the unusually able pupil who was honored by a certificate, if successful, and with the glory of a cap and gown. Now nearly everyone remaining in school can expect to graduate. However, it was estimated in 1962 that in the ensuing decade one out of every three American pupils would leave high school before graduating,[4] very often because of discouraging family circumstances. And surveys show that "dropouts" are usually doomed to a lifetime of low level jobs and spasmodic unemployment, if not worse, so exacting is the American labor market in its schooling requirements.

The typical high school is coeducational and completely comprehensive. Future lawyers, doctors, and clergymen are classmates with future mechanics, shopgirls, and farmers. This is because the schools normally allow a wide range of elective subjects in the upper grades. An attempt is made in most cases to ensure that a child has a really broad education, either by grouping electives in suitable patterns or by "counseling." A school of any size has one or more counselors or other ancillary educators whose job it is to personalize relationships for the children and to advise them on problems.

There is no doubt, however, that much of the counseling is done by ambitious parents who persuade their children to choose the "college preparatory" type of subject, such as mathematics, languages, and science. For these there is now some very good federally provided equipment. On the other hand, rather slow-learning children and those with worse advice or less farsighted parents can and often do choose very

[4] *Youth Service News* (New York State), Spring 1962, p. 15.

practical subjects with an immediate sales value. These include not only such subjects as bookkeeping, agriculture, journalism, and auto mechanics, but even bricklaying, plastering, shoe repairing, and hairdressing in extreme cases. In poor areas, especially in segregated "separate but equal" Negro schools, the proportion of practical subjects taken grows. In other words, selection by social class or future is discernible; but we must note (a) that these children are still at school and subjected to a wide range of humanizing influences when many other nations' children would be hard at work, and (b) that in association with these practical subjects it is often possible to develop both personal qualities and really sound understanding of conventional subjects.

Home economics and "industrial arts" are usually, though not always, admirably taught and studied. Moreover, a great deal of overlapping occurs. Your future teacher or doctor may include "shop" (that is, mechanical work or carpentry) and home economics in the round of school subjects. Some of these may be taken for only one year, or even half a year. American history and some form of literature are the only subjects all pupils will take, though the core curriculum of general interest subjects has had a wide vogue.

On the other hand, it is rather misleading to talk as though children's futures were settled. The majority of them come very late to specialization. Many of them do not know even after high school graduation what they will ultimately become. This has its severe drawbacks; but it has the great advantage that many of them have a very wide range of future callings still open to them.

Among the obvious drawbacks to such a system, which is not only comprehensive but usually "unstreamed" into differing grades of ability, was the longstanding reluctance to make a challenging opportunity for the really bright or eager child. Another has been that of securing full attention for the profitable if somewhat unpopular subjects, such as mathematics. This is aggravated by the acute shortage of specialist teachers, who are drawn off by higher pay elsewhere; but even if the teachers were there, the intrinsic difficulties of a free choice would raise problems. It was stated in 1954–1955 by the United States Office of Education that 23 percent of the high schools in the country did not offer courses in the basic sciences or in mathematics. Though this statement could easily give the wrong impression, because the figure of 23 percent really refers to small rural schools catering to only about 6 percent of the total high school population, it does suggest a wider neglect of the very subjects that are basic to the future of a technological society. General science, physics, chemistry, and biology—to say nothing of foreign languages and information about foreign countries—do not come high in the popularity poll. When they are taken, it is usually at a very elementary level. Though "enriched" and presumably more demanding programs now appear more frequently and prominently, foreign observers should not expect anything very spectacular in most cases. They might class such programs as "normal"; though if the present example of some federally prompted intensification prevails, the standards of the whole country might alter conspicuously. Many districts, however, and whole states, remain unconcerned and unaware; and all too many professional educators are complacent.

Therefore it is not surprising that in his school subjects the young American is still usually two years (or even more in special cases) behind his European counterpart. Many subjects must in fact be postponed until college, though in Europe a very high standard in them would be required before there could be any possibility of entry into a college. An extreme critic of American standards, R. M. Hutchins, has declared that early in the twentieth century every young person holding the leaving certificate of the French *lycée*, a German *Gymnasium*, or an Italian *liceo* had acquired at the age of 18 (i.e., after 12 years' schooling)

> "approximately as much knowledge of subject matter as three modern college [i.e., university] graduates together will have acquired in the United States after 16 years' schooling, at about age 22. If a college student in America specializes in mathematics he will have arrived at the age of 22 at such branches as differential and integral calculus, analytical geometry and differential equations. The fundamentals of most of these fields were, however, known to 18-year-old graduates of the old-fashioned European secondary schools, who also knew equally well three other subjects at least: Latin, Greek, and their native tongue." [5]

Every outside observer, like the American Dr. Hutchins, experiences continual shocks from contrasts of this kind. There are signs that better informed Americans generally are feeling them too. The more reputable universities are becoming increasingly selective on the grounds of attainment. Many firms offering scholarships at the university level are insisting on certain minimums before awarding them, and in some cases are unable to find takers for what they offer. Moreover, recent comparisons with the redoubtable achievements of the Soviet school system are

[5] Hutchins, R. M. *The Conflict in Education*. New York: Harper & Row, Publishers, 1953, p. 38.

making patriotic and sympathetic American leaders wonder if too little has been expected of the high school in the way of solid work. Once they have left school, Americans work very hard indeed—and at a pace which it is almost exhausting for some foreigners merely to observe; but for many American children the shock of the career world's competitive ruthlessness is postponed until they leave college at the age of 22.

Still, criteria of attainment are not the only valid ones to apply to a folk institution not altogether designed for the purposes of intellectual training. Much attention is paid to socializing activities in groups of every conceivable kind. A surprisingly frequent word for a democratic country is the ever-recurring "leadership." On the other hand, much trouble is taken to ensure that everyone can hope to be a leader in something (as long as he is not too radical or intellectual). The very wide range of interests and skills found in the normal large school secures a high standard of work in such things as school newspapers, celebration pageants, and so on. Moreover very many children have some experience of paid vacation work during their summer holidays, or travel widely. The American child usually "knows his way around," and has confidence that he can get where he wants to go. Perhaps most other educated children in the world are deficient in this sense of adventure and personal dignity. On the other hand these admirable qualities in the American child might be enriched if combined with a greater readiness to learn. Such readiness may indeed be induced by the "sales pressure" not only of educators but even of advertisers, who no longer commiserate with "eggheads" but glamorize them. That is a great change.

In addition to the public high schools, about 4000 private high schools enroll more than 930,000 children. This is about 12 percent of the high school population. Most of them are denominational schools; but a few resemble the English Public Schools in demanding very high fees and in specially preparing their students for the universities. The influence of the "college preparatory" school and of the "ivy league" university in securing privilege for a few is much stronger than Americans care to realize; but it is nothing like so powerful in this matter as the English Public School. For one thing, the ordinary high school is the training ground for most of America's really successful men and women. Secondly, the inquiries of selectors are much more directly concerned with present excellence than with antecedents of parental position and one's own school. Thirdly, society itself in the United States does not exclusively venerate particular occupations, but tends to have a real admiration for any boy or girl who makes good. Lastly, the standard of the ordinary high school (taking in everyone, and not just the average 20 percent or 25 percent of the population found in the English grammar school) is recognizably similar to that of nearly all American private schools, though it must be admitted that some of these are impressive by any standard. A few cities (New York, for example) are experimenting with advanced public schools for especially gifted children, and some universities help to speed up progress for such people in ordinary high schools by admitting them very early if they have reached an appropriate standard. This is the advanced placement program already referred to.

The next stage after high school, and following naturally from it, is "college." That word and "university" are practically synonymous in the United States. More than 1940 colleges enroll above three and a quarter million students. The majority are coeducational and many colleges are state supported or city institutions. A large number of these charge no tuition fees to residents of the state, and the fees of the other publicly maintained institutions are often very small when taken in relation to American earning power. Any high school graduate has the opportunity to enter a university, though not any university, if he can pay the fees requested. Many students earn their way through college by securing employment either in the college (for example, as a waiter, switchboard operator, gardener, or clerical assistant), or outside. Some find it possible to earn enough in the long summer vacation to pay most of the cost (including residence) of an inexpensive university; but this means hard work. Sometimes college timetables are arranged on a sort of shift system—partly to accommodate those who come in before or after a half day's employment, partly to accommodate married students who alternate studies with baby-sitting and other domestic chores, and partly to cope with the enormous numbers of students. The dropout rate is, however, very large indeed.

It is obvious from this description that a representative American university is unlike anything of the same name anywhere else in the world, except perhaps in postwar Japan, the Philippines, and other spheres of American influence. The standards of academic work required in Europe and Asia would be unattainable in these circumstances. But then the American college is not intended to do the work that the world's universities consider to be their special distinction. It is not so selective of intellectual quality, taking in almost one-third of the population of university age, and in some districts more. In some cities with "junior colleges" (that is, to age 20), the majority go. College is therefore not so specialized a place, not only because it has to follow a comparatively unspecialized high school but because it has itself a much broader base of study for the individual student. Many courses are on a level familiar in foreign high (or selective secondary) schools. They may indeed be much lower than that, though, as is proved by the still frequent provision of remedial reading courses and elementary mathematics or comparable basic subjects during the freshman year of a state college or university. The range of the typical college includes many courses that would be prepared for by less grandly named schools in other countries, or even by professional apprenticeships not given the name of "school" at all. Such colleges freely award degrees in subjects that would be doubtfully awarded a much lower certificate elsewhere. Far less emphasis is placed on independent, critical study than in foreign universities, and far more emphasis is placed on attendance at lectures. Of these there is often a heavy and somewhat repetitious load.

Foreign professors generally find American students too docile for their taste—a surprising thing in the land of liberty. More importance is attached to terminal grades and "credit hours" than to searching examinations or critical reading as expected of students everywhere outside North America; and not even the most loyal champion of the representative American campus could claim that the extracurricular pursuits of undergraduates effectively supply real, critical compensation for intracurricular passivity. The students' whole experience (very often with only "objective" answers in any tests they may have undergone) has all too frequently left them unschooled in criticism or detachment, and often left them unprepared with the basic knowledge. Their university career does not always help them. The more advanced or graduate students will often work methodically, for example, at "term papers" or essays which must be abundantly documented with annotations and sources; but there is so much of the archivist and so little of the scholar in them that they will not infrequently ask an instructor whether "research" or "original work" is required! Outside North America such a distinction would be quite meaningless. In extreme cases it is easy to get by with only the professors' handouts or the "book for the course," and one can hear idle or perversely able students swear that they "never cracked a book." Hence, shrewd American critics now sometimes say that the "custodial" function so recently characteristic of the high school has now passed over into college. However, increasingly selective admission requirements and the competitive recruitment of talent (indeed, of already developed talent) are already aggravating the academic and social distance between the prestige-enjoying minority of colleges and the still complacent majority. Many small "liberal arts" colleges and the highly selective "prestige" colleges have long set very high standards.

This is the negative side to a massive achievement. Though Americans persist in saying these young men and women are in "college" and therefore to be compared with university students in other lands, they thus put them at an absurd and unnecessary disadvantage. The majority of American college students are getting something that is not available to most of their foreign counterparts—a taste of the elements of academic learning, and a foothold on the ladder of social esteem and advancement that is elsewhere restricted to the learned professions. Everybody in the United States must have this chance; so all professions, more or less, must be "learned" and suitable for a university degree. This is an exaggeration of American regard for the romance of learned status; but like all caricatures it bears a recognizable likeness. Nursing, accountancy, catering, local government service, advertising, commerce, and journalism are typical graduate careers in America, though not elsewhere.

An extended period of general education is afforded to young Americans by the special characteristics of their undergraduate life. This usually consists of four years in a "liberal arts college" or its equivalent, though a growing proportion of students now major in "applied" subjects such as business administration and commerce. In 1961 these were the major fields of interest of 12 percent of all American first degrees. So many students want to have some college experience (preferably at little expense and near home) that an increasing number of junior colleges start them off for the years 18 to 20. There are now over 500 of these, many of them also serving as community education centers for the adults of the neighborhood. Teachers' colleges now total about 200. Some have gradually expanded into liberal arts colleges, and in a few instances they have been transformed by accretions into full universities with several "colleges" (British "faculties") and postgraduate departments. Teachers' colleges and "colleges of Education" in many universities, especially in their practical departments, have already been criticized for the uncritical and repetitive emptiness of many of their courses; but the best of them are fine institutions with outstanding scholars and international reputations. Graduates of teachers' colleges, or those who are halfway to graduation after two years in a junior college, can proceed to further study in universities at the appropriate level. Because they have not really specialized so far, even at the age of 22 with a bachelor's degree, students are frequently able to begin genuinely professional

Children playing in a Danish schoolyard.

(Copyright Royal Danish Ministry for Foreign Affairs.)

Rest hour at a new school in Copenhagen.

A woodcraft project at Nørre Saltum School, North Jutland, Denmark.

A dormitory at the university in Aarhus, established by royal decree in 1931. Denmark's other university, in Copenhagen, was founded in 1479.

(Copyright Royal Danish Ministry for Foreign Affairs.)

A corner of a classroom at the *lycée* in Sèvres, near Paris. This is one of the six fully experimental *lycées* in France.

A scene in the courtyard of another French school.

(French Embassy Press and Information Division.)

An art class at the *lycée* of Saint-Germain-en-Laye. (*French Embassy Press and Information Division.*)

A class in technical drawing at the Lycée Technique d'Etat at Montlucon.

The monumental proportions of the reading room of the library at the Sorbonne contrast markedly with the crowded laboratory at a college of dental science in Paris.

A first-year student at Eastbourne Teachers' Training College observes the methods employed in an Infant School classroom.

(*British Information Services.*)

A demonstration in a class in "mothercraft" at Coston Secondary Modern Girls School.

An art class at Kidbrooke, a London comprehensive school for 1700 girls.

(British Information Services.)

Dissecting a fish in a biology class at Priory Secondary Modern Boys' School, London.

A four-hundred-year-old classroom in an endowed grammar school is the scene of a geometry lesson. Note the ushers' chairs on each side of the master's desk, not used now.

(British Information Services.)

A chemistry demonstration at Brymore Secondary Technical School of Agriculture in Bridgwater.

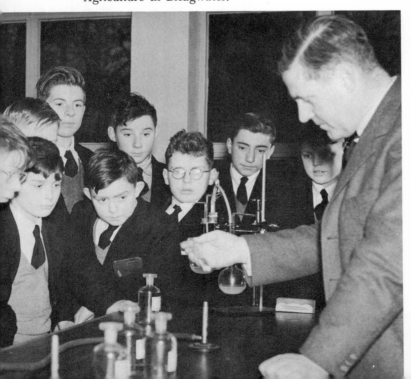

A kindergarten class in a Kirkwood, Missouri, public school (*photo by Francis Scheidegger*), and a second grade class in a Texas school. Note the variety of activities taking place at once in both of these classrooms.

Some of the exhibits at the annual science fair at **St. Gregory's**, a Roman Catholic high school in Chicago. (*New World Photo.*)

A class in ladies' tailoring and patternmaking at the High School of Fashion Industries in New York City. New York is unique in having such highly specialized schools within the public school system.

Small liberal arts colleges, such as Dickinson in Pennsylvania, attract students from all over the world to their friendly and informal campuses. A group of foreign students is shown here with Dr. William W. Edel, President of the College.

An aerial view of a portion of the campus of the University of Washington in Seattle gives an idea of the physical extent of a large state university. (*James O. Sneddon, photo.*)

Lunch hour in a kindergarten attached to a factory in Soviet Armenia. The children are looked after while their mothers work.

A dance program at the Moscow Municipal Pioneer House.

At a Moscow children's club these girls learn fancy embroidery. Note the near-religious picture of Lenin and the conventlike atmosphere, which is heightened by the dark uniforms and severe hair styles of the girls.

A botany lesson in one of the new boarding schools in Moscow. The children all wear the red scarves of the Pioneers.

Third-year students in a soil mechanics laboratory in the geology department at Moscow University.

At a teachers' college in Stalinabad, in the Tadzhik Republic, a second-year student gives a talk on the mechanics of a motion-picture projector. The diagram of a projector on the blackboard has a Russian caption.

A village secondary school in Madhya Pradesh, India, has a demonstration lesson on an "open day." Note the sharing of books and the absence of alternatives. (*Press Information Bureau, Government of India.*)

An adult literacy class held at night. Note the wooden writing tablets. (*Information Service of India.*)

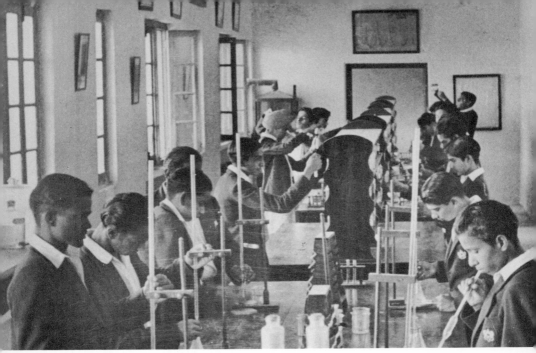

A science class in the Scindia School, Gwalior, India. This type of school, modeled on the English public schools, is unrepresentative.

(*Press Information Bureau, Government of India.*)

A section of the Calcutta University Library. Indian education is greatly hampered by huge classes and a shortage of books, but some universities have fair-sized collections.

training (for the master's degree) in one of their previous subjects or a new one in "graduate school." Of over 2030 "colleges," under 150 are officially listed as "universities" proper—that is to say, institutions with graduate schools and research facilities. These could be more truly compared with the universities, technical colleges, and commercial institutions of Europe in their intellectual and professional standards. Though only a relatively small proportion of Americans enroll in a graduate professional school, it probably represents more than 10 percent—at least twice as high a percentage as reach comparable standards in Britain.

At this level, too, "teaching fellowships" and other ladders to the academic life encourage many a young scholar of talent to persevere with his research and serve a university apprenticeship under very favorable conditions. The library and research facilities available in the better American universities, and indeed in some departments of many which are not so distinguished, are outstanding by any international standard. For such exceptional young academics, too, careful teaching and patient guidance are provided—often on a friendly and stimulating seminar basis that can put to shame the struggling isolation of researchers in many of the world's universities. However, we must remember that here we are considering the minority of university research students, and not the typical undergraduate or indeed the typical "master's" candidate.

If we except many of the masters' and doctors' degrees in "Education," American higher degrees are very often comparable with similar degrees in Europe, at any rate in the more selective and exclusive American universities. Graduate schools often have a sound and searching professional curriculum. It is impressive to find that although a bachelor's degree obtained by a scientist, for example, may be little more advanced than a *baccalauréat*, *Abitur*, or General Certificate of Education at Advanced Level, the doctorate is very often quite up to the standard of a Ph.D. in Britain. This cannot, however, be said of colleges in general. Yale, Harvard, and Princeton and some other notable institutions are magnificent universities by any standard. The great technological universities are models for the world. Many other research institutes and universities have outstanding specialist departments that attract the cream of America and academicians from all over the world by their incomparable resources. (American salaries have something to do with it too!) But this cannot justify an unreflecting and blanket defense of what passes for higher learning in many places.

It is especially important to make this point in connection with an increasing tendency to parade scholarship under the trappings of annotation and documentation drawn from any sources that seem appropriate. This particular fad was rejected in large measure by most of the universities of the Old World toward the end of the nineteenth century, when the heavy artillery of German professors bombarding each other over the interpretation of Classical texts was shown to contribute so little to real insight or humanity. The almost compulsive scholium of over-documented yet often unreflective "library research" now so common in those American university departments uncertain of their academic respectability (particularly in the great search for quality since 1957) should not be taken as proving the presence of critical scholarship. It can actually be a token of a "climate of distintegration" (to borrow an expression used by Professor Ulich in describing the decline of creativity in the medieval University of Paris); and it certainly may inhibit not only creativity but indeed original interpretation.[6] Sober, well-grounded scholarship needs no salesmanship; it would fare better with less counting of documentation and doctorates.

One understandable consequence of the prodigality and experimental diversity of American higher education, particularly, is that many leading scholars who ought to know better are tempted to make pronouncements based upon the institutions and departments they know, and then suppose they have made universally valid declarations. No other country has quite this problem, because no other has quite this diversity or such chasms. The author has made six extended study and teaching visits to the United States, has had the advantage of participating in two nation-wide surveys and one international evaluation of American higher education by unimpeachable American scholars, and has also benefited by numerous well-informed but down-to-earth discussions in nearly all parts of the country—not to mention meticulous preparatory inquiry and continuous follow-up research. Yet nothing is more common than to encounter pseudocomparisons or defensive manifestoes put out by self-confident professors who are just not effective students of their own system. As the turmoil attending the National Defense Education Act has shown, such ostrich-techniques neither serve

---

[6] R. Ulich: *The Education of Nations*, Cambridge, Mass.: Harvard University Press, 1961, pp. 27 & following; see also my *World Perspectives in Education, op. cit.*, pp. 38–39 and 173–174, for a fuller examination of these techniques in relation to the encouragement of scholarship.

the United States nor truly represent the wishes of well-informed Americans.

It is fairer to America and a more genuine appreciation of its genius to admit that a college education is still for most of its recipients a social experience more than an experience of work and scholarship. On the typical American campus young men and women destined for all kinds of profession, and of many different origins, mix freely to discuss their responses to many of life's problems. Normally, the faculty (that is, the academic staff) consider it their duty to be accessible to the students for all kinds of consultation. In addition, a "dean of men" and a "dean of women" are in charge of the general well-being of the future citizens of one of the most fluid societies on earth. Medical and psychological services are also available, and vocational counselors help with careers. It is also of great value to most young people to make personal contact with real scholars and the originators of progress. Perhaps this splendid opportunity would be appreciated more if all students realized that knowledge of facts and a willingness to undertake independent inquiry into original sources are essential constituents of a proper discussion. In a small minority of universities or colleges, and in some enterprising (but as yet untypical) departments of others, this realization has been achieved. In speaking of Denmark we noted the value of the folk high school as a kind of retreat house conceived in secular terms. In America the campus is not quite that; but it serves a comparable purpose in some ways, and it similarly mixes up young men and women drawn from different localities.

Of course, the extremely lively campus life is an integral part of a college education. It is not quite as crazy as the films show, but near-professional football and basketball and baseball (mainly pursued by student athletes recruited for this very purpose and with little regard for other qualities) are a staple ingredient of the typical college. Many functional societies and a large number of fraternities and sororities (often associated with professional interests) claim the attention of students. Some of them are socially exclusive; but that is not typical. An initiation into a fraternity is a kind of blend between a religious service and a Greek drama; but it is often taken seriously despite that, because belonging to a fraternity is very important. There is a comparative lack of the literary, political, philosophical and generally skeptical clubs familiar to European students. If anything, the faculty are more intellectually and socially critical than the typical student of today.

A somewhat disturbing indication of this was brought home to me in 1955 and five later university assignments. In lectures on social philosophy and a comparison of educational ideas I noticed that the traditional liberal assumptions of the Western world rang somewhat strange for American students (mainly graduates); so I joined forces with professors of philosophy and related subjects to draw up questionnaires and test discussion topics. These revealed among students a marked reluctance to recognize the basic claims of individuals and minorities in a multiple society. They showed fear of encouraging marked individual differences, even in complementary kinds of difference; they showed strong reliance on "leadership" and other kinds of worship for big men or "experts"; they certainly revealed an absence of real concern for separate and responsible personal reactions. In America this all sounds peculiarly ironical. It may be added here that nothing was said or directly implied in these questions about Negroes or communism. On the contrary, when notions directly quoted from communist sources or when details of educational or corporate activity in communist countries were tried on these graduate Americans, they were found to be more familiar and acceptable than most of the contrary notions of liberal Western democracies—the notions, that is to say, of the American founding fathers and of those who throughout the ages have championed the rights of man.

Once again, my implied criticism is no attack on American institutions. It is one more indication of the impact of mechanization and of industrialized relationships on democratic notions of personal dignity and responsibility. It is only more remarkable for being so clear in the one country founded on charters of human liberty, and dedicated to progress. Modern abundance is, of course, based upon the mass production of standardized wares. Commodities and opportunities are produced that way, even schools and books; but men's minds and freedoms are of different stuff.

One feature of American social life, which is also conspicuous at school, never fails to impress foreigners. It is the emancipation of women to something more than equal status. The American woman has not merely caught up with men; she has achieved her own special dignity and prerogative beyond those accorded to men, so that in some ways she is a "man plus." It is an unforgettable experience to attend a business or professional women's gathering, and to note factory managers, real estate agents, scientists, doctors, lawyers, and even ministers there. They are not all young either; many must in fact have had their professional education at a time when their European sisters were struggling to claim something beyond a mere rudimentary schooling.

It would be a mistake to attribute feminine advance to the schools, though they have certainly helped a really American advance to gather momentum. From the earliest pioneer days women have been at a premium. Simple shortage, combined with abundant opportunities for self-vindication (and for mobility or escape) perhaps gave women in frontier settlements stronger claims to equal consideration than women have usually had anywhere else. These unspoken but real ingredients in the background have long been rationalized, so that Americans take them as "natural"; but they do not need to go too far back in their own history to find college coeducation mentioned as a sort of utopian madness. Now coeducation is almost the only conceivable method, from kindergarten to research.

In circumstances of complete freedom and abundant proximity, American girls have long had an opportunity to get to know boys well. They go about with them freely as companions, flirt with them, and go through all the preliminaries of love with no public disapproval. On the contrary. Americans probably do not know how amazed most foreigners are at the extent and frequency of this adolescent play. Most overseas observers are little short of scandalized, and to them juvenile American clothing itself may seem naïvely and therefore innocently indecent. On the other hand, foreigners seldom realize how vital a part all this is of the American legendary virtues of self-recognition, self-expression, freedom of choice, freedom to find one's own frontier and so on, all in the rather unique circumstances of their long preadult tutelage.

For modern Americans this dance of the sexes is not merely permitted; it is, in their own idiom, a "must." The near-universal practice of "dating" ensures that girls and boys learn a personal and social routine that is of the greatest importance to self-adjustment. It is both a token of personal acceptability and the means to further acceptance by the group. Boy-girl relationships, though certainly not a formality or inhibited, are highly stylized. They come under close supervision (seldom with an eye to disapproval) by parents, elders, and also one's peers. They are prompted by advertisements, by one's sisters and brethren in sororities and fraternities. Parents can be as anxious as the adolescents themselves if a week, and above all a week end, goes by without "dates." Dating could in large measure be describable to foreigners as parent-sponsored.

Since about 1945 a marked change has come about in the pattern of dating. Whereas for at least a generation it had been supposed that boys and girls would have a succession of different dates, ringing the changes perhaps twice a week, the custom has grown up of "going steady" not just as a direct preliminary to marriage but in the very early teens also. I have often heard highly respectable matrons warmly defend their own adolescent practice of successional dating as an experience which not merely brought them into contact with a wide circle of friends of both sexes but also allowed them more clearly to discern personal virtues from merely masculine attractions. By the same token these people view with regret the change of fashion which prompts 12- and 13-year-olds to ask their parents how soon they should "go steady." Of course, many parents are very anxious about such premature "going steady" both for obvious reasons and because they are reluctant that their youngsters should form an inexperienced attachment to an unsuitable companion. The youngsters themselves, even under the age of 14, have keenly examined me about comparable practices in other countries when I have invited "any questions" during visits to their classes.

It might be supposed that going steady would imply a less socialized form of juvenile courtship than successional dating. That is not really so. The rules are elaborately if tacitly drawn up by one's contemporaries; performance is often thrashed out in a sort of open confession in sororities and other clubs; and there are many books to advise, some soundly. It is still too early to form firm judgment, but young people are marrying earlier. Many are married in college; some leave high school to marry. This might have happened anyway. The outside observer should be content to observe rather than judge this American innovation in juvenile freedom. Although at the time of the first edition of this book in 1958 the phenomenon described above could have been named as typically American, it has since then become more common in many other countries (particularly Britain). The question of young love and early marriage is hedged in with all kinds of economic and social problems; but the juvenile expectation or dream is surely there. It is interesting (though not altogether profitable) to speculate how much of this change is directly attributable to popular records, films, and television suggestions—for these are the voice of America most avidly listened to abroad, educational and political differences notwithstanding—and how much is due to a world-wide change of a subtler kind in the expectation of youth now more than ever cooped up in school and having its powers and desires denied an adult fulfillment. But that raises questions of social reorganization, of working challenges, and of significant participation in the exacting struggles of adults, while we are simply thinking of youth's emotions.

Like every human innovation, early dating brings its attendant problems. Despite Hollywood and canned television, American adolescents are neither more salacious nor more depraved than those in other places. It must be said that most of them are well poised and very agreeable indeed. But greater freedom (as in Britain, for example) permits a more overt disregard for the older proprieties among most people; it would be very hard to say if it causes more wickedness, because in the heyday of real wickedness it is often fashionable to hide it. Dating also stimulates a higher expectation of marriage and a readier dissatisfaction if things do not come up to it. This brings about more divorces; but once again it would be hard to say if by the same token it blemishes more marriages than were imperfect in previous generations. By all accounts, however, it does provoke marked anxieties about being up to standard, true to type, and so on. On the basis of American statistical surveys and spontaneous comment by Americans whom I have addressed on this topic, I feel that anxiety about conforming is perhaps more marked in premarital relationships than in any other potentially socializing activity. All over the world freedom between men and women is growing, as a necessary consequence of permitting women to be judged by male standards; but it is usually a freedom (like religion or politics) that seeks a relatively unsocialized and private area for its fullest development. All sexual behavior is more socially determined than anyone cares to admit; but manifest American socialization in this matter often surprises well-informed foreign observers.

This last comparison once again raises the important question whether the American pattern of living is not also the "shape of things to come" in other countries. If Americanization, as most other people see it, is almost indistinguishable from industrialization and urbanization, it is most important that others should study its blessings and pitfalls with their own future in view. In fact, few cultures have had a wider publicity at any time. Not merely are American examples (and not always the best ones) broadcast through the world by books, film, and advertising; they are also implicit in programs of technical and economic aid—even in the very instruments and staffing arrangements that help modern industrialization to run smoothly. Truly we may say that modern American assumptions are built into modern technology, which in one way or another is as full of educative suggestions and rehearsal systems as the round of daily school and life at home. Whether these assumptions are the same as those consciously striven for by parents, teachers, and educators is another question—one that it is crucial for Americans no less than foreign observers to answer. An increasing number of significant American publications reveal profound misgivings on this score.

Why should it be so important to decide whether modern "Americanization" is automatic or a matter of consciously chosen values? The whole philosophical foundation of the American republic is one of European liberalism nourished in an atmosphere of free growth, free experiment, and tolerance for others. The "great experiment" of all time has been the building of a nursery for individual human enterprise amidst abundance, not in conditions of uniformity or automatism but in conditions that assure the basic minimums of social justice and economic sufficiency. As a matter of principle rather than of actual practice these "inalienable rights" are the very heart of American education in schools, in homes, in public life. It is American insistence on equality without identity, on differences that can be complementary, on accepting qualities as "right" if they can justify themselves pragmatically, that have differentiated the American way from pure intellectualism in the past and from Soviet-style standardization in the present. It seems of primary importance that the same distinction should be made now. The private decisions of American life are front-page news for the world. They may in fact be decisions for the rest of mankind.

Well over half the human race is yellow or brown, and a considerable proportion of the rest are black. Most of them are still literally hungry a large part of the time. Even liberty and the rights of man take a secondary place in their preoccupations. Industrialization seems the god that will rescue them from servitude and poverty. They know America not as the land of liberty but as the Mecca of abundance. Yet by the same token the USSR is also remarkable. Its stupendous machine is just at the beginning of its work, and also in an imperfectly exploited territory. Marxian preaching of equality and democracy (which may be "double talk"), in any case means little to those who have never understood democracy. But Russian technological excellence, Russian raising of living standards for tens of millions, Russian standards in scholarship and research are likely to be persuasive messengers even where no communist has infiltrated. In our next chapter we shall consider some of these redoubtable achievements. Only the enemies of our type of democracy waste time denying them. To round off this chapter we have to ask once more what it is that essentially differentiates the Western way from the Marxist, and what are the problems that this examination poses for Americans.

The essential difference is the claim and the guarantee for a full and self-determining life for each person irrespective of origin, race, sex, or belief. It is written in glowing terms in the preamble to the Declaration of Independence, and also in the preamble to the United Nations Charter. Americans need to decide whether their colossal achievements so far can be added to by reconsideration of children's access to education and well-being throughout the highly decentralized and unequally equipped territories of the United States. Arrangements that suited the thirteen colonies and the English villages before them may not be suited to today. Though this fact has little to do directly with domestic American decisions, hundreds of millions of black and brown eyes are watching all over the world. In addition, Americans must decide whether the youthful delights of the American school can also permit the brilliant or simply different American child to enrich himself and his country more fully and more quickly than at present, even with the help of the National Defense Education Act, the national programs, and the great foundations. In the field of science this is becoming an urgent question. It is also a basic problem in social philosophy.

The whole complex of problems arising out of industrialization, urban life, and automation is transforming the educational arena in the United States. As a pioneer in this field, the United States is bound to make critical decisions which will affect the whole world. I said earlier that automation's full force is being checked; yet in the decade ending 1957, factory output was increased by exactly 50 percent with an increase in factory workers of only 2 percent. Farm output was increased by 20 percent, with an actual decrease of 25 percent in the number of workers. The problems of life's tempo, of how much a profession itself is educative, of leisure, of "custodial" education are all bound up with this development. Mankind has never really needed a conscious solution to this range of questions before, because technological and social change has been piecemeal and evolutionary. Now it is impossible to "let things happen" for, as we have seen, the machine can take over control and produce a state of pretotalitarian standardization, or at any rate the passive receptor-mentality which is equally demoralizing.

Therefore the outside world, already heavily indebted to Americans for technical aid and much material assistance, looks anxiously toward the development of another kind of "know-how." The material aid given by the United States is without precedent in history. Readiness to help mankind in education (as distinct from technique) is made manifest by all the scholarships awarded to foreigners, by all the grants given by American foundations to foreign institutions of learning, and by fundamental education projects throughout the underdeveloped lands of the world. Not even the most cynical could whisper that these activities are designed only to defend America, though they certainly help in that direction.

Americans increasingly recognize that civilization and the humane solution of recurring human problems (like health) must be available to all mankind if they are to be firmly enjoyed by any of mankind. But no technique for living—not even the American prescription—can be exported like a "package deal." Every solution needs to be worked over repeatedly in its own context and studied in the light of comparable experiments. For this reason, the age-old hunches of the Old World may still have valid suggestions to make to those shaping the New— indeed, to those helping that still newer world to shape itself where a choice must somehow be made between the Old World, the New World, and the advancing techniques of their totalitarian competitors.

The choice would be easier for the rest of the world, and for Americans themselves, if Americans took stock realistically of the immense achievements of their country and its educational system within the present century. The greatest of these has been to provide a high all-around minimum standard of education and consumption. Not everything is admirable, to be sure; but of what human institution could that be said? To take another example, this time of a noneducational achievement within a field of endeavor which is universally regarded as being distinctively American—the colossal superhighways accelerating motor traffic across the continent, and the less spectacular but equally admirable highways which preceded them, are revolutionary creations of this century and indeed of the present generation. Yet it now seems so inevitable to think of American life as based on them that no one thinks of boasting about them and comparable achievements in the way that Russians boast about their spectacular technological advances, or as foreign scholars pay tribute to Japan's rapid modernization after the Meiji Restoration in 1868. That road system and that technology *are* America as we see life in the United States now, though in the period of "dirt roads" during the 1920s and later they would have seemed unimaginably revolutionary. The revolutions of one generation become the commonplaces of the next. The role of world leadership has fallen upon the United States somewhat unexpectedly; but it is nevertheless a direct consequence of revolutionary advance in some fields of ingenuity and enterprise. That advance did not come from regarding the status quo as sacrosanct. Neither can education now become static or base itself on familiar norms.

The United States now stands particularly at a world crossroads of educational decision. The whole period since 1945, and especially since 1958, has been marked by an amazed stocktaking of previous deficiencies and inequalities; it has shown accelerating intensification of effort, with an ever harsher condemnation of those would-be "educators" who for two decades or more reduced the level and purpose of the nation's educational upsurge, often by the punctilio of "process" and "methodology," but more often by isolating "progressivism" from the true progress that sharper eyes could already see under way in the more advanced parts of the national endeavor. Sometimes plain ignorance was to blame; but this can be remedied by the careful study of Comparative Education as a basically analytical assessment of systems at work—at work over problems which may seem local and peculiar but which (like all great poetry and music) communicate something of universal value and edification. Thus, peculiarly foreign systems are not just so many statistical items or factors or solutions, important though these may be. Those systems are significant parts of the human drama, to be studied for their universal import and indeed for their relevance to the very place where the observer is undertaking his study.

In the tumultuous self-evaluation of the United States, therefore, the most far-sighted of Americans are aware of the critical importance to the world of their domestic decisions. They are also aware of the domestic relevance to them of the world's decisions. The radical boldness that made Americans part with European assumptions when technologically produced abundance made another estimation of mankind seem possible and desirable can once more bring about a reassessment of their own interwar values and mechanistic shibboleths in school practice. Recent developments have shown these to be but technical phases in the nation's historical development. So America's world responsibilities in education are no longer a matter of generous disbursement only, or an unprofitable one-way traffic; they inhere quite as much in that stocktaking process which loyal Americans so assiduously practise even when some entrenched "educators" retreat behind accusations of sacrilege. The determined progress of the United States is likely to depend for the future, as it depended in the past, on the deliberate utilization of all the opportunities that the school system can offer, including those revealed by the fuller cultivation of rare abilities and by a deeper all-round evocation of purposeful endeavor.

chapter 6

THE SOVIET UNION

The Claims of Communism

The Union of Soviet Socialist Republics covers about one-sixth of the earth. A glance at the map of Europe and Asia shows that the heart of that land mass is comprised by the Soviet Union, with free Europe and the Indian peninsula and Japan seeming like dissident fringes, while all the rest is of temporarily indeterminate status. China, though separate, is politically akin. India, though not too friendly, is impressed. Japanese opinions and emotions are torn between the Soviet Union to the west and the United States to the east. This picture of Asia and Europe is roughly as the Soviet citizen sees it.

The present area of the Union's territory is over eight and one-half million square miles. The population in 1962 was estimated to be roughly 218,000,000. This figure means that there are perhaps four Soviet citizens for every three Americans, or for every one Briton. Nearly 70 percent of this population is in Europe, although less than a quarter of the Soviet territories are there. The vast and still mostly undeveloped resources in Asia place the Soviet Union in approximately the same position of "unlimited possibilities" as the United States enjoyed in the early days of the republic. The population is increasing rapidly. Industrial and urban development might be compared with that in Canada—but on a vast and radically planned scale.

The fifteen Union republics and twenty-two autonomous republics of the USSR are not a federation like Canada or Australia; nor do they possess in practice those "state's rights" so cherished in the USA. For governmental purposes there is tight centralization; but in some aspects

EDUCATIONAL SYSTEM IN THE SOVIET UNION

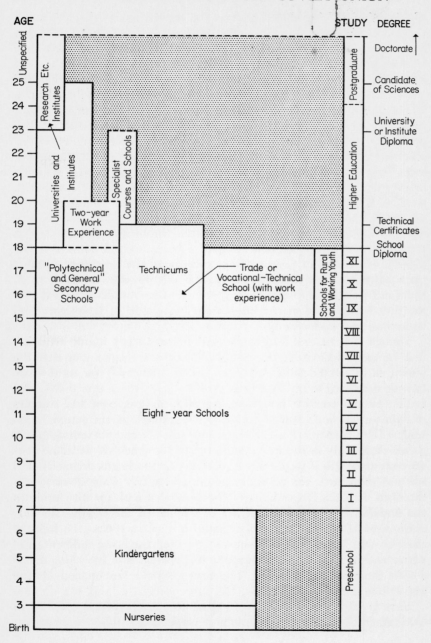

of education and in cultural matters the regionalism of the USSR can still be strongly felt. Only general education (not vocational or higher instruction) is administered by the several republics, and even then Communist party centralization makes for uniformity. A little more than half of the whole population either speak or easily understand the Russian language (for the Soviet Union is essentially based upon the territories of the Tsarist Russian Empire), and the Russian republic (RSFSR) is of course the most populous and influential of all. But up to 180 languages are spoken in the Union. Several are of Turkic affinity, being spoken by 11 percent of the population. Of the others, some have ancient literatures, whereas several had no proper grammar or even alphabet until after the Soviet Revolution in 1917. Although Russian is the prestige language, and although no educated Soviet citizen is likely to lack real proficiency in it, it is possible to find vigorous linguistic and cultural nationalism throughout the constituent republics in all except the political field. For example, at Tiflis in Soviet Georgia students can proceed from infancy to the university through the medium of their mother tongue. It is not possible, however, to go so far in the regional tongue everywhere, and therefore Russian is taught to every Soviet child as the international language of technology and higher cultural opportunity.

Though it is natural and convenient for us to talk about "Russia," it is far more helpful to our understanding if we remember that the Union of Soviet Socialist Republics means something far more emotionally gratifying to millions of its subjects than Russia ever did. Under tsarist rule the minority territories, especially in Asia, were like colonies of Moscow. Though Russian is gathering strength as the international tongue (and rightly so), and though Russification and Sovietization still go on (especially in the economic and technical fields), we blind ourselves to the truth if we do not recognize that the linguistic, racial, and cultural minorities are generally proud to identify themselves in enthusiasm with the Soviet Union. The faces that look up with pride to the remarkable phenomena of Soviet science in the heavens include millions of Mongoloid features or aquiline Turkish types—the faces of children who know that they are not despised for being different, and whose enthusiasm is proportionate to the change that has come about within their parents' lifetime. The Soviet system has opened up the universe to them.

That is why the startling success of the first artificial satellite in October 1957, was such a triumphant vindication of Soviet education in the eyes of Soviet citizens. Its solid evidence was a sort of cement for identification. If tractors and dams have been hymned, how much more Sputnik? The flight around the moon, and the highly successful space flights of other kinds, have reinforced this pride. It is a mistake for us outsiders to think that practical or material considerations alone are involved in such triumphs (though these are of huge importance). Two other aspects must be constantly borne in mind, one psychological or social, and the other ideological. The psychological or social victory so richly prized in Soviet education inheres in the knowledge that an extremely vigorous and arduous school system evidently justifies itself— not only in being successful at the top but in the broad social basis of its recruitment, enlisting the capabilities of nations and classes once thought to be of inferior caliber. The ideological triumph which the Communist party leaders capitalize on is associated with their belief that all human progress can be "scientifically" studied and planned in accordance with perennially valid principles; material and scientific progress therefore confers conceptual justification on the orthodoxy of the new interpretation. The sense of being right, of having a genuinely new civilization to offer—based upon a truer philosophy and deeper interpretation of humanity—this is a conviction extremely widely and sincerely felt throughout the Soviet world and its satellite fringe. We do not accept these views, of course; but we are guilty of the most crass purblindness if we do not recognize their widespread existence, their fervor, and their evocative or cultural power. More than any other nation, perhaps, the Soviet Union is "sold on education" both for its manifest results and also for its inner virtues.

It follows from what has already been said that the republics and peoples making up the present Soviet Union differed profoundly in their degree of advancement at the time of the Revolution. It has been fashionable in most Western circles to suppose that most of the Russian Empire was backward anyway, and became perhaps more retrograde after 1917. This is ridiculous. The Soviet achievement has really been to bring the eastern and southern regions up to and beyond the former standards of its own western republics, where most of the population were in a state of education comparable perhaps with that of much of the Austrian Empire or certainly present-day Spain and Portugal. The well educated people even before 1917 were cosmopolitan gentry and scholars like those of other countries. Despite large-scale emigration and liquidation, the majority of these stayed behind under the new regime. But this must not obscure the magnitude of Soviet changes. Though

Russia proper had a long tradition of scholarship even in science and technology (as well as the arts) in its schools (so much so that the United States was glad to copy), nevertheless there were grave inequalities of education and opportunity within Russia itself, and in most of the former imperial provinces there was real backwardness. The Russian revolutionaries themselves in the early days seem to have agreed with Marx that the Russian Empire was the last place in which communism could be expected to triumph. Germany or Britain, with their high industrialization and their urban proletariat, seemed to be much likelier ground.

In the chaos, famines, pestilences, civil wars, and the foreign interventions which followed the 1917 revolution and persisted until at least 1922 there seemed little chance of building up a new and educated nationhood with any prospect of economic stability. Foreign capital was withdrawn, and trade was at a standstill. Many of these terrible misfortunes persisted until the late 1920s. Moreover, in World War II the Soviet Union sustained losses and damage more severe than any other country. Yet despite a poor start and all kinds of interruptions, the Soviet educational recovery was such that in 1955 the USSR was turning out 60,000 university graduates in engineering a year, compared with 22,000 in the United States and 3000 in Great Britain. Since then the pace of technological learning has accelerated. Engineers are not everybody, of course; but these figures are paralleled in other Soviet education activity—and the quality is without any doubt very high. Americans equate Soviet "diplomas" with their own "master's" standards, and British observers make similar comparisons.

Making all allowance for the fact that a higher proportion of Soviet diplomas and degrees are in engineering and technological subjects, we are still left with the conclusion that educational achievements are phenomenal. They are already outstripping the prowess of the free world and the West. Yet it is not a generation since Soviet educational standards, in all except a few favored areas, were judged by observers to be regrettably low. How has all this change come about, and what lies behind it? We must not make the mistake of supposing that educational advance has only been at the highest level, and that the lower grades have been neglected. Illiteracy, formerly very widespread, has almost entirely disappeared not only from the younger generation but from among the old people also. Boys and girls do not merely go to school nowadays (more than 36 million of them); they also tend to stay

on. In 1955 over three-quarters of a million finished their tenth year of
intensive schooling.

In that year it was confidently expected that by 1960 between two
and three million children every year would reach the school year before
university entrance. (The corresponding figure then estimated for the
United States was 1,700,000; that for the United Kingdom was 70,000).
In fact, so nearly successfully was this goal pursued (without being actually reached), and so strongly academic was the schooling provided,
that changes were introduced in 1958 and subsequent years to divert
the majority of children away from the universities and formal higher
education which seemed so nearly within their grasp. At about that
time increasing competition and an academic bottleneck created difficulties to be reviewed later in this chapter. Since 1958–1959 the majority of pupils have been headed away from universities and toward
work-linked education or technicians' careers. This change of emphasis
does not, it should be noted, necessarily curtail *education*, though it
diversifies *schooling* and career prospects. It certainly makes some concessions to scholastic ineptitude or plain dullness; but the reiterated and
well argued dedication of Communist educators to a high standard of
genuine all-round education (within the confines of fidelity to their
faith) leaves no doubt of their intentions or of their positive planning
to elevate and not debase the academic and cultural level of all their
peoples. Just what does it all mean in terms of children, teachers and
parents?

Though the peoples of the Soviet Union have their long-standing
local ideals, the mass propaganda of the government officials and of the
Party has substantially produced a new ideal for Soviet Youth. Children
are very much to the fore, smiling in photographs and cheerful in
reality. Like Junior in the United States, young Ivan is expected to be
well fed, husky, and "normal." He must be, and usually is, public-
spirited. The future belongs to him, and he is expected to play a great
part in developing it through participation in many juvenile activities.
Many of these, like some American youth programs, subtly wean the
young people from the folkways of their parents; as a rule they are far
more thoroughly manipulated than in America. The Party sees to that,
whereas in America the public mores and community expectations are
less direct or effective in their socialization. Russian children are well
disciplined, by their peers as much as by their elders. They will not get
far even in youth organizations unless they are good at school work, for

example. A private as well as a public passion for education possesses Soviet citizens, and is very noticeable even in young people. The Soviet system has offered it to them in abundance, and the Soviet system (which seems good to them) is the only one they know.

Obviously, the emotions that the very different types of Soviet citizen experience when they think of their country and its system cannot be altogether the same. For one thing, its territories extend from the Arctic wastes, barely clad with stunted bushes, down through the forests and wheat plains to the Black Sea and the Caspian shores, where tea and rice and palms are grown. The distances the other way are far greater, spanning the earth from the Baltic to the Sea of Japan. The country, in its physical diversity as well as in its climatic fluctuations, is one of extremes. Extremes of wealth and poverty, privilege and servitude prevailed within living memory under the tsarist regime. Only two or three forces made for real unity—the centralized bureaucracy of the imperial government, the difficulty of free communication with the outside world, and the sense of "being right" indulged in by rulers and clergy under the dispensation of the Orthodox Church. It will be obvious that the peculiarities of the Soviet government of today have evolved in large measure from the special features of Russian imperial rule. The methods and mystique of godless communism are very like those of "Holy Russia." But added to the traditional emotions there are others of a very significant kind.

Despite present harshness, and a standard of living lower than that of continental Europe (to say nothing of Britain and America), most Russians and most other Soviet citizens are conspicuously better off than their parents and grandparents. Their material living and working conditions are much better, on the average. The absence of real freedom is not felt by those who have never known it. Indoctrination is not much different. The differences mainly result from the highly mechanized controls exercised by propagandists and supervisors in these latter days, and in the dwindling of those private oases of free thought and discussion once available to liberals and the "intelligentsia." (There are, however, signs that since Stalin's death more latitude is being successfully claimed.) If we are to try and understand how the average Soviet citizen feels about his country's achievements and controls, we have to concentrate first of all on his material gains and still more on the material promises held out to him. Party privilege, party interference, and universal regimentation are not so much resented (being historically familiar) as some other things are appreciated: the abolition of hereditary castes and privileges, the closing in of economic extremes, the offer of first-class opportunities in education and careers. Moreover, non-communist observers have frequently commented on the exhilaration often sensed in gatherings of Soviet youth. It seems they feel they are working together for a future which they can make for posterity if not for themselves. Youth is required to contribute to the future, practically and culturally. It is helped, in so doing, to realize an inward happiness and sense of personal fulfillment in "the collective"—one that can only be compared in fairness to a religious sense elsewhere. This sense of dedication has been described as a "YMCA" feeling.[1]

A comparable "forward look" is discernible among young people in less developed areas of the United States, and still more in western Canada. There they often endure harder conditions and more loneliness than they are accustomed to, though the material rewards are greater; but the sense of a beckoning future is one of the strongest experiences of their lives. In the Soviet Union the "virgin lands" of the eastern territories exercise a similar pull; and if it is not a physical horizon that beckons, there is a promised millennium. Undoubtedly there is drabness and sometimes dreariness in Soviet schools, fashions, and cities; but observers should not underestimate the contentment and perhaps enthusiasm with which people generally support a regime that is planning a better future for them. (For that, after all, is the way *they* have been taught to look at it.)

The essence of Marxism is in its suggestion that the future is scientifically controllable through an understanding and manipulation of the rules of economic progress. It teaches that ideas, emotions, and political experiences are only a manifestation of the environment as it controls human development; the environment itself, according to Marxism, can

---

[1] This expression is not used lightly. Lenin once said: "The whole of education and upbringing shall be directed to their training in communist *morals*." Youth organizations of all kinds carefully watch over the behavior not only of their members but of their neighborhood. They discourage slack and dirty habits (including smoking). They vie with each other in "socialist pledges" to maintain the proprieties, order, and productivity. So do the trade unions, neighborhood associations, and so on. All this is officially encouraged by the Party, of course; but in large measure it also seems to arise from eager cooperation. The communist faith, and also the practical business of social reorganization, are served by dedicated bands not altogether dissimilar in spirit from Catholic guilds and sodalities, except that the Soviet organizations ramify in their activities throughout the whole of civic and industrial life—including adult activities. Hence all those quasi-voluntary "brigades" engaged on civic projects, or on the tidiness campaigns which make Soviet streets, public buildings, and transport so immaculate.

be bettered by improving the methods of production and distribution and the sources of driving power. The young Soviet citizen sees plenty of evidence of such change around him. Questioning and disquiet come less naturally to him than they would to an American or a Briton. They seem like questioning the basic principles of faith—always a difficult and lonely thing to do. If we appreciate how the Soviet peoples have been "sold" the Marxist assumptions of dialectical materialism, and if we also bear in mind the authoritarian and self-righteous patterns of pre-Soviet Russian life, we shall be better able to understand the hold that the present Soviet upbringing maintains over its young people. They usually feel they know how their bread is buttered; many also feel near-religious dedication; and in any case the outside world is pictured as less advanced and hostile.

It is foolish to imagine that advances achieved in production and education by communist governments are prompted by tender concern for individual citizens. According to the environmentalist view, these individuals are little better than puppets or manifestations of the economic pattern; it is that which you are trying to manage. If personalities are difficult, they can be altered or put out of the way, much as we might train a tree to a desired shape or even uproot it. The "cult of personality" is adjudged to be a defect not only when it entails a glorification of Stalin or another fallen deity but also when it attempts to justify personal claims by you or me. One crazy revolutionary (Tkachev) in the early days suggested exterminating everyone over the age of 25, so that a clean start could be made. This criminal brain-storm was only a *reductio ad absurdum* of a widespread attitude—that in shaping the future it might be necessary to disregard not merely many people but even whole generations. Instead of disregarding them, however, the Soviet dictatorial board from the very beginning sought to reshape the older citizens into a favorable matrix for the future. Only the intractable were exiled or liquidated. Techniques of influencing people had not been developed to their present *expertise*, and time was short. After a while the system could be left to take care of itself except in unusual circumstances.

The "bourgeois" institution of marriage was among the first to be attacked by Soviet leaders, for three reasons: it perpetuated the continuous cultural exchange between parents and children, cemented by emotional ties; it was linked with the inheritance and accumulation of property; and its taboos were associated with religion. Therefore the importance of marriage was minimized, and divorce became a mere matter of form-filling. Casual relations and abortions were encouraged (though they are now very strongly discouraged). The Church and its workers were persecuted. However, children were well attended to—not just by parents but overwhelmingly so by the state. Crèches, nurseries, and the like took care of babies while their parents worked, and schools too took away not merely the duties but also the authority of parents. An abundance of preschool and extracurricular care for children is still characteristic of all communist countries.

In the early days of the Revolution, especially in the mid-1920s, the emphasis was on emancipation and equality. Women became equal to men, and received identical treatment in official matters. Children too were made to feel real partners in their own and public development—of no less consequence than parents and teachers, whom they were not afraid to defy and criticize or even denounce if need be. This was the phase of Soviet thinking exemplified by the story of Pavlik Morozov, a 12-year old "Pioneer" who denounced his own father as an "enemy of the people"; the father was condemned to death, and the boy widely acclaimed as an example for all young citizens. During those days army distinctions were reduced to a minimum too, and officers did not receive salutes or special uniforms. School subjects and books and timetables were adopted and discarded by children in the most "progressive" way. Until the early 1930s children often chose their own teachers. There were no examinations, and the standards and curriculums were those that seemed justified locally by "life adjustment." Pupils could expect to advance from grade to grade each year in accordance with their own personal standard, and those who wished to proceed to higher institutions could do so without having to satisfy predetermined criteria. The only real barrier to advanced education was being the child of a former aristocrat, professional person, priest, or other suspected opponent of the regime.

As part of self-determination, education was in those days entrusted altogether to the constituent republics. There was no federal Ministry of Education. Centralized control was limited to that implied by the power and solidarity of the Communist party. Local notions and needs determined what should be taught, and children were encouraged to plan and regulate their own school life. Though there was a shortage of schools and teachers, and though fees were still charged in schools (which did not have compulsory attendance until 1930), there were good opportunities for young workers and older underprivileged people to attend evening schools. These attempted to give them a "middle school" (that is, American high school) training and even to offer them university studies. Obviously the system could not work; it was bound to result in gross lowering of standards, and in an assumption that everyone had as good judgment as anyone else. (Soviet educators hold that everyone, given the right opportunity, is equally educable.) Anti-intellectualism was rife. Of immediate practical concern was the poor quality of workmanship in the Soviet factories and in agriculture.

Low standards in practical matters were rather surprising. Ever since the 8th Communist Party Congress in 1919 the new pattern of prole-tarian education had included much experimenting with the "work school." The idea of learning about life and of developing personal culture through work was recommended by Marx in 1848, and further recommended by N. K. Krupskaya (Lenin's wife) in her very influential writing from 1917 onward. At its best the "work school," as developed by Georg Kerschensteiner in Germany, may be compared with the very finest of the "industrial arts" programs of the United States. In the Soviet Union it had long been popular on account of its name; but by the 1930s it was obvious that it was not helping toward the successful education or industrialization of the Union. Lenin had, of course, been an avowed admirer of this and other "American" methods; but Stalin had already struggled to power, and in 1928 the first Five-Year Plan was proclaimed, to begin the following year. It was marked at every level by increasing centralized control and by its great thoroughness. By implication, of course, the old slapdash methods of education, which had served well enough during the period of casting off shackles, were doomed. Thus we come to the end of the first important phase of Soviet education (from 1917 until about 1929) and pass on to the second.

During the second period, the years from 1929 until about 1935 were spent on the consolidation of elementary education, and the years from 1935 until about 1941 were devoted to the stiffening and coordination of intermediate and higher education—all with a view to the strengthening of Soviet power and the establishment of an efficient hierarchy in industry and government. Less rather than more concern seems to have been felt for the interests of persons and subgroups in Soviet society—a tendency paralleled by Stalin's ruthless collectivization of farms and industries, and his suppression of local cultures (though he himself was not a Russian, and spoke the language with a strong Georgian accent until the end of his days).

At this point it is helpful to explain a few simple terms used in writing about Soviet education. Until 1959 the *four-year school* meant the elementary school period from the beginning of attendance (at 7 years of age) until 11. Village schools were usually of this character, and many still are. The *seven-year school* meant the elementary 4 years with an additional 3 years spent either in the same establishment or (frequently) in another building, which might be in a larger village or convenient center. The *ten-year school* meant a provision for the whole period between the ages of 7 and 17 or later. Since 1959 the term *eight-year school* is being used for the "general education" years until 15, and an *eleven-year school* is one reaching the university threshold about the age of 18. Similar terms are used in other European communist countries. It has always been customary to make children "repeat a grade" (as in many European countries) if not considered satisfactory. Therefore many might have had 10 years at school without completing "ten-year school."

Even if they did complete "ten-year school," that did not necessarily mean formal classes in conventional subjects during the whole of that time. Even during the most typically Stalinist period the last three years might be spent (and certainly were for the less "academically" suitable children) on projects closely associated with work,[2] and particularly linked with the current Five-Year Plan. It was during this period that the "Labor Reserve Schools" and "Trade Schools," with very utilitarian instruction linked with basic general education, became firmly established to guide future thinking about adolescents' scholastic potentiality. (A fuller description of them and their successors will be given later.) Like many Americans, most Russians like to have practical consequences from schooling. Much more even than Americans (especially in the later stages of education) they like to present basic principles in relation to utility and action. Soviet children and their parents are particularly responsive to this form of presentation. The over-strong emphasis on academic talents and attainments before 1958 was itself utilitarian—part of the determined drive to produce top-level scientists and administrators in unprecedented abundance.

To initiate the second phase of Soviet educational development, after 1930 school became compulsory from 8 to 12 years in rural areas, and in towns from 8 to 15. At first there were too few schools and teachers; but compulsion was soon reasonably effective. The old "self-determining" methods were promptly abandoned, and by 1936 were nonexistent. Teachers were reinforced in their traditional authority.

[2] It must not be supposed that the attainment level in these schools was necessarily low. Major Gagarin, the world's first spaceman, was trained as a youth in one of these "Labor Reserve Schools" before passing on to higher technical training.

Textbooks had to be used systematically, and became official. Each word and each definition in every book was henceforth scrutinized with the utmost care on ideological grounds as well as for accuracy. Pupils were ordered to work hard in school, or leave and work hard outside. The "work school" idea was left out of general education, to become the lot of less successful children after the age of 14. Far less was heard in "middle school" (i.e., American high school or British grammar school) about "polytechnical" education. Proper attention to *subjects* was insisted on; and the traditional "liberal" ingredients of European schools (except the Classics) were restored to the curriculum.

A Federal "Committee for Higher Technological Education" established in 1933 (now the Federal Ministry of Higher Education) has maintained strict control over higher education ever since. It therefore effectively controls the academic curriculum immediately preceding higher education. Co-ordinated with its interests are the programs of other Federal ministries concerned with different aspects of further education (e.g. Agriculture). The research and planning of the Soviet Academy of Sciences, of the current State Plan, and of the Party all systematize the aims and functioning of higher education and everything below it. The researches and publications of the Academy of Pedagogical Sciences of the *Russian* federal republic (not the Soviet Union) are also increasingly influential in directing school developments throughout the USSR.

In 1944–1945 the period of compulsory attendance was changed to begin at 7 years, and to last until 14 for those in the country, and until 17 for those in towns and cities. It was planned to make a ten-year comprehensive school period compulsory by 1960; but the new law of December 24, 1958, demanded that a universal eight-year period of general schooling should be followed by either more academic training or work-oriented training for at least 3 more years, becoming a compulsory work-linked 11-year total by 1970. In 1964, this total was again reduced to 10 years, perhaps to restore attainment levels impaired by work-linkage, or to prevent loss by premature employment. But let us return to the historical sequence. The second phase of Soviet educational development secured universal elementary schooling, developed substantial "middle" schooling, and made the Soviet Union one of the most thoroughly schooled of nations. During the second phase special care was taken to ensure that village children went to school. It was a step toward the intended industrialization of agriculture itself, as well as a means of preparing more workers for urban industries.

It should not be imagined, either, that school is for juveniles only. Extensive adult-education programs accompany it, sometimes undertaken by school children and young students as well as by their elders. Elaborate and highly successful campaigns have swept illiteracy out of farms and factories. The Soviet people are avid readers, and in some ways perpetual students of a sort that Western Europeans find it hard to understand. Therefore museums, planetariums, and the general harping on "culture" are really popular manifestations, and not just hackneyed gestures. That is not to say that everyone is always satisfied with communist handouts; but the general zest for educational opportunity expects "culture" from somebody, and the Communists have full control.

The "middle school" or "general" period still reflects Stalin's formalization. Its curriculum includes much mathematics, physics, and chemistry in addition to Russian, foreign languages, history, geography, and physical education. (Half the children in the Soviet Union learn English.) The going is hard, the presentation formal; but progress is sound, and steady. "Work experience" is still gradually introduced during the years 14–15. That included, the children attend school six days a week. Before the recent reforms, some hours of "socially useful labor" were already required every week, and this continues. Children often devote their Sundays to quasi-voluntary work in the public interests—for example, in harvesting, or in work brigades keeping the town or parks tidy, or similar operations. Yet they have spent 32 hours already under instruction, and they have a great deal of homework to do—not to speak of youth organization activities. (In the elementary school there are 24 hours a week of classroom instruction.) We should remember the Russians' previous heritage of agricultural history, when many of their ancestors were serfs. There is habitual emphasis on work followed by more work, just as in the United States the popular picture of the young American at work on the farm or in the kitchen or garage is an honorable one. In the old days most Russians had the children of the petty gentry, the clergy, and the educated classes lording it over them while they worked; now, therefore, they do not mind so much what appears to us the dull insistence on work as a means to emancipaton, to good jobs, and to the tickets to the theater and ballet that once were others' prerogatives. Where many of us would flag they still seem

enthusiastic. School holidays are still short.[3] A good performance and
high marks are so important that marks and grades are publicly announced. It is impossible to do well in social life or in the party without a good scholastic record. The children are under supervision and
subject to prodding all the time in more ways than we might suppose.

Control is ensured not only in the schools themselves, but in the
actual or virtual monopoly of books (including the hero stories that
have replaced many of our nursery tales), in the censorship of newspapers and radio and films, and through the various youth organizations. It is impossible to avoid the constant "plugging" of the party
norm.[4] Only a very small percentage of Soviet citizens are members of
the Communist party, for that is a real privilege often keenly sought
after as a steppingstone to promotion. It cannot be achieved without
a careful scrutiny, about the age of 27. In order to be acceptable to the
party, or in order to be admitted to responsible membership of the
Pioneers (ages 10 to 15) and Komsomol (Young Communist League,
from 15 upwards), boys and girls must not only live exemplary party
lives but be able to prove excellent performance in school or factory.
When candidates are proposed for office, one of the first questions concerns marks in examinations.

Even outside party affiliation, the prestige attached to the work of
these youth organizations is enormous. They offer all the community

[3] This does not seem literally true when we learn that the schools are closed during
June, July, and August (except for the final examination classes, whose ordeal takes
up nearly the whole of June), and that there are two-week vacations also at New
Year and in the spring. But the buildings are constantly used for youth clubs and
other extracurricular activities (in which the teachers help for long periods). There
are also camps, harvest work, and other kinds of "socialist reconstruction" to
claim the children's energies, quite apart from directly academic studies undertaken either privately or in association with a Pioneer House. Many or most urban
children now spend up to three months under looser supervision in camps
(organized by Party youth groups or by trade unions etc.). These are often at the
seaside or by lakes or in forests. An increasing number too spend their six-day
week in boarding schools, going home only on Sundays.

[4] This is all the more effective in the absence of alternative influences. Just think
what our city life would be like without advertisements constantly urging us to
buy this or that, to conform to some fashion, or to dream of something gorgeous
beyond our proper expectations! Soviet propagandists in particular point somewhat primly to their own freedom from "sexy" advertising and other "decadent"
influences that might distract or demoralize the young. All radio and television
programs (which seem to continue incessantly) are also vehicles of approved
enlightenment and taste. It is really surprising that there are so many concessions
to popular preference—in the circumstances!

services available to young people in other countries. They also provide facilities for sports and extracurricular activities of an academic kind. Some additional instruction is given, and especially such things as foreign language clubs attract the participation of young people who are not Communists. The real emphasis of communist education is in fact placed on activities outside school. In school the dreary brown tunic with a black pinafore worn by girls may be relieved only by the red scarf of the Pioneers. One way and another it is not surprising that 90 percent or so of the children wish to belong. Many who are not admitted to real party status nevertheless take part in the activities of these organizations.

This general pattern of elaborate control through school and party was confirmed during the Stalin period, and deviation was ruthlessly eradicated. A fair number of intellectuals who had weathered earlier storms found the means to escape from the Soviet Union. Some of these have written about intellectual standards and behavior in Soviet schools and universities during the admittedly chaotic inception of the second educational period, when young teachers and students who had grown up during the 1920s were passing into adult life. Their memories are doubtless true; but they are certainly not a true picture of the period immediately before the war, and they are still less true of today. The rigidity and vigor of formal schooling under Stalin's control has really established the structure as we see it today, though with some modifications in policy and practice. Some of these are intentional, and others were introduced almost willy-nilly from wartime experience. The German attack on the Soviet Union in 1941 meant the abandoning of all but the war effort. Teachers were withdrawn from schools; many pupils were drafted for work of national service; women took over still more of the professions. Tuition fees which had been abolished were reintroduced (1940–1941). They were not removed from higher (that is, university or "institute") education again until the end of 1956.

The third and present phase of Soviet educational history may be dated from the end of the war in 1945; but it is probably truer to see the postwar period until Stalin's death in 1953 as one of reclaiming what had been lost, and as a fuller development of the plans enforced immediately before the war. Purges and party maneuvers were not allowed to affect the general building-up of a heartlessly efficient training at school, at work, and in public organizations of a well-disciplined and well-informed totalitarian citizenry. A new political aristocracy arose, and these and the economic heroes were given rich personal rewards; but for the rest there was little expectation of diversified opportunities through school, any more than there was decentralization of control. "Frills" of all kinds were embargoed; there was a shortage of consumer goods, and a denial of variety in everything from classrooms to clothes. Therefore, although the late Stalin period may be characterized by the mass production of "capital" goods for the future in the shape of numerous well-trained scientists as well as in vast development schemes, the present or third phase of education can be described as beginning after Stalin's death.

Since 1953 there has been a natural reaction against many activities associated with Stalin. Old plans have been cautiously and then more generally revived. Controlled experiments of many kinds are taking place. The greatest is the radical school reform diverting the majority of pupils into vocational education (of which more will be said later) after the age of 15. The supply of top technologists and researchers is well assured, and more technicians are needed. The "polytechnic" idea is being revived in all education; training for automation and its consequences is beginning; boarding schools are named as "the schools of the future"; and much attention is given to education for a Communist millennium instead of the mere "socialism" of the present.

The overcrowding of schools adds to the importance of extracurricular work. Numerous schools visited very recently in Moscow, Leningrad, Baku, and elsewhere were on a two-shift system. A school building may be an elementary school in the morning and a middle school in the afternoon, or vice versa. The premises are in continuous use. The simple fact introduces another aspect of Soviet school life— the standardization of presentation. Young children and adolescents are expected to use the same desks and classroom arrangements. Also, the great emphasis on the theoretical and social (i.e., dialectical materialist) study of physics, for example, is not matched so far by a full provision for practical work at this stage. Standardization is such that there is a completely undifferentiated school program from the Baltic to the Pacific, except that in Lithuania and Georgia, for example, the "eleven-year school" may take 12 years because of difficulties of learning additional languages. All pupils take the same subjects. Beginning in the first year with Russian language and literature (or the mother tongue) for 13 hours, with mathematics, physical education, singing, and some practical work, they eventually reach a grand total of seventeen subjects in which they have received instruction. In an article published in February 1957, Dr. George Counts of Columbia University calculated that the ten-year school offered 9962 hours of classroom instruction, some 10 percent more than a Canadian child got in 12 years of school. This in turn is more than the American average. We must add to it the strong extracurricular influences at work.

Children do not have a choice of subjects, though there is specialization at university and "technicum" or college level. All middle-school teachers are specialists, and responsible in detail for the "correct" presentation of their speciality. Methods officially approved at one time are changed at another, and subjects such as history or biology are re-edited from time to time. There are no private or independent schools. No religious teaching is permitted in schools. Schools are prevented from having much individual self-consciousness, quite apart from party considerations, by the fact that they have numbers and not names, as a rule. They are all coeducational, and apart from the period of paramilitary training for boys and that of domestic science for girls there is no basic differentiation of the curriculum, either as between boys and girls or between children or varying interests and abilities. Superficial modifications may be found; for example a majority of children aged 12 and over learn English, while others learn French or other languages. Supplementation for the slowest and brightest children (and for aesthetic taste or practical skill) is abundantly supplied in the youth organizations.

A high standard of proficiency and diligence is demanded by the children's own "collective will for advance" no less than by the teachers. The children are taught in groups—*never* selected according to ability—in which the forward ones help their slower brethren. As much as is consonant with predetermined standards, children are made responsible for the organization of their progress through the curriculum. Character training of a somewhat puritanical austerity is very much part of the school's atmosphere. No experimentation in education is permitted at the school level; but there are many research institutions at the highest level. In particular the Institute of Defectology in Moscow had paid special attention to remedial reconstruction of a child's learning environment, and claims good results with those who in some other countries would be considered hardly educable, or at any rate unsuited to a bookish education.

Though there is no selection of children for schools, nor any "homogeneous grouping" into streams of equal ability, there are state grade examinations at the end of the fourth, eighth, and final years;

there were also yearly examinations until 1957. Children whose performance is not satisfactory are kept back. If they repeatedly fail their grades they may then be sent to a special school. Learning includes much memory work and repetition of facts. On the other hand, the subjects are presented as scientifically as possible. For example, in the learning of English, student-teachers who have never been outside Russia acquire a sound intonation and perfect accent by means of oral diagrams, intonation graphs, and records. They also undertake a comparative study of Verner's law and learn Old English. In personal contact they are found to have a remarkable command of the language, which they are eager to use in discussion. English is perhaps the third language they have learned. In schools a similar though less advanced technique is used.

Though fees were abolished again after the war (even from higher education in 1956), education at the middle-school level is not entirely without cost to parents. They must pay for books and stationery; and children wear a sort of uniform, which must be paid for if possible. On the other hand, differences of social and economic origin, and those of race or color, are not allowed to handicap the promising Soviet child. (An exception must be made for the kinder consideration given to party officials' children for selection into universities.)

A typical lesson observed in 1960 may be described as follows. The teacher gave an almost unbroken lecture for about 45 minutes, with but little feeling for his class. He was a purveyor of information, and a subsequent assessor of pupils' achievement. (There was a slight variation in this technique for science and languages; but even then little give-and-take took place.) During the lesson a child was called up to show his homework. He wrote on the board for several minutes. The others watched silently, with hands clasped on their desks. A mark was given on a five-point scale. This was recorded with much public interest. Teachers who push on fast may make things difficult for about a third of the children, and nearly impossible for the slowest third. If teachers are slower bright children may be bored, but will find plenty to occupy them at the Pioneer House (school subjects as well as recreation). Russian children aged 16 or 17 are about British "ordinary level Certificate" standard in knowledge, though below it in practical work in science subjects. This means that in knowledge they can be more than favorably compared with most good American high school graduates. That is a fairer comparison, for the Russian school is, like the American, a "common school." We should note here that the classroom atmosphere just described is still entirely character-istic of those European continental schools in which progressive meth-ods have not taken hold.

Countries with great educational arrears to make up, or with diffi-culties arising from geography or a shortage of teachers, often rely more strongly than others on standardization and official programs. This "keeping up to the mark" is of service to the ill-informed or un-imaginative teacher, especially if he is isolated. It is found, for example, in Australia and parts of Canada, and is at the basis of the French insistence on a unified program for city and hamlet. It is in marked contrast to the practice of many American states which give people high school teaching certificates without specifying what subjects they are to teach, and without making sure that they really have a sound enough background for the various duties they may be called upon to undertake. English certification is much more lackadaisical still; but at least it may be assumed that the teachers have had a sound grammar school complement followed by specialized academic "subjects" as well as "how to do it" in college or university. As a complete contrast to Soviet uniformity we may refer to a publication of the Fund for the Advancement of Education, *Teachers for Tomorrow*,[5] it says that 49 percent of American high schools did not then offer a foreign language, that 23 percent taught no physics or chemistry to anyone, and that 24 percent taught no geometry. In the Soviet Union these subjects are taught universally as the basis for a Soviet child's understanding of the material world; but they are also of very practical value to Soviet statesmanship and technological advance. Mathematics and science subjects take up nearly 40 percent of a middle-school pupil's time.

When the "seven-year school" was the most that the ordinary child could hope for, the threat of possible rejection in the seventh year was of great importance in keeping up the tempo of work. Now gradual differentiation by abilities demonstrated in lessons or "life-linkage" before 15 is equally important. Performance at 18 is more critical still. Once, all obtaining middle-school certificates could enter higher educa-tion. More recently, only "gold medalists" with outstanding results could be sure of admittance. Now even these prodigies have to submit to tests and interviews. Those chosen immediately for universities and higher institutes are the top 20 percent of an already selected group. The 1958 reform law required all others (i.e. 80 percent of the academic

---

[5] Fund for the Advancement of Education, *Teachers for Tomorrow*. 1955.

18-year-old school graduates) to take jobs of any sort for two years before entering higher education—if they were qualified. Many thus begin their university work with evening instruction or correspondence courses. Again the best of this latter group may be admitted to full-time study about the age of 20; but in 1962 half the students in higher education were on a part-time basis, and of these a large proportion continue so. Courses then take a minimum of six years instead of the usual five.

An outsider might perhaps suppose that the exclusion of so many potential students from full-time university courses is a regrettable and temporary expedient. Some American commentators say so. Yet this is quite a mistaken idea. An official Soviet publication in 1962 stated that the future trend in higher education would be to have the majority of students beginning their university-level studies on a part-time or correspondence basis, in combination with a factory or agricultural job. (We must remember that, wherever possible, tuition facilities may be provided in state enterprises or close to them). Some ideological justification underlies this plan; it is undoubtedly the intention of communist educators to emphasize that academic experience is not so much a lucky alternative to work as an alternative kind of work. In any case, full-time students in higher education now have to do their stint of "socially useful labor" too, for the good of their personalities and for the furtherance of the current productivity plan.

Moreover, we shall draw naïve conclusions if we fail to take note of the increasing selectivity of all Soviet education. Just as work experience before the age of 15 is a valuable indicator of suitability for this or that future career, particularly when combined with class records daily reckoned from 1 to 5 marks for every piece of work done, so the work requirement now imposed upon the great majority of even the more academic 18-year-olds is a sort of filter too. Only the best and most persistent are likely to get straight into university or institute at 18; and only the most diligent and deserving of the others will go full-time into higher education at 20 or so. In observing these trends we must not envisage the customary European dichotomy between work and study. Communist countries often closely relate higher studies to the practicalities of work (including their humanizing perceptions and a sense of professional responsibility). In Soviet higher education, the equivalent of American "term papers" or British essays may also be closely related to some industrial or agricultural problem as experienced by the student "in production."

The selection at 18 years of age is therefore harsh and relentless. No fees are charged in higher education; and most students get scholarships or grants, which are conditional upon progress. Only the best scholarship holders have quite enough to live on, though; the others need supplementation from their "work experience." University students proper have many advantages, especially considered in relation to the housing shortages and other hardships of Soviet urban life. They are exempted from military service. They work very hard for the five-year course, but they once again are enthused by a sense of future promise. Though the number of university and institute (college) places is proportionately higher than in most other countries, it is not enough to meet the demand. Add to this the fact that Soviet public opinion is in favor of intellectual distinction, so much so that people (nonstudents) read textbooks freely on public conveyances, and it becomes easier to appreciate how much it matters to be excellent. Some indication of this same esteem is given by the relatively high status of teachers. Engineers and miners or those who work in dangerous occupations are given the highest rewards. University teachers and researchers, followed by other teachers, come next. The medical profession, consisting largely of women auxiliaries to specialists and researchers, come about fifth. The whole of public opinion thus supports a systematic attention to work and intellectual training.

When a seven-year school life was still normal, many quite able but nonacademic children thereafter entered the Labor Reserve schools already mentioned. Instituted during 1940 to train a million boys for major industries, they were immediately popular. The war halved their numbers; but until 1959 they still trained hundreds of thousands of teen-age boys and girls for 1–3 years, making them skilled workers. Many such schools were residential, with tuition, board, and clothing provided by the state—especially for war orphans and refugees. These schools are now called Trade Schools or Vocational-Technical Schools (*remeslennoye uchilishche*), and offer a tough utilitarian course to boys and girls who have finished the eight-year general program. Though they offer a basic nonvocational supplement too, they do not yet complete the eleven-year school curriculum. For this, bright children are urged to go on to the next stage in day or evening study. (It should be noted that Trade Schools may actually be on factory or farm premises; and it should also be noted that *all* eleven-year school pupils of every kind must now learn a trade, including the "academics.")

A Technical School or Technical College proper (*tekhnicheskoye uchilishche* or technicum) offers either a four-year course (usually) to 15-year-old entrants, or a shorter course to 18-year-olds with a middle-school certificate. For the former group the "technicum" offers training as a medium-skill specialist, together with a general education up to university entrance level. For the latter it gives technical training and a preparation for intermediate management positions and the like. In 1955, *Izvestiya* declared [6] that half the students in technicums had already completed the ten-year school course; and until 1959 the proportion with a complete secondary education increased. In any case there is an exacting entrance examination. On completion of the course, students may apply to universities or institutes, and about 5 percent are admitted; but the technicum itself is the "college" for music, ballet, art, nursing, medical auxiliary work, and most ordinary teaching, as well as for technical skills, business administration, journalism, and the like. Some 3340 technicums in 1961 trained more than 2 million students for well over a thousand distinct careers. They include thoroughgoing practical experience "on the job" during their later years. A new-style "factory college" at this or a comparable level was also initiated in 1960. Foreign observers should not underestimate the importance or attainment level of this "intermediate" kind of further education, which, to say the least, overlaps much that is called "higher" education in some other countries.

An interesting sidelight is thrown on the academic standing and social prospects of schools in this range by the fact that in some rapidly industrializing districts in some communist countries there is a tendency for boys to go into the technicum as an alternative rather than the more formal academic school after the age of 15; so girls may predominate in the latter. That is surprising anyway; and it is the more surprising when we recollect that in the Soviet Union engineering and similar professions have been successfully colonized by women.

In addition to these school-day preparations for the lower and intermediate ranks of the vocational hierarchy, there are many supplementary offerings. Not only are there evening high schools and extramural courses; it is also possible to make use of a wide range of correspondence courses. It is largely by means of evening opportunities and of factory schools that illiteracy and ignorance among older people have been combated. Trade unions, cooperatives, collective farms, and community organizations all have a share in them.

---

[a] See A. G. Korol, *Soviet Education for Science and Technology*, Boston: Massachusetts Institute of Technology, 1957, pp. 101 and 127.

The Communist party also covers the country with a network of propaganda centers which hand out much general information on the side. Library and museum services have always been vigorously developed by the Soviet government. Ballet, theater, music and opera are generously subsidized, and immensely popular.

It follows from the description of technicums given above that the old European division of the teaching profession into two or more parts has for the time being been accepted by the Soviet government, though there are many signs of change. Abolishing illiteracy and universalizing elementary education demanded many teachers immediately. Now there are more than seven times as many teachers as existed in 1914. Until 1957 some teachers' technicums offered a four-year course from the age of 14 (or 2 years after completion of the ten-year school). Since that year, elementary school teachers are trained in four-year pedagogical institutions or technicums. They enter at 18–20 years of age. There is an admission examination and the course is hard; but the leaving certificate does not count as graduation. Such teachers are never specialists. They teach all subjects in the first four school years, and move up year by year with the children. They are paid on a basis of 4 periods a day, for 6 days a week. In-service training is common, and the best elementary teachers are urged to proceed to higher institutes of university standing, where since 1958–1959 more than 1000 places are reserved for them. This is said to be the goal in all teacher training for the future.

The higher pedagogical institutes just referred to are part of the higher education system. Over 200 specialized *institutes* (or colleges of advanced technological education) in the USSR run parallel to the universities, in some cases exceeding the prestige of the latter. Their difference lies in more specialized or "applied" courses. Not all the buildings are impressive architecturally; but they are often superbly equipped and have magnificent library facilities, with numerous copies of individual titles and dozens of photostat copies of current learned periodicals from all over the world. So in attending a pedagogical institute a future teacher shares an experience comparable to that of most Soviet graduates, the vast majority of whom were institute students. There are also general universities (40 in 1961), with over 200,000 students. Moscow and Leningrad Universities each have more than 20,000, and enjoy all-Union prestige, though each of the separate republics has at least one university fostering its regional culture as well as serving utilitarian purposes. Students in all higher education must now take some courses in Education (except advanced theoretical scientists and mathematicians). A good supply of excellent scholars thus enters teaching. Since 1960 courses in pedagogical institutes have been extended to 5 years, like those in other institutes and universities. Teachers trained in them are specialists serving the academic 15–18 classes and other senior grades in the middle-school; but an increasing number of them are found lower down the age range and also in more practical subjects.

Many institutes can be compared for subject intensity with American graduate schools, or the Honors specialization of British universities and specialized research institutes. On conclusion of the course, the student obtains a "diploma." The term should not be misunderstood. It may be equated with an American master's degree or a British Honors degree—and not just in terms of technical knowledge. Eyewitness evidence and personal encounter leave no doubt of the extremely high quality of Soviet students. About 60 percent of them are technologists (compared with 56 percent in Britain and 25 percent in the USA.)

Specialized in its application and orientation though Soviet higher education usually is, nothing could be further from the truth than to suppose that its alumni are little better than super-technicians. Those institutes or courses devoted directly to the humanities can boast a degree of scholarship and sensibility not to be dismissed lightly.[7] It has in fact been greatly admired throughout the civilized world—no slight recommendation when we reflect on the isolation Soviet scholars have had to endure, imposed by restrictions at home no less than abroad. Moreover, the average level of all-round cultural development manifested by Soviet specialists is admirable. What other countries have worried about as a "two cultures" cleavage is less apparent in the Soviet Union in consequence.

Testimony to the excellence of Soviet higher education has come from many sources in recent years; but none has been more striking than that of Lord Robbins [8], who gave his name to the Robbins Report issued by the committee on higher educational reform which visited the United States, France, West Germany, and the Netherlands before

---

[7] See D. Grant, ed. *The Humanities in Soviet Higher Education*. Toronto: University of Toronto Press, 1960 and C. L. Wrenn, "Higher Education" in *Communist Education*, ed. E. J. King. London: Methuen, and Indianapolis: Bobbs-Merrill, 1963.

[8] Interview reported in the London *Times*, June 12, 1962.

proceeding to the USSR. He declared that he had "tremendous respect" for the way in which the Russians had combined quality with quantity in education. Some non-Russian observers are foolishly misled by the names of Soviet qualifications, above all, the "diploma." Non-Russian comparisons will remind us that in several western European countries a "diploma engineer" is the most highly qualified of engineers. Incidentally, in this field, Soviet higher institutions have in several years been training as many technologists as the rest of the world put together. Of course, the more settled economy of the United States or Western Europe could not absorb 60,000 graduate engineers a year; but the expanding development of the Soviet Union and its friends can.

The whole educational system of the USSR is in full evolution; but nothing is changing faster than technical and higher education. Conventional distinctions between subjects, or "levels," are being superseded by new arrangements—always to make the most of the human, scientific, and productive potential. Graduates in each specialization are trained in the numbers anticipated to suit the State Plan; and on graduation they can be directed to particular jobs for 3 years, after which they are free to move elsewhere. Not only directive powers but financial and promotion incentives too ensure the full deployment of skilled resources. Teachers (especially in higher education) are well paid and highly esteemed. This fact should be assessed against a world background of teacher shortage. In the USSR, not only ideology and patriotism but sheer industrial realism make leaders of the country's enterprises realize that education is an investment that can never be skimped.

Much attention is paid to higher education in the arts. There are 47 institutions of this kind, for music, visual arts, theatre, and cinema. The correspondence departments of higher education exceed 500, with about a million students. Such students can usually get time off work for summer schools, examinations, and the like.

No real difference is made between women's and men's access to the professions. Some 25 percent of the engineers, about one-third of the physicists, and 75 percent of the doctors are women. There have been women generals. Coeducation is once again the rule, as it was until 1939, when it was discontinued during the war years.

Since Stalin's death there has been a crescendo of interest in "polytechnicization." This includes a return to the old idea that work or a career prospect gives life-interest and realism; it also suggests that a truer perspective on all life is given through working experience, especially when oriented toward the communist millennium in which all will be workers together, giving according to differentiated abilities and receiving according to need. (The crusading value of this slogan is everywhere evident in the USSR.) Therefore polytechnicization has its moral and aesthetic side as well as utility; it is absurd to represent it as disguised "child labor." Though it certainly entails hard work, there is little doubt of its evocative success—for the average child at any rate. General as well as technical education is obviously secured, and the children seem to like it. About two-thirds or more of them above the age of 15 are now trained directly for occupations while receiving a general education; yet the formal content of the *schooling* received by at least one-third of this number during their 4 vocational training years is as substantial as if they had been in a Stalin-style ten-year school, and indeed may go well beyond it. For the more academic 25 percent or so selected for preuniversity courses between 15 and 18, there is still a craftsman's trade to be learned in school workshop or public enterprise before higher education is embarked upon. (This is done part of 2 or 3 days a week during school time.) Moreover, all except a minority of university or institute entrants have now had 2 years' working experience beforehand. They are said to be much better students in consequence, in terms of learning as well as of character.

Though the undoubted bottleneck in the approaches to Soviet higher education before 1958 certainly made diversion of would-be students necessary on merely numerical grounds, the hangover of European disdain for "dirty hands" occupations was felt even in Russia. Such bourgeois immorality obstructed the building of a collective spirit, of course; but it also was a nuisance when technicians, maintenance men and supervisory people were needed rather than more pioneers of research or teachers—abundantly supplied by the ten-year school. Middle-grade occupations are those predominantly needed by contemporary society, and even more by the automated world of tomorrow. Soviet society is as planned as its economy. A Marxist must believe that patterns of production and distribution provide not simply the material basis for life but its very roles and perceptions; they are therefore the stuff of culture and the web of sensibilities. This is much nearer to medieval Christianity and to Dewey than the nineteenth century traditions of European schooling. Stalin's formalization of the curriculum of the ten-year school, therefore, though the foundation of Soviet technological triumphs, was a reversion to continental assumptions and also a departure from the "American" ideas Lenin had admired. De-Stalinization reintroduced more "learning-by-doing"; it also combined what had become necessary for the next stage of industrialization with what was thought socially desirable as the next step toward communist culture. Previous *ad hoc* attempts to retrain academic half-successes for practical work were not popular or satisfactory as this one is.

One universal reason for inattention and absenteeism among older school children is boredom. The inclusion of subjects of more obviously practical value, especially when the training is given residentially away from home, will probably help to cut down the uneasiness and disaffection of youth. The Soviet Union, like most other nations now, has its problems of juvenile delinquency and the type of borderline behavior that produced beatniks and hot-rodders in the United States and Teddy boys in England. No one is so likely to be a public nuisance as a young person whose abundant energies are unabsorbed while his ambitions are frustrated.

It is a mistake to imagine that polytechnicization need necessarily be a whittling-down of the liberalizing possibilities of education. If more insight or conviction is gained by linking studies with practical considerations, well and good. Yet, however praiseworthy the plan may conceivably be, the sudden change found the teachers unprepared. They have been, as we have seen, trained as specialists eager to be correct; they were at a loss to know how to be correct in an application of their studies that was unfamiliar to them. Still, sudden about-faces are part of Soviet history, and no doubt teachers will both survive and comply in due course. The outside observer is more interested to discover what underlies the initiation of this third phase of Soviet education. First it was *laissez-faire* and self-determination; next it was the austere formalities of the European curriculum, but with a much stronger scientific content; now we are witnessing the development of a "polytechnical" and more socialized move toward communism. "Socialism today—Communism tomorrow!" is a familiar slogan. "Children, think, speak, and work like communists!" can be seen in many a classroom and workshop. "The task of our school is the creation of a new communist humanity" does not ring so strangely in eastern Europe as the more work-oriented new variants upon the reiterated theme of "Study, study, study as Lenin studied." Lathes and other equipment, some quite elaborate, now appear in Pioneer houses and recreation centers more obviously than before. The same evocation to "school" is given a more workaday complexion in this way.

Other changes inside the Soviet Union may perhaps be associated with this one. In the disorientation and jockeying for place that followed Stalin's death, western European liberals tried to discern a stirring of independence that might have loosened the shackles of communist dictatorship. Undoubtedly something of the sort seems to have occurred. There have been violent repressions in East Germany. Poland seems to have come as close to emulating Tito as her Soviet masters were prepared to allow. Hungary went too far in the direction of liberalism, and was ruthlessly quashed with violence and bloodshed. Such violent eradication of "counterrevolution" is quite in keeping with communist philosophy; but what prompted this anxiety abroad was perhaps the inner disturbance at home. It has been credibly said that the communist regime's hold over its own youth was at stake. Much emphasis has been placed since 1956 on the establishment of increased numbers of boarding schools, presumably for greater control and discipline, and, since 1958, on the disciplinary value of work.

Reference has already been made to the difficulties experienced by school-leavers in getting into college. At the universities and colleges themselves it has become fashionable to cultivate independent attitudes, read "dangerous" books, discuss heterodox ideas, and generally to become "decadent." In free countries this sort of puppy-play is no more than a trial of strength against what is old and traditional. In the Soviet Union it could be a challenge to the communist way. The affected Western European clothes and hot-jazz records of the *stilyagi* (Teddy boys, beatniks) are certainly more than a matter for critical cartoons in the comic papers now; the Soviet authorities go out of their way to denounce the disaffection of these youths. Dissatisfaction has probably not so far reached the stage of serious criticism, however, and some criticism or heterodoxy (at any rate in poetry and music, and perhaps in the interpretation of the Marxist canon in relation to similar things) can apparently be accepted. Striking evidence of this is shown in open debates in Soviet periodicals, and still more in the visits of Yevgeny Yevtushenko and other "angry young men" to Western capitals.

Yet undergraduate excesses must not be considered in isolation. At the working-class, less intellectual, level in the Soviet Union, there has been hooliganism, delinquency, and "even religion!" Even in the communist world opportunities and rewards are evidently so unequal that a kind of brutal repudiation occurs. Sometimes there is good reason for frustration. That is no doubt why, after Stalin's death, a great decentralization of management—or at least a devolution of responsibility under the central, watchful eye of Moscow—has been initiated. As one writer put it, the immense beehive of Moscow bureaucracy has been overturned. The safe jobs are no more. Managers are to be more effective and responsible in their sphere. Remote control can evidently become too remote even for Communists. The dispersal of industrial responsibility is not only for strategic reasons, we may be sure. It is at least partly caused by a need for greater public contentment. Admittedly it coincides with an announced determination to open up the east and north more effectively. The twentieth Congress of the Communist party in 1956 published plans for the irrigation of large stretches of arid land in Asia. There has long been a movement of the young people to the "virgin lands" either before or immediately after their college careers. This migration is semivoluntary, and those who participate usually find it a rewarding experience. From the point of view of the top administrators, it must undoubtedly be a safety valve also.

Communist orthodoxy has in the past clamped down on literary and artistic deviation no less than on political sacrilege. In recent years there have been unprecedented strayings from the party line. Before the door is shut once again it is worth recording that, in 1960, university professors could publicly listen without fear to broadcasts in English from British and American radio stations—not just in their homes but in the faculty club. Strangers meeting casually in bars and public places would freely discuss such programs, either initiating a conversation or willingly taking part in one when started. They clearly had read and listened widely. They also took anticommunist visitors to their homes, though 1957 was the first year that teachers had been permitted to do so.

It is impossible to state or even to guess what the future will be, at any rate in the matter of politics or of liberal evolution in literature and art. One thing is quite certain: the Soviet Union is planning the full development of her vast federated empire with every foreseeable human device. Every day sees the building up of vast capital resources and the founding of real human wealth—good land conservation, fine crops, material advantages. This, of course, could well be done without communism; but it so happens that those doing it now are com-

munists, and claim they do it because they are communists. The
masters of the Soviet Union are able to lend technical assistance to
countries in desperate need of it. They would without doubt do so
even if it meant injustice to thousands of their own citizens, and
perhaps this does result. However, the technical and educational
prowess of the Soviet system is now so well established as to be
beyond controversy; it is unremittingly watched by the governments
of the United States, of the Commonwealth countries, of every free
nation. It is the envy (or the lodestar) of emergent territories.

A writer on social and educational backgrounds will not meddle
with political futures; but since 1957 Khrushchev has repeatedly declared that the Soviet Union's "inexorable" technological advance toward a higher standard of living for the world was a more potent
weapon in her armory than all the nuclear weapons ingenuity could
devise. It is possible he means it. It would be true even if he did.
Most of the world is too backward, hungry, and ignorant to be fas-
tidious. It sees real advance in science, technology, and production; it
sees educational advance far beyond the dreams of man half a century ago; it cannot stop to consider the political price because it has
no experience of freedom whereby to measure what has been sur-
rendered. The only effective counterblast of the free nations is to show
that, in equal circumstances, they can achieve an equal or superior excellence which will spill over all the same material abundance—together with a richer political, social, and personal experience.

To sum up, what does living in the Soviet system mean to its millions of men, women, and children? To outsiders it seems a gray and
repressive life. Congested housing, mainly poor quality consumer goods
at high prices, regimentation, dull fashions, and conventional art—these
are what we see, even if we forget the grim political side. What does
it matter that full-time working hours are being steadily reduced to a
maximum of 40 in 1962, 35 in 1964? What is it to outside observers
that Soviet maternity leave is now 112 days of paid absence, or that
sick workers get holidays in fine hotels in the Crimea, when they miss
the subtle taste of freedom? But then we are judging by inappropriate
criteria—our own, and not theirs. Those who, for example, are accustomed to being packed like sardines in Indian trains, or to riding
on the top in the dust and heat, do not object to third-class travel in
European trains. They may think it luxury. So it is with the Soviet
citizen, as a rule. But education is fortunately a discontenting thing in
itself—and at its best a potent source of "divine discontent." It is to be

hoped that the evolution we have experienced, and that Russian liberals experienced in the past, may repeat itself. Whether this happens or not will certainly be decided in part by the educational and technological successes of the noncommunist world.

One undoubted prerequisite to a genuine growth of humanism within the Soviet empire will be the free interchange of persons and ideas. This has hardly reached even a token level yet; but if it does become a reality we may once again find that "you can't fool all the people all the time." Until such exchange can take place over the Soviet boundaries, it seems doubly vital to ensure it among people in the nations outside, whether we like their politics and manners or not.

In this chapter every attempt has been made to point out the comparative austerity, if not drabness, of private expectations in the Soviet Union. But people who are living in what they feel to be an emergency out of which they will triumphantly emerge will often put up with the rationing of what we consider essentials but they consider desirable luxuries. Therefore what we think of life in the Soviet Union is irrelevant; the only sensible criterion is what Soviet citizens and their neighbors think. The neighbors are very important in this case. They are more than half of mankind. Much of what they see under the hammer and sickle seems more attractive than their own present lot even now. As Soviet productivity approaches American productivity, and American-style material abundance comes closer to the reach of the hungry world, the growing admiration for Soviet technology will know no bounds. Education on the Soviet plan is recognized as the foundation for Russian development.[9]

Many of those neighbors who see plainly the perils of communist authoritarianism are harried by their own extreme underdevelopment. There is great underproduction of food in the world, and bad distribution of what is grown. Part of this imperfection arises from the inability of poor nations to buy other people's surplus or even their waste. They cannot acquire purchasing power until they develop industrially or build services (such as shipping, works of art, precision engineering, or mercantile and administrative skill) that other nations

---

[9] Detailed information about Soviet educational reforms, ideology, and institutions is given in my *World Perspectives in Education, op. cit., passim.* A more extensive survey dealing with educational assumptions, practices and institutions in the U.S.S.R. and several similar countries is provided by *Communist Education op. cit.* Other references are given in the bibliography at the end of the present book.

want to buy. None of this can happen without educational developments, preferably very inexpensive developments.

In this connection the world role of Soviet education is of extreme significance. The first stage in education is having enough to eat. Then a man must have a home for his family, and keep them free from starvation and disease. It is a vital step when it no longer becomes necessary for a whole family to labor relentlessly from dawn to dusk (or longer) in primitive agriculture or some noisome factory. Repressive class stratification can be questioned. So can its supporting superstitions. Even half an hour a day to one's self is a humanizing instrument of the greatest importance—a chance for self-recognition, for conversation, for cooperation.

The most remarkable item of knowledge for anyone is that he is a man and that he matters. To attain this beginning of self-help all kinds of reforms are helpful: a more prolific strain of seed, a finer breed of cattle, a better marketing organization. Even a different pattern of hoe can be educative if it allows its user to stand upright and talk to his fellows instead of being crouched almost double like a beast. When we think of present needs in education for a very large part of mankind we are thinking of life at this elementary level. Perhaps a quarter of mankind, though above this utterly depressed status, are still barely at subsistence level. Providing them with an effective chance of further advancement depends on the skill of their governments in securing the benefits of modern technology and the opportunities for more education. The future of education depends on a material change now; children cannot go to school if they are exhausted in the fields or the kitchen.

Therefore, to appreciate the importance of the Soviet Union's influence in world affairs, especially in its cultural influence on desperately poor countries, we have to feel as vividly as possible what it means to have a neighbor who has done all these wonderful things, and apparently made them available both to its own subjects and to others, irrespective of nationality and color. Our own objections to the Soviet system then seem trivial, compared with the multiple gains held out by using Soviet methods. In wartime, as we ourselves have seen, even convinced liberals and democrats accept curtailment of freedoms and privileges. Greater things are at stake, things upon which peacetime privileges and opportunities are based. For the majority of mankind, the mere acquisition of the material basis for what we call civilized living is still a long way off. The winning of it is a war more desperate than we have ever known, because it is lifelong and merciless. Empires, besides inflicting certain injustices, have also shown formerly subject peoples what riches can be envied and now in these latter days be obtained by emulating western technological and scholastic excellence. Those very empires have passed on to their subjects the educational and administrative foundations necessary for the building of indigenous progressive societies. But it is not surprising that, where a speedy and gallant emancipation has not been permitted to former subjects, there should remain an impatience of occidental hegemony and a doubt whether democracy really means what it is supposed to do. All the nations with many overseas representatives export some poor specimens along with their worthier examples.

Therefore those who want success quickly, and who want it without the seeming wastefulness of inequality and "muddling through," are usually attracted toward a planned rather than an evolutionary society. Not even Soviet inhumanity seems less humane than destitution and former repression. The things that seem central and fundamentally objectionable in a communist or near-communist system when we look at it, may seem to others merely an accidental disadvantage, like fumes and heat from a highly productive furnace.

The main hope for the liberal and evolutionary societies, which have so long been privileged, is that the underprivileged may come to know that western democracies also have educational, political, and technological skills that will work out just as efficiently and more humanely in the long run. When all is said and done, human societies everywhere have in the course of ages evolved their own humane perceptions. Their well-informed leaders are no more eager than we are to surrender those subtleties of life that make it more enjoyable, that distinguish living from mere existence. Very often, however, they object to the universal extension of such urbane opportunities to their compatriots. When productivity, distribution, and the arts of living depended basically upon human muscle power, only a few could attain full, cultured stature. Mechanization brings a prospect of an urban standard of living for most people. It makes some old-style educational and social assumptions as antiquated as the water mill or even the treadmill.

Material development is of prime educational importance. That is why agencies like UNESCO devote such energies to fundamental education, food production, the elements of government and commercial administration. The Colombo plan for the development of south and southeast Asia is another agency of paramount educational importance, on a world view. The unprecedented generosity of the

United States government in the postwar period has helped the painful stages of pioneer industrialization or agricultural reform in many countries. Capital investment by private persons and corporations is also of great value; but it needs to be done with extreme sensitivity if it is not to be misconstrued as "economic imperialism." Not one of these activities can be effectively assessed without reference to the influence of the Soviet Union as a potential alternative.

The example of life in the Soviet satellite countries has not been conducive to an unreflecting adoption of the communist overlordship. There, as seems clear, everything is geared to the needs of Moscow. Yugoslavia is an exception, because it is undertaking a national experiment with communism. It is true that living standards in "Iron Curtain" countries in Europe are noticeably higher than the average in the Soviet Union itself; but some of those countries are being "creamed off" or even "bled" economically. In education, an abject submission to Moscow is much more marked. A careful study of education in East Germany and Czechoslovakia, (except for minor adaptations which are certainly not enough to change the schools' character appreciably) shows that the Soviet pattern prevails almost down to the last detail. To take one absurd example: books (in German) on biological subjects intended for use in East Germany take their illustrations from birds and animals not familiar in Germany at all. They have been approved in Moscow, and after their *imprimatur* they are presumably right for communist youth elsewhere. In fundamental matters too the Soviet pattern is in force— a communist monopoly of education, without private schools or religious instruction; [10] a uniform curriculum; the same structure (with "polytechnic" and working experience where appropriate, and so on). It is just as thorough and just as illiberal; but once again it generally shows an improvement on what average children were treated to before.

The position of China is difficult and peculiar. It is far too vast a subject to treat here. But communist history is mainly repeating itself, at least in public works and in schools. There is immediate concentration on capital development. Major works of reconstruction are undertaken. Communications by rail, road, and cable are being revolutionized. Rivers are being spanned for the first time, and power resources are being exploited with great speed. Schooling is groomed (or trimmed)

[10] Poland, strongly Catholic by tradition, was a notable exception. Until 1962 religious instruction was given under difficulty—and only by priests paid for the purpose but not allowed to teach anything else. There is still some religious instruction in Czechoslovakia and in Hungary under similar or less favorable conditions.

to serve immediate technological and political ends. Its recipients are obviously enthusiastic and prepared to tolerate hardship. They work hard in return for their benefits. Uniformity or regimentation is so little resented that it is patriotic and cooperative to wear blue overalls. The neat blue suits and blue caps of Chinese delegates in Moscow present as sobering an appearance as the clerical garb of a latter-day Puritanism. The Chinese, besides being the most populous nation on earth, are also proud and unpredictable. Their future may show their old independence leading them along a road of socialist development deviant from that approved by Moscow.

To return to the USSR, we should carefully consider Soviet educational achievements not only in terms of material abundance or military strength (important though these are for the moment) but also in terms of a new view of human potentiality, especially as that may appear to hitherto underdeveloped countries. That is to say, we must heed Soviet claims to have produced not only an efficient technological apparatus but a new and fairer prescription for civilization, with a more fully developed conscience and sensibility as well as opportunities for a rich life. For this, no less, is what Soviet educators mean when they talk of a communist society. We shut our eyes to the inner driving force (and the "sales value") of Soviet education if we limit our appraisal to plain politics and economics. Economic improvement and social justice are the bait dangled by communist propagandists before the underdeveloped people outside. Inside the Soviet Union it is very widely felt that these things are already assured, that the present stage of development has made Soviet citizens more civilized than those in capitalist countries, and that the next stage is one of even greater intellectual, aesthetic, and moral perfection.

How much this program owes to ancient Russian messianism, how much to religious Orthodoxy, how much to Marxist ideology, and how much simply to a firm commitment to education is a problem we should ponder.

But rather than venture here upon a purely speculative and hazardous study that could not in any case be profitably undertaken in a small compass, it would be better to consider the case of India. India has similar economic difficulties in some respects; she also has a vast and mounting population; for the first time she is able to control her own destiny as an independent country. The solutions with which she is experimenting may ultimately be of supreme importance to Asia and Africa, and in turn to mankind.

chapter 7

INDIA

Development and Democracy

A hundred years ago it did not seem altogether likely that either the United States or the Russian Empire would be in a position of paramount world leadership within a century. In some ways, despite their real achievements, they must have seemed rather like the relatively undeveloped countries of our own day such as Brazil or Argentina; their future had so many uncertainties. Looking forward from our own time we can hardly be sure what countries will ultimately have most lessons to offer mankind, even though we can see that some (like Canada) are likely to have a future of great material prosperity. The present position of a country like Canada represents one extreme of the human situation —a vast territory with riches still to be developed, and a small but enterprising population. In these circumstances there is ample opportunity for continuing and improving on the educational successes of either the United States or the Soviet Union. Seen from this standpoint their educational problems and responses might seem to have some affinity.

But when we turn to such a country as India we feel unable to forecast either prosperity or world leadership. The land is so poor, the population so vast, and the present situation so depressing. On the other hand our own nineteenth-century forebears were unable to foresee our world, and we may be making just as serious mistakes in our own calculations. It is stupid to see the future in contemporary terms. It is also misleading to judge other people's educational problems by our own frame of reference. The children of India are undoubtedly being

EDUCATIONAL SYSTEM IN INDIA

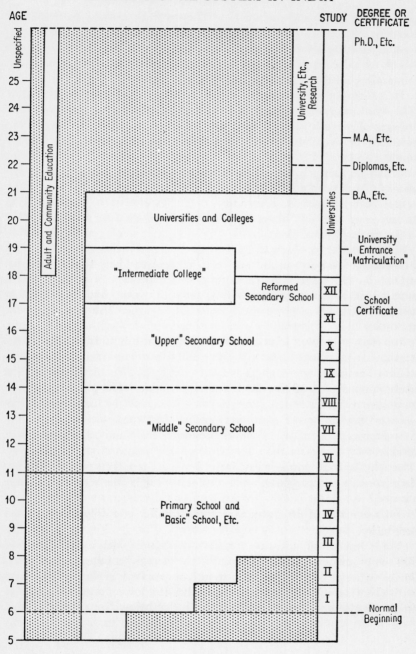

taught in schools and universities. They will be trained in fields and factories and offices. But to see the crux of Indian education we have to look beyond these familiar institutions and come down to fundamentals which we take for granted but which in India are suddenly revealed as demanding all the educational skill we can muster.

It is time for us to consider children on a different plane of reality. The whole world's problems of food and population, of class, of superstition, of poverty and disease are gathered together in the Indian peninsula in an acute form. (Most references to India in this chapter might also be applied with minor variations to Pakistan.) The solutions which India can achieve for these ancient problems may well place her among the nations which have most benefited mankind. We must also reflect that no human community so far has effectively suggested how to safeguard the old "liberal" or "rounded" humanities in a world that is increasingly specialized, industrialized, urbanized, and proletarian. This is a matter in which India feels vitally concerned. Any solution she can even tentatively suggest will help to save the health and sanity of mankind. The educational and economic problems of India seem at first glance to be in another world from our own; but in truth they epitomize the ancient terrors of mankind, and they may also comprise its future.

No country is more in need of radical reshaping than India, for several reasons. India, though the seat of the Hindu way of life for thousands of years, achieved a new beginning only in 1947. She then ceased to be a dependent part of the British Empire, and became instead a self-governing member of the Commonwealth of Nations like Canada. She was the first nonwhite dominion, and the first republic to stay in the Commonwealth. India had never previously been united, except under British rule, and even then several princely states had large autonomy. Though Pakistan broke away from India as a self-contained Muslim federation in two parts, the remaining territories of the republic of India survived as a great nation knowing unitary existence for the first time. It now consists of 16 states and some smaller centrally administered territories.

Yet it was not only its newness that faced India with a challenge. She has many profound problems, each grave enough to be urgently critical in its own right, but each even more complicated by being bound up with the others. The first is that India has the lowest standard of living in the world, and that standard is really far below the comprehension of those who have only experienced destitution in Europe. There is just not enough to fend off starvation from time to time, not to think of health or (even more remotely) prosperity. The majority of Indians know what it is like to be hungry—not merely in the sense of missing a familiar meal or two, but in the sense of being undernourished to the point of disease and the risk of death. Nothing happens on a small scale in India—great droughts, great floods, burning heats and torrential monsoons are aggravated by plagues and hostile insects or animals. When your peasantry are skirting subsistence level, or when you are sinking all in a cash crop, any one of these visitations can bring irreparable disaster.

Food shortage is not a simple risk unconnected with other things. It is immediately bound up with the problem of overpopulation. Since the reader first started on this chapter, some thirty or forty new Indians have been born. India is one of the most outstandingly prolific countries in the world. It is estimated that in 1800 there were about 50 million inhabitants in the country, roughly the same as the present population of the British Isles. In 1951 there were rather more than 359 million. By 1961 the census showed that the population had risen by more than 79 million. Moreover, we should add to India's total of 438 million the 85 or 90 million in Pakistan if we are to assess the increase over the Indian peninsula as a whole. India's third economic plan for 1961–1966 reckons on more than 8 million additional mouths per annum to be fed. A yearly increase of 2.5 percent is an anxiety, when there is already insufficient food to go round for the most meager standard of living. This calculation says nothing of other social needs such as health and education.

Too many babies are not the only problem. Because of starvation, malnutrition, disease, and other misfortunes, India long had an almost incredible mortality rate. No Indian baby could expect to live much more than 20 years in the not too distant past. Advances in the control of malaria and other tropical diseases have increased life expectancy by more than 10 years in a comparatively short time. More mouths to feed! Fewer deaths in childbirth! Longer parenthood! So the spiral rises.

Rising population is not a problem confined to India, or to Asia. It is most rapid in South America; but as the population of Asia is so immense now, the actual increase there fast outstrips that anywhere else. It is worth reflecting on these figures. Out of a total world population of over 3000 millions, nearly half are found in China, the Indian peninsula, and Ceylon. The world population is *increasing* by 80 persons every minute; some 170 babies are born, and only 90 people die. The total human race counts 120,000 more than yesterday, and at least 43 millions more than at this time last year. At this rate the number of human beings will be doubled by the end of the century. In fact, with medical advance, the rate may be stepped up, because the death rate is being quickly lowered while the birth rate stays fairly steady at 34 per thousand per annum. India in particular is a country where a diminished death rate is likely to increase the population enormously. It was the reduction of the death rate even more than large Victorian families that brought about the sudden increase of population in nineteenth-century England. In India the increase has been appropriately called an explosion.

Before considering the measures taken to cope with this and related problems, it will be as well to complete our picture of the total situation. The total area of the Indian peninsula is about half that of the United States' mainland territories; there are roughly 1,265,000 square miles in India, and 365,000 in Pakistan. Yet the Indians and Pakistanis outnumber Americans by nearly three to one. There are no external resources, few raw materials such as minerals, little industrialization, and little expectation from trade. Much of the land is exhausted by centuries of cropping, and some is desert or mountain.

The Indians so densely crowding this large country live for the most part (85 percent) in villages, which number about half a million or more. The majority of them are self-contained units, where subsistence agriculture meagerly supports peasant families and innumerable small craftsmen serving rural and domestic needs. Recently Jawaharlal Nehru estimated the total of these underemployed and penurious craftsmen as 100 million. Their earnings are unbelievably small; but they are higher than those of the peasants, for whom it is a comparatively rare thing to handle money. Even then that is usually in coins worth a mere fraction of a penny. Though village life is hard, and fraught with incessant labor, it has traditionally enfolded the population in the security of the Hindu way of life. The very caste system helped to ensure easy acceptance of status for the present in the hope of promotion in another life. To us it seems deplorably unjust; but then we should reflect what human beings have endured without much or any complaint in the interests of stability. Security is a basic human need. When it is associated with re-ligions it is sometimes encouraged as "resignation."

The Hindu way of life is not so much enjoined by religious dictation as practiced out of habit.[1] Its codes are those evolved for self-sufficient and isolated villages. For example, the veneration of the cow originated in an unwillingness to kill or harm the constant supplier of milk and butter and cheese. After its natural death the animal yielded hide and other products anyway. To this day the life of the village is regulated by ancient custom and the rural round of ceremonial, linked with crops and animals. Its pivot is the local temple or shrines. Secular life moves round the well or pond (usually contaminated), and the local stores. The villages are feebly linked with each other and the outside world by earth tracks or muddy roads; along them the pace of communication is that of the oxcart or the pedestrian. When epidemics and natural disasters took an unchecked toll, the population did not increase beyond the native resources. Now there are far too many hands to till and harvest crops for the landowner,[2] and far too many mouths to feed. In the old days the crops were consumed locally. Now modernization has increasingly made familiar the notion of the cash crop, garnered and sold for profit (not the villagers') in some distant town. Less stays behind, and the standard of living is worsened, at least by comparison with that of others.

Though toil is relentless from dawn to dusk, yet the human surplus is such that many are unoccupied. They seek employment or beg, or just sit around in the vain hope that someone will hire them. Between about 1951 and 1955, four million new jobs were found; but in the same years natural increase added another seven millions to those looking for jobs. It is obvious that unemployment and underemployment depress wages to an almost incredibly low level. To give an example: teachers are paid much higher wages than the average; but in 1955 some of them received 8 rupees a *month* as wages in rural districts— worth $1.50 or 10 shillings; however, properly qualified teachers earn up to ten times that amount. The huge population and ensuing cheap-

---

[1] In addition to the influence of example itself, the tradition of oral instruction is very strong in the villages to this day, and this is a powerful force in education (sometimes very conservative) that must be reckoned with in our assessment of other methods of instruction. In a village, respect for the *guru* or wise man may be paramount. Besides, rural people everywhere (especially in a preliterate state) set great store by proverbs, riddles, and the like.

[2] Though this is widely true, and likely to remain so for a long period, the establishment of industries in some areas during the 1950s and 1960s has led to local shortages of adult agricultural labor. This change is sometimes a disadvantage to children, who must help out; and it does not often help to raise living standards appreciably for those who remain.

ness cause human muscles to be used where Western people would hardly credit. It is much cheaper to use manpower to empty wagons of railway ballast, or to carry baskets of earth from excavations, or even to carry massive steel girders, than to use machinery. Thousands, including women, can be seen helping to pile up a railway embankment or working on a housing site. Recently 12,000 workers were employed on one double-tier bridge in China, and between 100,000 and 200,000 manual workers were engaged in laying a single stretch of railway track. A similar labor situation is typical of India.

Though ruinous strain and muscular effort are so often demanded, human energy has frequently been sapped by malaria and malnutrition. Weakness and cheapness have made it no uncommon sight to see two men digging with one spade—one to press the blade in the ground, and another to pull on a cord for leverage. Men, women, and children work together in order to scratch a living. Some are refused access to these scanty means of livelihood because they are restricted to certain occupations by their caste (hereditary class). Some actually belong to no caste, and are left to do the filthiest jobs such as attending to sanitation, which is of the most rudimentary kind. Such outcaste people were formerly called "untouchable." Though untouchability is now illegal, many village people keep up the old forms of segregation. Those discriminated against, for example, are not allowed to approach the village well for water, but have to get a higher-caste person to draw it for them. Hindu religious custom forbids a high-caste person to eat food contaminated by low-caste or "untouchable" people. Even their shadow is enough to make food unclean. Though untouchability is disappearing, it is only an extreme illustration of the low value put on other poor human beings—who are the great majority in India.

It is therefore clear that the low standard of living cannot be considered apart from the problem of overpopulation. Even if there were enough food to go around, the wage structure is not such as to enable workers to buy enough. Nor are there enough jobs to provide wages of any kind, no matter how miserable. Any prospect of industrialization is also bound to raise the question of reducing the demand for crude labor still further below the level of that now available. On the other hand, India needs better health, more skills to turn into cash, more money for capital development, more industries. None of these aims can be realized without improved education. Here again the population problem appears. The number of literate Indians has been rising for some time; but the *proportion* of these actually decreased in relation to the whole for several years.

In India's circumstances, information about health and nutrition and better crops is of more immediate significance than literacy. People who have learned to read soon forget about it if they have no books or lack the time or energy to read them; but basic education in the skills of health and community well-being is likely to last. It will bear fruit cumulatively. Unfortunately for India, it may also result in more babies. It is obvious that one fundamental step must be the limitation of India's fertility; but Indians are so poor that the cheapest known contraceptive is at present too dear for those who need it most. It is sometimes said that it is cheaper simply to have babies if the mother can, and to let the mother or the baby (or both) die if she can not. Puerperal deaths from various causes are still appallingly frequent—a consequence partly of economic destitution and malnutrition, but also of feeble education.[3]

Supposing reliable means of family limitation were available without any cost, it would still be necessary to bring information. It would also be necessary that the information should seem to matter, and that it should be properly used. We take it for granted that it matters to reduce the strain on young women, to save life, to improve standards of education and social prestige, to save India from self-suffocation. But that shows how little we appreciate the problem. We fail to have insight in exactly the same way as an Indian would if he were to advise us to reduce our road deaths (more numerous than those in a typical war of recent years) by abandoning private motoring or reducing speed. To many an Indian peasant it does not seem unusual or unnatural that there should be so many babies. It seems inevitable that women should begin to have them at an age when all our girls are in school, and that near-starvation and degradation should be the consequences. Every leading Indian educator and statesman is committed to campaigning for contraception; but first factual knowledge and social education must be widespread enough so that population control will seem important. The most significant point of contact for this education would be among young women and girls; but here we find grave difficulties.

The social status of girls is low. They are usually expected to bring a dowry—a great nuisance to their fathers, and then after marriage they traditionally belong neither to themselves nor to their childhood home but to their husband's family. In these circumstances it is not surprising

---

[3] "Basic education" in the subjects of domestic and agricultural interest can easily precede formal schooling (and eventually lead to it), especially in a country like India where the communication of wisdom relies so much on oral instruction. But it is not always easy to secure sympathy in the villages or suitable instructors from the towns.

that only progressive parents bother much about education for girls even if they get as far as sending their sons regularly to school. The status of woman as a mere appendage to a man's life was traditionally recognized by the practice of suttee (now stamped out, though with difficulty). This custom required widows to burn themselves to death on the funeral pyre of their husbands. Girls and women in India now have a much brighter future to look forward to. A great many not merely go to school but actually become university professors, scientists, and diplomats. However, life in the villages is exceedingly slow to change. Western ideas of feminine emancipation seem to belong to another world. Well-educated and progressive Indian men often find it difficult to find an acceptably educated wife. We can imagine how much harder it will be to communicate emancipated ideas, like those of controlling a family's future, to women whose whole life expectation has been one of trailing behind. However, we must look on the bright side, and note that in some parts of India, as in Ceylon and other countries not too different, the education of girls is rapidly becoming a familiar practice. With the nation-wide extension of compulsory schooling (not achieved yet), a better chance of social reform will be secured.

We foreigners must not interpret too naïvely the signs we sometimes see of educational improvements for girls. The results may be admirable in the long run but the motivation is still sometimes primitive. One of the greatest disgraces for an Indian family has always been to be left with unmarried daughters. Therefore, prosperous parents of lower or middle caste will frequently give a daughter some extended schooling so that they can arrange a better marriage for her. That is to say, the whole family (and not the mere girl) will thus obtain a more profitable investment. Such perspicacity is more often shown too if the girl in question happens to be a bit darker than usual, or has other disadvantages. Girls in these circumstances may have their education continued later too, (under orders), by their husbands' families, for the same socio-economic reasons and not out of personal consideration. Maneuvers of this kind are particularly common among those prosperous and highly placed enough to be able to go to college and university. It is ironical to think that many Indian women graduates in western Europe and the United States owe their chances to such inegalitarian prompting. Lack of equal consideration is also abundantly shown in the many household and family demands placed upon Indian women, who must undertake them in addition to their career responsibilities or onerous studies. So the mere experience of education and the unfolding of career prospects other than the traditional ones do not in themselves automatically emancipate Indian women or change their status greatly. It follows from what we observe in these highly exceptional women that the educational and social prospects for ordinary girls in India still leave much to be desired.

At this point we must observe that no educational or cultural change can ever take place without profoundly altering the social context. Many hallowed ideas have to be challenged. It may be necessary, and often is, to alienate the generations from each other. We may begin our experiments on a small-scale and tentative basis; but sooner or later the whole social system will be leavened or challenged. It is not so disturbing a process when the historic background is such that the shocks can be absorbed, or when social advance has already proceeded so far that an evolutionary and free society is flexible enough for further, easy change. But when a tradition-bound country like India becomes involved, it is necessary for those who supervise reform to take an exceedingly long view and to maintain a detailed and comprehensive vigilance. Otherwise frightful rifts will gape, uprootedness and bewilderment will be found everywhere, and existing resources will be dissipated before new ones can be developed.

India has so little in the way of economic reserves, so little educated capital on which she can draw, that the strictest budgeting and planning must be maintained. Therefore it is not surprising that one of the first acts of the new government was the establishment of a Planning Commission, and that India is making her way toward a better future through a series of Five-Year Plans. Though education in India is a state responsibility and not a federally administered activity, nevertheless the Central Advisory Board of Education exercises great influence, and the All-India Council for Technical Education is planning scientific and technological training on a wide scale. Only thus can the domestic and personal problems we have considered be tackled in accordance with India's prospects of evolution. Change must be realistic in terms of the resources and opportunities available.

The difficulties reviewed so far can be listed as follows: those arising from India's recent emancipation, and from her newness as a sovereign nation; those provoked by the need for forward evolution without the chaos that might result from a sudden disruption of the old systems of social rehearsal; problems of social inequality; those caused by an acute shortage of capital and the terrible destitution of India's people; those of a rapidly growing population in a land so crowded that men are cheap; the low status of women; and general ignorance and superstition. This is a formidable enough list, but we have not finished yet. There are also to be considered the disadvantages of geography and climate; problems arising from food habits (associated with religious beliefs); acute language difficulties; outmoded ideas about schooling and the aims of education; and finally anxieties about the political future of the country, especially in relation to democracy at home and to peace abroad. It would be a desperate situation for any nation to have to clean up.[4] It is a particular testimony to India's determination and resourcefulness that so much headway has already been made. We can proceed to examine plans and progress, not according to the logic of India's needs but in the order that seems simplest for our purposes in this chapter.

Hinduism has been the main framework of Indian life and values for many centuries. Nearly all Indian leaders of note, though determined to win for their country the material opportunities that are enjoyed by western countries, and which depend on western education, are also eager to retain many of the virtues and graces of the Hindu way of life. Therefore it was a very bold decision to declare India a secular state. Such a declaration does not mean that it is an atheist state, or for that matter indifferent. It signifies only that the state takes no part in religious controversies. It will require no views and forbid no views on religious matters. This is in contrast with Pakistan (which at first officially proclaimed itself an Islamic state), with Indonesia (also founded on Islam), and with Burma (Buddhist). Hinduism is one of the most tolerant and assimilative of religions; yet it was considered safer for the people as a whole to declare India secular. Thus we may hope that the sectarian disputes which disrupt many countries, and have frequently resulted in massacres in many parts of the world, may be avoided. On the positive side we may hope also that the reform of the caste system and of food habits will be made easier. Some 85 percent of Indians are Hindus by faith; about 10 percent are Muslim, including a distinguished Minister of Education and many of his advisers; 2 percent are Christian; 2 percent are Sikhs; and approximately 1 percent are Jains, Buddhists, Parsees, Jews, etc.

To anyone reflecting on the acute shortages which bedevil India, it always seems strange that cattle (which are sacred in Hindu belief) ramble about unmolested and are only very imperfectly used. They may

---

[4] The social, economic, and technological problems of India and other developing countries are reviewed in my *World Perspectives in Education op. cit.*, chaps. 4, 5, and 13, with particular reference to educational development and culture conflicts.

be seen interrupting the traffic in big cities; they eat much-needed crops; they are not bred systematically for dairy utility; and their meat is just wasted though it is greatly needed as a source of protein. Indians vary in what they will eat; but the majority are vegetarians living on a very poor diet. Yet their religion does not actually forbid them to eat meat, and those who come to cool countries like Britain can easily be persuaded to build up their resistance with meat, even with beef and veal. However, strong religious scruples must be overcome by anyone taking such a step. The onlooker sympathetic to India's future can only be patient and hope that a very important food reform will one day be achieved. After all, at one time it was considered shameful (if not sinful) to leave one's village—still more to cross the sea to another land, or to eat in the company of unbelievers and outcastes such as Christians and westerners. International travel helps to convince Hindus that such notions and customs are not really essential parts of their religion's ethos, but more in the nature of symbols that can be dispensed with in due course. Habit dies hard, though.

Also the monkey population of India is absolutely enormous, and eats or wastes huge quantities of food desperately needed by human beings. Monkeys are sacred, and must not be killed. They are not even driven off as they might be. Apart from the conspicuous hindrance to progress constituted by beliefs about cows and monkeys, there are many other items of religious conviction or habit that need to be adjusted to the times. Some of these are conspicuous, like those of caste; some are more subtle and difficult to cope with. As we have seen, untouchability is now illegal, and it is difficult to imagine how the development of industrialization could possibly allow the caste system to survive. After all, the essential characteristic of industrialization is the standardization and interchangeabilty of services and parts. In India industrialization will be a potent agent for democracy if it does not result in an uprooted and irresponsible proletariat unschooled in the positive performances of an educated democracy. In that event the urban population would undoubtedly be a ready prey for totalitarian ideas. The delicate balance to be maintained between old rigidity and new chaos exemplifies the difficulties besetting Indian statesmanship. In the matter under review, secularism seems essential; but careful cultivation of genuine, humane values in a new social matrix will also be as necessary as it is unprecedented.

Also associated with caste status and religious scruples is the method of distributing and cultivating the land. A great deal of land has been redistributed and entrusted to new ownership (or cultivation) after the expropriation of great landlords, who were often absentees from their estates. The next stage will be the establishment of a more self-sufficient peasantry, well educated in a range of technical skills transcending caste limitations, and with a balanced diet now denied to them by religious habits. It will also be highly desirable to secure the economic future for such peasants by organizing cooperatives for marketing, for the purchasing of requirements, and for insurance. Before these desiderata can be achieved, a great deal of education will be necessary. On the other hand, the gradual establishment of self-help organizations for agrarian reform will perhaps be the most promising vehicle of elementary education in responsible citizenship as well as in factual information. Indeed, an appreciation of this possibility was the mainspring of Gandhi's plans for "basic education." He urged the cultivation of "head and hand" together. UNESCO programs are very similar.

Reforms of the kind just mentioned seem inevitable in the case of India; but they are all too easily stigmatized by the ill-informed as irreligious and socialistic. They are certainly not irreligious, though they combat superstition which the ignorant confuse with religion. Undoubtedly they are socialistic. It is difficult to see what else could happen in the special circumstances of Indian difficulties. Not a penny can be wasted, so that the whole process must be publicly regulated in the best interests of all. There is no private capital available for investment on the scale required, and India has so far not enough external trade. On the other hand, Indian planning is a bulwark against precommunist chaos.[5] If India were to become communist, something like two-thirds of the human race would be under the red flag, and the chances of the other nations in Asia staying free would be remote indeed. Democrats everywhere need to appreciate how vital for them it is that India, by her radical planning for social justice, should succeed in a socialistic experiment. That implies no recognition of socialism as a valid commodity for export. It simply recognizes it as an alternative preferable to totalitarian communism. India is committed to democracy. Her statesmen, though many of them have proved their patriotism by being imprisoned as rebels, are also steeped in the liberal traditions of the west.

---

[5] One Indian state, Kerala, elected itself a communist government in 1957. The communist victory there may be ascribed to local confusion, and above all to the inability of the local factions (particularly of the rival Christian sects) to sponsor a joint program for social and economic reform. In 1960 communists lost control; but the risk here and elsewhere is never far away, unless a carefully planned economy and social and educational reforms build up a workable alternative.

Starting out on plans of reform, however, is not the same thing as having everything ready for change. The size of India and the difficulty of communication have already been refrered to. There are other handicaps of a geographic nature. Some regions are desert, and greatly in need of extensive irrigation. Most parts, however, are seasonally subjected to the swamping downpour of the monsoons. Later they will bake in parching heat. Climate cannot be controlled, but its effects can sometimes be turned to human advantage by such things as reservoirs, hydroelectric power, and solar-heat engines. All these things are costly. Even when they are built, there are some geographic difficulties that seem insuperable. For example, Kashmir has snow for four or five months of the year, is mountainous, and has extensive forests that because of transportation difficulties are not yet available for silviculture as we understand it. Yet the valleys and plains are rich in crops and fruit during the summer, and even Kashmir's ruggedness is potentially a tourist attraction to wealthy people from many countries. For full exploitation, though, capital development is essential. It is far beyond the resources of the indigenous population, who in any case need educational and financial help before they can effectively help themselves on a small, local scale. At the other extreme, India has swampy, malarial plains, jungles, and the enervating heats of a tropical summer. To make the best use of her more temperate regions and seasons she is sorely in need of railways, roads, and other communications. Under British administration these arteries of the western way of life were extensively built; but an independent and self-sufficient India will need many more to support a higher standard of living.

People of widely different racial origins inhabit the various regions of India, as can be clearly seen by looking at them. It is not only that the Mogul invasions brought in conquerors of Persian and related affinity down from the northwest into northern and central India; the nations and tribes long settled in this huge country make up as many recognizable ethnic variations as we find in Europe—perhaps more. It is only to be expected that, despite certain common sympathies engendered by the great religions (Buddhism formerly, and now Hinduism), local ways of living and looking at life should be full of individuality. Diversity of idioms in practical matters is sometimes a barrier to national cooperation; but an even greater obstacle to common effort and understanding is the great variation in language found in India. If we include the distinct dialects that have enough idiocyncrasies to make them difficult to understand by those who are not native to an area, we can count well over 200 different languages in India. Some are spoken by tens of millions, and some only by thousands. (To correct a false impression given by some writers on Comparative Education, it is necessary to point out that the number of speakers has nothing to do with the distinctness of a language. Romany (the Gypsy tongue) and Basque are not widely spoken in Europe; but they are nearly unique. Nothing more easily divides people from each other culturally than language).

Fourteen of the Indian languages are major regional tongues. Several of these have fine literatures reaching back into remote antiquity; others have a much humbler literary status, though they are governmental languages and widely used for commerce. Of the other 200 or so minor languages some have not yet developed an alphabet. In mixed linguistic groups it is often an important principle that children should be given primary instruction in their mother tongue, and proceed to instruction in a major regional language later. However, in India's formative stages this raises the question whether these marked local variations should be crystallized by being accorded literary form in books. Let us take a comparison from Europe. If during the sixteenth century the Scandinavian languages (which are mutually intelligible to practiced listeners), had not been written down in distinct literatures, a common "Scandinavian" for literary use might have evolved. In Switzerland, vernacular Swiss German is very different from the literary High German of the Bible, the pulpit, and the radio stations (even as it is spoken by Swiss); but it has not been stylized in written form until very recently for use in elementary classes. Indian reformers, who are likely to set a precedent for many generations to come, are faced with a difficult choice between sympathy for the vernacular (which coincides with the general practice of professional educators) and a realistic outlook for the future.

The Dravidian languages of the south are notoriously different from the Sanskrit derivatives in the north, and there are other linguistic families too. But in one form or another, about 47 percent of Indians could understand the languages of the northern (Sanskrit) group. Hindi and Urdu are very closely related, so much so that during the British administration a kind of lingua franca blended from them and called Hindustani was current. Though this is (we should perhaps says "was") really a colloquial language, it could become a unifying force in India and develop literary force. Gandhi recommended this. But since emancipation and partition, Hindi (with a more Sanskritized vocabulary and in the Devanagari script) and Urdu (with a Persianized vocabulary and in Perso-Arabic script) are growing farther apart. The purely linguistic patriotism maintained by speakers of these tongues is accentuated by the fact that Hindi is more closely associated with the Hindu faith, and Urdu with Islam, though this is not exclusively so. Hindi has been chosen as the official language of India, and Urdu that of Pakistan. Because English is very widely used in India (having been formerly the language of government, being still the medium of instruction in all but a few universities, and having international importance in every way), there did seem to be a chance at one time that it might be chosen. But only about 1 percent of Indians speak it (the educated ones), and it is understandable that an indigenous language should have been preferred.

On the other hand, the social value of the English language continues very high. In the larger towns and cities, affluent Indian parents who are eager to set their children off on the right foot are prepared to pay what locally seem exorbitant tuition fees to Anglo-Indians or Christians who have a fairly high standard of English. Schools have sprung up to cater to this trade—sometimes in the teachers' modest apartments. Ambitious parents will often make a habit of speaking only English in the family. Others make great sacrifices to send their children away to English-language boarding schools, and in fact the number of such schools vaguely or directly imitating the English Public Schools has rapidly increased since independence, though the number is still small.

The reports of postwar Indian commissions on language usually agree on the following recommendations. Ideally, primary instruction should be given in the mother tongue. Sometimes, especially for linguistic minorities of small size, it may be necessary to supplement this with instruction in a very simple form of the regional language, such as Urdu in Kashmir. At the secondary stage, however, the regional tongue should increase in importance. In some cases it might be the medium of instruction, though where a language minority exists in sufficient numbers it might be possible to continue to use the mother tongue at this stage; nevertheless, the regional language should be learned compulsorily. At least a modicum of Hindi should be taught, at least in secondary schools. As times goes on it is anticipated that Hindi will be more widely and thoroughly used. Three stages of proficiency in Hindi have been recognized and recommended for schools, depending on the pupils' own linguistic proximity to that tongue.

At the college or university level English is still the medium of instruction as a rule, partly because that has been usual, and partly because of the supply of English and American textbooks and publications. Prospective university students and others who are ambitious therefore need to learn English in the secondary stage. Despite its prestige, proficiency has fallen since emancipation. It has been seriously suggested that the university is one place where English should be retained; but popular opinion is in favor of using Hindi as the university language everywhere as soon as possible instead of English. However, for various reasons that does not yet seem feasible. A third alternative, already enforced by law in some states, is the use of the regional language in universities. This could be dangerous if it limits intercourse among scholars; there is also the problem of the exchange of students, teachers, and textbooks. India, which is after all a vast and highly diverse country, might conceivably be split linguistically and culturally if too strong a regional patriotism developed. Some educators have recommended the adoption of Hindi as the university language in the North (where it is either spoken or easily understood by the majority), in the hope that its use may spread southward in due course. Southern Indians, however, continue to campaign in favour of English for government, business, and universities. They declare that English to them is no more foreign than Hindi, and no more difficult to learn. English, too, is established in business and educational circles already. The strength of their position is shown in the declared all-India policy that Hindi will become the "official" language in 1965, but that English will be the "subsidiary official" medium.

From what has been said already it is obvious that many an Indian child even at the ordinary school level may well learn four or five languages: his mother tongue, a regional language, Hindi, and English, together with either an additional modern language widely spoken in the vicinity or else one of the ancient languages associated with particular religious scriptures (Sanskrit, Arabic, or Persian). Among Indian students at the University of London such linguistic *expertise* is common. The strain may be even greater if, for example, teachers or public officials or even tradesmen find it necessary to deal professionally with linguistic minorities of various affinities living close together.

Whatever happens, it is obvious that the curriculum of any child is bound to be congested on the linguistic side before anything else is learned—both for the child's own "life adjustment" and for reasons of Indian unity. It would be much easier for everybody if Hindi (or English) were universally understood. For this reason it is required that Hindi be offered in all schools; but it is so far an optional subject for the children. If everybody learned it, communication would be easier in any one region as well as nationally; in no region or province do all the communities speak the regional language(s). In Bombay, for example, there are three of these. A courageous attempt has been made to redraft state and administrative boundaries throughout India on linguistic grounds. Any relief of this sort will ease a grievous burden now lying heavy on school curriculums and community relationships. Those who attempt to belittle linguistic problems in India either are ignorant of the facts or ignore the powerful emotions aroused by linguistic dissatisfaction.

Distinct from language problems, though sometimes accentuated by them, are those of race. Marked cleavages also exist between communities and groups not only according to caste divisions but in respect of their varied degree of social advance. For example, some communities still live a tribal rather than a village or urban life. Others, because of their economy, consist of seasonal migrants. Linguistic factors here again can accentuate human differences. Welcome though these are in some ways because they enrich the total Indian view of life, they are nevertheless potential causes of serious discord if not handled with great sensitivity. Moreover, if books and instruction are at all unfamiliar, they are likely to be forgotten at the earliest opportunity. The problem of wastage has always been serious in India, and is certainly aggravated by linguistic and community idiosyncracies.

It is not surprising that most responsible Indians are convinced that it is impracticable to deal with Indian education wholesale on a uniform plan. That is the reason for devolving the organization of it upon the several states, subject to central supervision and advice. The Constitution of India directed that universal, free, and compulsory education for all children from 6 to 14 should be established within 10 years of its promulgation; but it may be many years before that aim is nearly achieved. Plans were all ready before the outbreak of war in 1939 for a radical reform of Indian education under British auspices. The scheme drafted by Sir John Sargent envisaged that universal free education would be provided in 40 years. After independence Indians ridiculed the length of time estimated; but they now realize that 40 years may well have to elapse before all their children do receive the 8 or 10 years' education hoped for.

It is almost impossible to paint a representative picture of the Indian school. Even in a progressive and populous city like Calcutta it is easy to find wide variation even at the primary level. Municipal schools, aided schools, and private institutions are bound to differ greatly from one another according to their clientele, the teaching staff, the fees charged, and the amount of equipment. From area to area in any town, from district to district throughout any state, circumstances completely alter what has to happen. After all, the main concern is to get the children to come to school, and to keep them there and profitably occupied. In many country towns of reasonable size (to say nothing of the villages characteristic of Indian tradition) parents may find it necessary or preferable to keep the child at home or in the fields. Many adults are lucky to earn one rupee a day (if they earn money at all), and if a child's labor brings in one rupee a week or even one a month there is a temptation to make use of it. This is the background we start with, and we must never forget it when considering absenteeism and failure to "make the grade." Moreover, it has not yet been possible to provide free tuition everywhere at the elementary level; therefore many parents who would wish their children to be educated just cannot pay for it.

On the other hand, those parents who can get their children to school and who know that school is the most potent means to a more comfortable life are pathetically eager to do so. In practice the teacher does not ask too many questions about the ages of the children she has to instruct. Though the expected age of entry is 6, the majority will be 7 years old, whereas a few from more ambitious homes may be only 5. Girls may not give their age at all. So any "first class" may have boys and girls of the most heterogeneous mixture in every way. In theory the elementary classes have no more than 30 children in them, though there may be many more. In a city they will probably be closely crowded together on straight wooden benches; in country towns they perhaps sit huddled on mattresses; in poor villages they just sit or stand, the little boys naked from the waist up. Great numbers of schools are operated on the principle that there are three teachers for every four classes. Much use is made of monitors to help the teacher; these are usually children of the same age as their classmates who can do the work better. The school premises range, of course, from modern buildings to the village structure consisting of a roof on four poles or even the proverbial Mark Hopkins log. It is the same with the equipment. Town teachers have a blackboard and books, while the children have slates or a painted tin rectangle for their writing. "Basic" schools in remote villages may have to practice their writing in sand. The same wide range can be found among the teachers; we may encounter a very cultivated young lady in a beautiful sari, a cadaverous elderly man imperfectly shaven, or anything in between. It is not unknown for a teacher to be a part-time farmer, or earning enough to live on outside his school in another way. So manifold and so intractable are the problems facing Indian educators!

The children may come to school at 9:00 or 9:30 A.M. in winter in the cities, but sometimes as early as 7:00 or 6:30 A.M. in the stifling heat of the summer. The teacher, like teachers everywhere, has a repetitious task in teaching reading; but with her material equipment she can seldom hope to do better than use the "chalk and talk" tradition in front of the blackboard—writing the letters, saying the sounds, and getting a chorus from the class. At the end of the first grade the children are able to read the difficult Devanagari script, which is made all the more complicated because in using it the words have to be run together phonetically to show the actual practice of daily speech rather than the mere theory of what the separate words should sound like. No mean achievement! There may not be too much practice in writing. Yet the children include several whose eager example in passing the grades with a view to "double promotions" is a spur to the others. Parents and teachers understandably push these children on. The full range of ten classes in the primary and secondary schools should clearly take a child to the age of 16 or 17; but it is not at all unknown for bright youngsters to be ready for the final examinations at 14, 13, or even 12. They are not officially allowed to reach the leaving certificate before the age of 14 (a regulation which is itself significant!); but, as we have seen, a child's age is not always accurately given.

When we bear in mind the fact that two classes, and even two teachers, may be in the same room together, we realize that problems of management no less than tradition weigh heavily in favor of formalism. In the "middle" school, after the primary years end at 11, classes of 40 and more are authorized in districts where primary classes are kept smaller. In the top "matriculation" class, 50 children may be found. This very tendency to let the top grades become larger shows to what extent bookishness and formal discipline prevail in the traditional training ground for the white-collar occupations. Rote learning and an unrealistic curriculum are only to be expected in such circumstances— the whole business being epitomized for one observer in the fact that the senior girls in one exclusive academy occupied themselves on a hideously hot afternoon learning (in English) Shakespeare's sonnet beginning:

> Shall I compare thee to a summer's day?
> Thou art more lovely and more temperate.

It is not therefore surprising that a large number of children who succeed in making their way through the primary school do not pursue their studies after the age (or standard) of 11 years.

In 1956 there were approximately 220,000 primary schools with rather less than 20 million children in them. Secondary schools numbered 24,000 (mainly private), with about 6 million children. Colleges up to intermediate level numbered 158, and there were 32 universities, some but not all of which were of good quality. Since that time there has been such a proliferation of universities that statistics have little meaning. All that can be surely said is that quality has not kept pace with the expansion. Many university students are much below the standard India requires, and pursuing unsuitable courses of study. The extent to which it has been possible to apply compulsion for schooling, even elementary, is of course varied. In Bombay province it was universal by 1953 except for villages with under 50 population—a fine achievement. It is important not to delay the provision of education in villages and small communities, in order to check the drift to the towns. Yet it is very hard to recruit teachers for work in backward villages. Though salaries have been increased in some cases fourfold, costs have also mounted. In 1958 a trained teacher might begin her career in a government primary school at less than $9 a month. Very recently, in a great and prosperous city a trained university graduate teacher earned as little as 75 rupees ($16) a month in a secondary school. Village elementary teachers get far less. Securing 30,000 to 50,000 new teachers a year is therefore an achievement. They are mostly boys and girls with secondary education, or a little better, though few are of first-class quality, or enterprising. Their morale and social status often leave much to be desired.

When independence was gained in 1947, barely 30 percent of the children between 6 and 11 years of age were in schools of one kind or another. Five years later the number had risen to 40 percent. The proportion has continued to rise. In 1941 the literates in the age range 5 years upward numbered 14.6 percent; in 1951, after years of war and difficulty, they had risen to 18.3 percent. If we confine our attention to persons over 9 years of age, which is more sensible, the figure in 1947 was approximately 20 percent. In Bombay about 30 percent were literate; in Delhi about 40 percent. There are great variations between regions and cities. Universally many more men than women can read; but accurate figures for literacy that is really retained and effective are very hard to obtain. The *total* literacy percentage in 1961 was 23 percent (a substantial increase in view of the juvenile population explosion); for women it was 12.8 percent, compared with 7.9 percent in 1951. Village census takers or teachers have sometimes accepted a "Yes" without verification. Some authorities have therefore taken a stricter view of literacy problems at the time of emancipation, stating that on the eve of independence only 25 percent went to school, only 15 percent were able to read, and only 10 percent were really able to read and write.

Many of India's misfortunes are blamed on the British, an attribution not surprising in a newly emancipated country, though opinion now recognizes that many advantages arose during the British India period— not least the impact of technology and science, of a world language, and of liberal and critical ideas. It is indeed surprising and edifying to see how appreciative educated Indians have become since 1947 of some British contributions, a development that does them quite as much credit as the British. But education as it grew in India under the Empire is rightly criticized for being defective in its aims and methods, and for having done too little for the Indians. It has usually been characteristic of British imperial rule to let indigenous populations develop their own culture. Religion and other life systems were left with a minimum of interference provided that these seemed consonant with peaceful rule. Such tolerance has its drawbacks. In 1835 (before India belonged to the British Crown, be it noted) Lord Macaulay introduced English as the medium of instruction into schools intended to provide the administration with Indian clerks and subordinate administrators. Ever since that time Indian education has been predominantly a white-collar, bookish and data-packed schooling intended to give social and professional status rather than to foster understanding or develop character. It has been a schooling for civil servants.

Bookishness and uncritical self-preparation for place-seeking, however, are not confined to any one system of schooling. They have indeed been characteristic of Indian and some other Eastern schools almost from time immemorial, as Indians themselves are quick to recognize in their attacks on classical pedantry, Sanskritists, and the like. However, it is unprofitable to look about for scapegoats. We must frankly recognize that until the time of emancipation there had been little escaping from the white-collar and conformist submissiveness of the complaisant pupil. There was a great need for a revitalized and Indianized schooling especially at the elementary level.

Since 1947 an enormous impetus has been given to Gandhi's schemes for a "basic national education" of "heart and hand." Humayun Kabir well describes the main aim as being integration with daily life, and the development of educational experience around a socially useful activity like a craft. Correlation and unity are striven for by seeing the items of the curriculum as constituent parts or complementary aspects of each other. The children are taught to cooperate as members of a community. In the strict interpretation of the "basic" plan they are expected to make the school pay for itself by selling artifacts. This last proposal has been criticized both as an old-world fancy and as an exploitation of an otherwise free learning situation. In 1937 Gandhi published a manifesto recommending basic schools which was then a bombshell but which has now become part of national policy. By 1953 there were 45,000 basic schools, mostly in the state of Bihar. It is proving increasingly difficult to get sufficiently well-trained teachers for them. "Basic" schools are still almost confined to children between the ages of 6 and 11.

What children learn at school between the ages of 6 and 11 (the usual age of compulsion in India so far, where compulsion is applied) is of particular importance in India. Quite apart from the natural responsiveness of young children that makes this period so critical in any school system, the Indian teacher has to take account of so many factors on which the future of these boys and girls will depend. For example, he may decide (often against parental pressure) not to push the bright ones on for examination purposes. It is still the usual practice in many areas to allow successful children "double promotions" so that they pass on to a higher class if they have mastered the work allotted to the one they are in. Thus a bright boy or girl might be ready to leave the primary school at the age of 10 or even 9½ years instead of 11. The lucky ones may proceed to a "middle" school (that is, American junior high school, or the lower classes of a British grammar school). On the other hand, many children will leave school at this time, because parents cannot afford "middle" school fees, or because they just do not think it appropriate and need to have the child working, or even simply because the child is a girl, and soon to be married and "off their hands." Even educators in India often talk in this way about their own daughters at an age when Western girls would just be beginning their secondary school careers. When we talk of Indian mothers, we are still often speaking of girls we would class as children.

So the outlook and teaching perpetuated by teachers in Indian primary schools is vital in determining or hindering social change. It is indeed greatly to be welcomed that so much progress has been made toward all-round and life-oriented education for both boys and girls under the age of 11. It is a wonderful thing to have boys and girls at school together. Mixed schools are often regarded (as in the Catholic parts of Europe) as less desirable than single-sex schools, and are there-

fore found more frequently in villages that cannot afford two establishments; but that is precisely where their effect will be greatest. Our
admiration for a more realistic and less bookish education must not
make us forget certain undesirable results that may follow from it,
especially in India. It may mean that children who have benefited by
it will stand less chance in the competitive life of the secondary phase.
Indian villagers might in fact think that their children are given only
the education that will perpetuate their status as laborers or poor craftsmen, while those who have had a traditional schooling are well on their
way to the job-winning and data-packed studies of the old-type secondary schools.

Many of the secondary schools of India have been missionary schools
established by Europeans, and attended by Indians of all faiths (few of
whom ever become converts to Christianity). The missionaries have
done wonderful work for Indian education, even if their schools are
frequently as scholastically formal as the worst in Europe. The personal
example of missionaries is a better testimony to western ideals than the
items taught. With rising costs and other difficulties it is hard for missionaries to meet the demand for secondary education. Government
schools (now operated by the state governments) and government-aided
schools financed partly by local taxes and by students' fees are increasing
in numbers, but not fast enough. The aided schools in any one state
are not likely to have a uniform salary scale for teachers with any given
diploma or amount of experience. Obviously therefore there is much
discrepancy in standards, though all of them try to give the same instruction because they are all looking toward the same public examinations and certificates. The tendency in Indian education is in this respect
toward more centralization, rather than less. But there is a long way to
go yet. For example, in Assam as recently as 1956 there were 64 possible
gradations of salary and status. And of course the 16 states and other
territories differ from each other.

After passing through the "middle" and "upper" parts of the secondary school (7 years in all), the successful prepare for university entrance.[6] Calcutta, Madras, and Bombay Universities were established

---

[6] The traditional arrangement has been to keep the children in secondary schools
until an average age of 17, and then to send them to an "intermediate college"
for two years in preparation for university entrance. Thus the universities take
them at the age of 18 to 19, or earlier if they have been pushed ahead by
"double promotions." Recent reforms anticipate the abolition of the intermediate
college stage. One of the years would be added to the secondary school and one
to the university.

in 1857; others of remarkably varied character and status have grown up to meet the ever-increasing demand. Some are residential; some teach on a day basis only; some do not teach but only examine. It is quite impossible to make any reliable comment on Indian universities as a whole, except that Indians themselves are dissatisfied with many of them. They are all overcrowded. The teaching is impersonal and distant. Professors and lecturers often think it beneath their dignity to talk to students. Examinations and "the subject matter of the examinaion" are typically what universities are for. Studies likely to lead to administrative and nonoperational occupations are the ones most eagerly pursued. Students may be very needy. Most live very meagerly if not in hardship. It is common to be supported during their four undergraduate years by relatives (often fairly distant kinsfolk) to whom they will be beholden for a long time. Therefore students often feel thwarted and uneasy; this helps to account for the frequently complained-of "indiscipline" which some mob-politicians turn to good account. It may be remarked in passing that even science is often regarded as a range of studies that will not make it necessary to undertake work with the hands. Unlike most American students, Indians think of it in terms of clean laboratories and white-coated leadership. However, despite their faults, Indian universities are in the forefront of their country's advance toward industrialization and modernity. The relaxed university atmosphere of the prosperous parts of the west must not be expected in a country where success is at the top of a precipice down which it is all too easy to fall to destitution.

Indians need only their eyes and noses to remind them of what academic failure might mean to them. They live in a country where the cruelest burdens are borne on human backs. The alternative to the dreary classroom may seem to them to be the village swarming with near-naked children under the hot sun; the green village pond in which the buffalo wallow; the stinking paddy across which the rows of laborers plant the rice, nearly knee-deep in the filth; or the rough hills whose streams turn prayer wheels incessantly praising "Brahma, the jewel and the lotus." It is not surprising that parents and teachers find it hard to reorient themselves, or that if they do, they still fear to hinder their children's success.

Moreover, as we saw in the case of France, and could easily see elsewhere, any reform in the direction of "life adjustment" is certain to encounter bitter opposition from those who have worked out the techniques of social success for themselves through the use of the old-fashioned schooling. The British have gone; but all too many Indians go on aspiring to the administrative positions even more abundantly open to them, and still think in terms of old scholasticism and competitions. They want an elementary education that will lead to the old-type secondary schooling, which will lead in turn to the university or professional school—and so on. If it is not a job that some of them are after, it is a good dowry or a good introduction. Recently there has been much frustration evidenced by those for whom formal education has seemed a "dead end" after all. Such men are politically dangerous.

Sincere Indian educators, however, are truly concerned that junior schooling should be a really personal experience for the child, and at the same time a social leaven or germ of new evolution. Secondary schooling they see as a self-contained and worthwhile thing. They call for a much stronger development of public secondary schools. During the years 11 to 18 they wish to sponsor clear thinking, with books as only a key; they wish also to pass on knowledge of practical value. These notions are commonplace in the west; but in India they are revolutionary. It is still an unfamiliar idea that the secondary school can be an experience of fundamental value in itself as distinct from a steppingstone to a much better place. A serious difficulty is that secondary education is still nearly all in private hands.

Community projects and extension centers are now to be found in over 50,000 towns and villages. These have received federal aid on an equal basis to match state aid. "Basic" schemes also have received a 30 percent subsidy from federal funds. Under both these plans the school is seen as a focus of community life. Increasing use has been made of radio and motion pictures. India is producing an astonishing number of motion pictures, which are very popular. Some of them are also very good. Without committing India to religiosity, statesmen and educators have encouraged a revival and elaboration of song, ritual, and art in connection with the village round of life. Some reactionaries fear the critical impact of science on this; but others mistrust only this mistrust, and feel that inner spiritual progress can accompany material advance. All that they are afraid of is "the hollow man." Of late there has been a widening interest in western philosophy too, as distinct from exclusively Indian or eastern mystic philosophy.

India is in some ways in a favored position. She can acquire many of the techniques of the west without suffering their "growing pains." Our mistakes have been social and philosophical as much as industrial. Indians usually believe that they can retain their traditional virtues of self-restraint, peace, and service, and still have the abundance and mass emancipation that western technology has made possible. That remains to be seen. The adoption of even one item from an alien technology is usually the beginning of altered human relationships. Some of these alterations would doubtless be welcomed by progressive Indians; but in the long run they might make the country and its system unrecogniz-able. But though the world seems to be growing more uniform in all respects under the impact of industrialization, that may be an illusion. It remains to be seen if Indian perceptions can add a further dimension. It will undoubtedly be a revolution in Indian education when scholars cease to be either the "withdrawn ones" of Europe or the "obedient servants" of the Indian civil service.

An All-India Commission reporting in 1953 made the following rec-ommendations: that one additional year should round off the secondary period (at 18); that a wider range of courses should be offered with a view to more diverse professions, but with retention of central or "core" interests; that multipurpose rather than distinct schools should be pro-vided for persons following different interests. The need to develop faculties of science, technology, and agriculture was also stressed. Thou-sands of Indian students are now abroad studying or doing research in these fields. In time they will raise the quality of what India is able to offer, and will also direct attention more practically to the needs of a predominantly agricultural country. Scholarships are being generously granted, especially when we consider the national poverty; and a chain of national laboratories has been developed. In the arts, national acade-mies are promoting excellent work.

The good work being done nationally is distributed as fairly as possible at ground level. Of course, when so little money can be spent it becomes vitally important to make sure that those most conspicuously able to profit from the few opportunities should have preferential access to them. Therefore it seems a matter of the utmost priority to train leaders for the next round of the educational struggle. Scholarships have been generously awarded; yet the Constitution has laid on the several states the responsibility for promoting also the interests of depressed sections of the community—particularly the untouchables, and girls and women. The latter must obviously be about half of all the Indians, and the un-touchables according to a recent count are estimated at 54 millions—more than the whole population of the United Kingdom. Since 1947 the scheme of postmatriculation scholarships for former untouchables and other backward groups has expanded some thirty- or fortyfold. At a precollegiate level an even greater effort has been made both to get the depressed people into school and to provide them with free opportunities of all kinds. Many civil service posts and even some high ministerial positions are reserved for them. Thus India's dilemma is being coped with at the highest level and the lowest. The nimblest brains and the most skilled workers are being trained to make their success India's success, and a sincere attempt is also being made to democratize opportunity.

The total public expenditure on education has increased more than fourfold since 1947; but costs have also risen, and in 1955 Professor Kabir estimated that India must further multiply her expenditure by three, even at existing prices, in order to provide a worthwhile and complete range of educational opportunities.[7] Some other sources formerly available (for example, private and missionary enterprises) have not been able to keep pace with increasing governmental expenditure.

As we have repeatedly observed, "education" is by no means to be restricted to schooling. In India's straitened budgeting it becomes doubly important to realize this truth. It is seized upon by the followers of Gandhi's doctrines; they recommend that rural productivity should be increased through the adoption of intensive cultivation on the pattern of Japan. Thus, it is said, a maximum number of people would be responsibly employed. They could be taught to become more self-sufficient, and at the same time their marketing and other arrangements would be made educative for personal and political responsibility. Such cooperative self-help is essentially decentralized, and that would suit India. Cooperative farming and trade are themselves educative (as in Denmark). They also cause participants to learn school-type subjects, such as reading, arithmetic, and elementary economics. Linked with this notion is the suggestion that without the disruption of the artisan system, power looms and other mechanical devices should be used more extensively. Though in some ways it looks as though any such tendency must inevitably lead toward greater urbanization and heavy industrialization, it might conceivably facilitate the retention of wholesome village independence and prevent the "uprootedness" so common in other rapidly industrialized areas. Actually, democratic copartnership could more conceivably permeate new industries if it were once to become habitual in preindustrial life. That is what many Indians hope. It would be a welcome alternative to communist-style centralization with direction from the top. A successful experiment of this sort, even on a small

---

[7] For a closer examination of educational investment in India, in relation to economic and demographic evolution, see my *World Perspectives in Education, op. cit.*, pp. 84–87.

scale, would be full of lessons for many of our enterprises in western countries.

An important ingredient in the whole process of leavening is the five-point program of "social education" for adults, partly through the community centers already mentioned. This has already produced notable results in the states of Delhi, Madhya Pradesh, and Mysore. Its aims are (a) to secure literacy; (b) to promote a life of health and hygiene; (c) to develop skills that will raise the standard of living; (d) to give opportunities for the learning and use of the duties and rights of citizenship; (e) to promote opportunities for and the enjoyment of healthy recreation. It is also assisting the social education of women along the lines already referred to, and is thus probably affecting the structure and educational relationships of the Indian family.

India has been well served by the monumental prestige of her statesmen in the postwar period. It would not have been altogether surprising if natural hero-worship had degenerated into something very dangerous to democracy in India itself and elsewhere; but fortunately there are few signs of leadership-disease. Even Mr. Nehru has to be actively sensitive to his people's anxieties about the niceties of democratic relationships. This is a very good thing for Asia as a whole. It is perhaps mainly attributable to the impressive self-restraint of Mr. Nehru and his postwar colleagues that India has become so jealous of the proprieties—a state of virtue which is admirable indeed. It has enhanced India's international prestige enormously. Yet it could conceivably be blemished by a blind spot or two, a sort of purblindness made harder to cure because the general moral outlook has been so high. That is perhaps why there has been so much difficulty over Kashmir, and so much costly defense expenditure with an eye on Pakistan. India not unnaturally still feels insecure. She perhaps does not realize her own real hegemony of free Asia, and the consequent need for her to be not only strategically strong but morally irreproachable.

During the past two hundred years or so the vast complex of the Hindu way of life has become entangled with the ways of the west. The Indians have come during that period to recognize the weaknesses of both, and to aspire to the advantages of both. As dark-skinned people and as subjects of an empire they have struggled to equality of status with the former masters of the greatest empire on earth, and have finally been welcomed to that status by their white partners in the Commonwealth. They have generously accepted, as free men, a partnership which (though long overdue) it took unexpectedly generous statesmanship in Britain to make available to them. Indians have shown abundantly their full title to their freedom. It remains for us to observe with the greatest of humble sympathy the uphill struggle of India to cope with such a tangle of difficulties. She has to establish the life of her own people (and by implication perhaps the lives of many underdeveloped peoples) on a basis without precedent. It is not just a case of restoring a former status, for there never was one. Nor, we hope, will it be a matter of dangerous, ready-made solutions from totalitarian neighbors. The experiments India will have to make will almost certainly seem to us rather hazardous from time to time; but desperate situations call for desperate remedies. We must not be so foolish as to prejudge, if only because we have no sense of India's distracting perplexities.

The ancient social problems are grievous; but on top of them come the new ones, such as the unanswered (perhaps never finally answerable) questions about the relationship of the individual to his family, or indeed of the small nuclear family, like ours, to the extended clanlike family on which Indian norms and economics have been founded for thousands of years. The critical question whether western civilization has much to offer to eastern nations (other than mechanical techniques) is bound up with uncertainties of this kind; for the whole notion of personality, with obligations and rights, depends to a large extent upon the limitations and opportunities of our social connections. The role of woman is also contingent upon the answers given to these questions. So are all the questions of schooling, travel, trade, careers, and personal ambition.

Indian schools themselves have difficulties of many kinds: material, pedagogical (that is, concerning orientation, content, and personnel), administrative, and social. They are weighed down with the legacies of history, politics, and ancient cultures. The child population is by western standards a phenomenally high percentage of the whole. The whole impact of technological change demands higher standards, and difficult readjustments; but it diminishes or diverts the potential supply of teachers. Moreover, educational opportunity has been, so far, very unequally distributed geographically and socially.

The whole question of the nation's world role in a time of international flux is a further crisis confronting the schools of India. In her case we see the immemorial problems of food, home, family, and future reduced to their starkest form. Observing Indian progress not only should jerk us out of complacency and pettiness; it may perhaps in time make us re-examine our own cultural or economic hierarchy, and our own notions of the relationships between home, work, and the process of learning.

chapter 8

Retrospect and Prospect

In thinking about other people's children we have found ourselves having all kinds of solemn thoughts. Some of them have questioned methods and organization; some have been concerned with the best subjects and interests to develop at school; some have assessed the schools in relation to social and economic change; some, indeed, have turned on the very problem of what man is intended to be.

Put in more conventional form, the items covered in our survey include the following: education as a function of the home, or of society as a whole, or of religious and similar bodies; education on a centralized or decentralized pattern; education of the elite, and the education of the whole community; education by instruction and authority, and education by involvement and experience; education by means of traditional lore and values, or education as an evolution toward an unresolved future; the liberalizing "essence," and vocational linkage; coeducation; the "common school"; the economics of education; and the whole problem of neighborly sympathy (especially international understanding) in relation to education. We have also thought about race, and language, and underdeveloped countries. We have assumed throughout that a major concern of ours was the development of personal responsibility in a democratic but highly specialized (and therefore increasingly automatized) society. The case studies selected in this book have enabled us to see the problems of other parents and children being worked over, and sometimes worked out.

In a concluding chapter it is a waste of time to attempt to summarize.

It is more valuable to stress that the various questions and anxieties affecting any one case study add up to something unique in that situation—a living complex as dynamic yet as personal as the relationships within any one family. The constituent persons and factors cannot be pulled apart without completely altering the context. No one item, even if it looks the same, can be presumed to have the same essence or the same effect everywhere. After all, a gift of flowers may cause a reconciliation in one family, but a grave suspicion in the family next door.

Having said all this, and having by implication warned parents and educators against assuming that what works (or does not work) somewhere else will behave in exactly the same way for us, I feel bold enough to urge a careful, comparative study both of the whole educational complex of any family (or community), and of the various ingredients in that complex. It does help us to understand one woman a little if we have read, heard, or discovered something about the others. Our comparative study does not deny to that one woman her uniqueness and ultimate unpredictability. It may enable us to encourage, appreciate, or even correct her; at the worst it should enable us to see our problems in the true perspective of human affairs.

That is just what parents and teachers are increasingly doing. For centuries, and especially during the past hundred years or so, educators of all kinds have been trying to pick up hints and methods from their neighbors. But as time goes on they all become a little wiser. They stop copying; instead, they think out their local problems in the light of others' experiments, and they learn to see their own involvement in a somewhat more detached way. In fact, it does us nothing but good to see just how involved we are. Those who set up and administer school systems tend to suppose that by fiddling about with them (and leaving everything else alone) they can alter the world. They can indeed, but not always in a constructive and rounded way. Education and civilization are no more matters only for the school than health is a matter only for the clinic. The school is simply the instrument that society (that is, people) select and perfect for a particular job in particular circumstances. The mistake of leaving it to the "experts" lies in the fact that no one view can see everything that is relevant; other people's complementary views may give a truer perspective. So it is when we think that *we* are experts, and that we know best; we usually are all the better for letting ourselves be judged (by implication) from outside. A school or family system is most successful precisely when it is exactly matched with its context. Comparisons help us to discern that context. In no case does the school exist as an absolute.

Each one of the experiments we see going on around us highlights some particular emergency. It may be that our own problems will stand out suddenly as in relief, or that our own methods will there seem cumbersome tools. Or perhaps the things that seem "natural" to us will be shown to need re-examination. Whatever else happens, we should be able to understand the basic human problems with the sympathy that comes of having worked them over with those most immediately involved, instead of knowing only about "issues" as though they were lifeless statistics from some dreary book.

The answer to "How much or how little can the schools undertake as their job?" is conditioned entirely by the background in each case. We have seen that it can depend critically upon questions of housekeeping, that is, of national finances in relation to the many needs to be satisfied. Sometimes our answer may be determined by political objectives, like the education of an electorate or the emancipation of women or Negroes. In this last connection we are reminded that the background of social psychology is an important factor in determining educational readiness. Fictions and obsessions can, through their practical results, become facts to reckon with. Technological changes too are full of vital influence on social relationships and on school objectives. In depressed countries they tell policy makers what to seek out first, and whom to educate; in the United States they entail the problem of how to use up material abundance to the best advantage. Finally, in addition to considerations of budgeting, politics, social climates, and technology, we now find we must give careful thought to our neighbors—international as well as domestic.

This all sounds very solemn, and it is desperately important. Conscious schooling must be brought up to date for our children's happiness; but we also need to take account of very many influences that school us quite as much as our lessons. Suggestions reaching us around school and after it must be reckoned with and seriously studied; they may fulfill school influences or contradict them. It will pay us to be on the lookout for educational pressures in unsuspected places. Let us compare police notices in Germany and Austria with those in Britain and in the United States. In the German-speaking countries we are simply told that something is *polizeilich verboten*; that sounds much more abrupt than saying it is forbidden by the police, and that is all the information you get. It is like saying, "Don't do it, or else!" In

Britain the form will probably be like this: "Passengers are requested to . . ." (perhaps even "not to . . ."), followed by an explanation. The notice will end: "By Order of the Police." In the United States the typical notice runs: "$200 fine for dumping trash on the highway." It threatens people; it assumes that people will defy the threat; and it indicates the citizen's most sensitive point. It is easy to visualize the whole hit-and-run drama, with states' rights and all that. These little notices are important chapters in any child's political education.

Such pleasant fancies could lead on to the sober reflections of scholarship if we permitted them. We need to do no more than notice that the motives of authority and fear in Germany gave rise to Marx with his brooding on the bloody overthrow of authority, to Hitler and his pogroms. In Britain the emphasis on responsible self-regulation (on the whole) has in one way or another contributed to the tradition of orderly dissent, of evolutionary statesmanship, and of personal freedom. When visitors say that the British police are "just wonderful," they might stop to wonder how that has come about. (Incidentally, British visitors often report that the police in many American cities are also exceedingly helpful.) Gracious officials both recognize that their public is cooperative and teach them to be more so.

All kinds of daydreams could be indulged in; but there is no time for more than a few selected at random. If boys and girls play happily together and go to school together, this simple fact is the best of all lessons in equality of personal worth without identity. If husbands do household chores and are willing not only to bathe the baby but to change its diapers when necessary, this again is a potential lesson in mutual regard between the marriage partners. If there is real personal appreciation, that in turn contributes subtly to more intimate felicity. So we pass on to realize why Robert Burns described the domesticity of raising a family as "the true pathos and sublime" of human life. The great passions and the rare perceptions of the most inspired poets are shared through actions around the kitchen sink—not only through black-and-white pages in the ivory tower. On the other hand, modern woman would not be what she is without the philosophic deliberations of the "highbrows." In education and culture no influence exists alone.

Sometimes rehearsal situations like the one described above may be considered to have universal force. Others are more local and temporary, even to the extent that they are questionable in the very places where they occur. In England the importance attached to accent is exaggerated beyond all reason, as is the value of a certain poise and mannerisms. However, the fact that these tricks can be learned, and learned by increasing numbers, is in some respects an emancipating factor although it is repressive in other ways. It also indicates, no matter how ridiculously, a very real regard for education and urbanity. William of Wykeham was not altogether wide of the mark in declaring that "Manners makyth Man." Behind all the frippery and folly there lies a regard for quality and values. Britain will gain if new vehicles for this appreciation can be devised, especially if any new rehearsal system embodies a real recognition of other men's essential worth.

In case anyone supposes that Britain has a monopoly of amusing folly among the English-speaking communities, we may note that in the United States a professor visiting a strange university needs to be very smartly dressed if he is to get a proper intellectual and material reception. Just as Americans usually ask "How big?," "How many?," and "How long?" when they visit European universities (and these are the last questions that the natives expect to hear), so they tend to think that a professor who looks like a rag bag must be a man of no significance. He evidently cannot be a "big" man, and is therefore hard to recognize as "important" (a dangerously favorite word in a democracy). By way of contrast, such a human scarecrow might be regarded with awe in Europe, and people would feel that he must be very distinguished. Quality counts, not dollars or productivity.

It is subtleties of this sort, so hard to pin down, that teach values and determine what the schools should or may not do. Though these influences are part of the structure of national character, they are neither unalterable nor fundamentally associated with any lasting ethical criteria. They can therefore be modified with the times. We have remarked that the Danes, once considered by their own spokesmen to be very boorish, and feared in centuries past as the fiends of the North Sea, are now a most highly civilized and gentle people. The once crude English are now criticized for being elegant "stuffed shirts." "Merrie England" is said to be a land where pleasures are taken sadly, and to be the home of that aloof arrogance called *la morgue anglaise*. Britons themselves are aghast at such unfairness, and believe that if there is any truth in the allegation at all it must be blamed on the Puritan republic of which Cromwell was the Lord Protector. (There is strong justification for this view.) The main point to notice is that national character and normative institutions can be changed by conscious or unconscious reconstruction. The most conspicuous changes in recent educational history are those which occurred in Japan during the past hundred years. The Japan of *Madame Butterfly* and the samurai was transformed in about 70 years into a powerful industrialized nation that could challenge the most highly developed country on earth, and come within sight of defeating it. Japan is now faced with a critical choice for her future, and rational planning no less than the socio-economic criteria already referred to will largely affect her decision.

Not all changes are planned, however, and many of those that are turn out unexpectedly. After World War II the United States was in a position of imperial responsibility quite unfamiliar to American political thinking, but conspicuous enough for some nations to accuse America of "economic colonialism." No one soberly believes that the United States government is imperialistic in this or any sense, no matter what some individual Americans or corporations may dream of. For our purpose it is important to see, however, that a position of world hegemony has been achieved because of America's technological success combined with external accidents, and that this combination of circumstances has very considerably reshaped the educative context of American life. It is certainly in a very different environment from that of the "little red schoolhouse" and the congregational meetings of old New England. In such circumstances there is usually a great time lag before the formal school system catches up with the true facts of life. Quite apart from human frailty and the legendary other-worldliness of many teachers, everyone's romantic attachment to old traditions hampers a realistic readjustment. People feel they should be loyal to something, or they feel guilty about abandoning their position. Yet abandoning the position may be the very thing that a real "life adjustment" and an imaginatively "child-centered" education require of parents and teachers.

When people really do readjust themselves in order to make the most of some new opportunity, they may find themselves transformed out of all true likeness. Sometimes the results may differ strangely from the original intention. Let us take an example very familiar to Americans. It is now recognized that the majority of the settlers who pushed out into the fertile black crescent of Southern cotton country were no gentlemen in any sense. Like any other frontiersmen they worked and fought furiously to win land for their crops; and when the cotton was ready they worked themselves (and their few slaves, if they had any) to the bone in order to build up a plantation economy. Like the homespun and ruthless Lancashire manufacturers these were hard men, and the struggle made them harder. Yet when they accumulated capital they set themselves up like colonial grandees and were determined to outdo the older rich in external elegance. This did not make them cultivated, any more than the same process turned the Manchester *laissez-faire* mill owners into the old landed aristocracy; but it did make it possible for their wives, children, and grandchildren to claim gentility with some justice. They had been to school; they surrounded themselves with fine things; they copied all the outward signs of refinement and some of the inner ones. Their comfortable paternalism did not, however, extend to a full understanding of the term *noblesse oblige*, limited though that concept always was in Europe, especially in regard to human rights. Southern gentility was unaffected by the intellectual inquiry which humanized so many "gentlemen" in Europe. It certainly did not lead to a local Enlightenment on the French pattern or to a regermination of the humanitarian republicanism that enthused the Virginian gentlemen half a century before.

To that extent, therefore, it was a fantasy. It has had pernicious results in so far as human rights are still extensively disregarded, not so much by the descendants of those Southern gentry as by that vast majority of Southerners whose ancestors never owned a slave and never rose above the social position of a rural "redneck." On the other hand, we must be very careful to give full credit to the positive and constructive aspects of the Southern legend. Now most Southern children in the United States strike the observer as being even better poised than the average American child, though their ancestors not too long ago were of the humblest order. There is a graciousness in their relationship with other white people that is truly praiseworthy; and if intellectual standards are still markedly lower than in the North, that is perhaps attributable to the economic backwardness of the South and to the many grave difficulties following the Civil War. Urbanity and a wish for refinement are very real in the South—not everywhere, of course, but on a wide enough scale to be a potential influence for immeasurable good in schools and homes when once Southerners see more clearly that their "peculiar institution" is still their own worst enemy. The elegance of Natchez need not be a hollow façade; it could transfigure American education in these latter days when all can aspire to be ladies and gentlemen. A myth passionately believed in can be a mainspring for reality. Even a backward-looking legend can be made to contribute some elements of progress to the future.

The very fact that the great majority of Americans everywhere claim to be of the middle class brings us to another illustration of formative influences that might not be given full recognition by professional educators. The United States is without equal in the development of technology for mass production. As we have already seen, the standard of consumption is higher there than in any other country, though the American situation is matched in parts of Canada and a few other countries where the same system is fast developing. Material abundance does not of itself refine humane perceptions; indeed it may do the opposite. Yet Yankee productivity has made slavery and the drudgery of human muscle-power unnecessary. This is potentially a releasing influence of great importance. It can free people for other things that are traditionally supposed to be liberalizing, not just for eating, drinking and making merry (though we ought not to forget that these have often been the concomitants of the arts throughout the ages). Above all, the cheap and easy flow of goods makes it possible for nearly everyone earning a reasonable wage to look like a lady or a gentleman. This is perhaps the beginning of thinking of one's dignity, and of cherishing aspirations. The mere accumulation of material objects will, given luck and proper education, eventually introduce questions of quality. Therefore the conveyor belt and the department store are potential instruments of education in so far as they provide the worker with material adjuncts to fuller living and may help his wife to widen her horizon with their products.

They do not do this on their own, however. Mere mechanization, even mere consumption, may produce wage slaves and dupes for the advertiser or expert. There is plenty of evidence that they do, and there is no need to go to the USSR to see the tendency at work. What transforms a negative situation into a positive movement toward good is the precious ingredient of value and preference. It may be that the first preference is for what is "bigger and better," or for what is "important," or what is "modern"; but any society that has retained some sense of values will reveal at least some citizens thinking about what matters *in the long run*. People are free to do this just because they are emancipated from an urgent preoccupation with safety and livelihood for today. Being relaxed, they may actually be open to ideas as well as values; but as ideas are always likely to be disturbing, men must feel reasonably secure before they will freely entertain them. Banishing real want and fundamental anxieties has always been a prime condition of civilized life. In the past it has always been thought that "culture" depended on the existence of a leisured class, and in primitive technologies it usually has. Nowadays the *nouveaux riches* of a highly mechanized society like that in the United States include the majority of the population. With some ingenuity on the part of those concerned with public education (not just school people), the population of such a country can become increasingly sensitive to the fine and lasting products of human ingenuity.

There is some evidence that this is happening, particularly as a result of adult experience rather than of formal schooling. More and more people demand high fidelity recordings, for example, with perfect reproduction of the recorded sound. This is just a fad, of course; yet in order to play with these toys their owners listen to the masterpieces of chamber music and the great symphonies. They actually listen to prose and verse readings too. It seems likely that a moderate connoisseur of good music today has a vaster range of great compositions and first-class performances at his command than many a composer in times past. The possession of "hi-fi" apparatus is a long way from being a participant in a string ensemble; but it is a modest step on the way there, and it is a gesture of identification with the humanizing tradition of sensibility. American orchestras are now increasingly made up of American musicians; and American composers and artists and poets increasingly claim world respect. None of these achievements are themselves factory made; nor do they come from believing that any kind of activity is equally worthy; but they have been made possible because those who enjoy them are materially emancipated from farm drudgery and the preindustrialization type of manual labor.

With the spread of modern industrialization over a great part of the world, many more people will claim for themselves those things that were once the exclusive privileges for "ladies" and "gentlemen." The way to the cultivation of civic and personal excellence is often devious and bizarre, however. The descendants of the rough and anti-intellectual frontiersman are now entitled to be genuine students in universities; but it is ironical that common parlance so often refers to them even during their university experience as "school kids." They have reached out for Olympus; they are relegated to the nursery. This is one consequence of standardization and of overlooking differences in quality. The typical American, whose grandparents can perhaps recall very hard days and still harder traditions, is very tolerant and gentle. By an odd quirk of history it was reported in 1957 that the sales of toilet articles for males slightly exceeded those for females in the United States. This news item does not prove a regard for the higher values; but it does indicate a progression in some kinds of sensibility, and it does suggest that that progression is on a nation-wide front. Once it is admitted that some things matter more than others, a most significant step has been made in aesthetics or elementary philosophy. It should not dishearten the culture-conscious unduly if their neighbors' advance seems too little or clumsy. Nor should the established intellectual aristocrat feel too smug if the new beneficiaries of social advance seem materialistic and vulgar; they think of good living instead of "the good life" simply because they have so long been neglected and starved of humanizing opportunity. All too often it has been the insensibility of the aristocrat that has caused that state of affairs; and if it has not been heartlessness, it has been the technological system that benefited the former elite at great human expense. There is no need for that now. It has become technologically possible for the first time for the mass of mankind to claim the Aristotelian "equal consideration in equal circumstances."

Therefore it is only likely that the schooling and aspirations of the "new men" (and women) will seem grievously proletarian and vulgar to the guardians of many countries' culture. That does not matter. It has always been the case. Most of our present ruling classes were vulgar a century ago. Some of the most aristocratic families in Britain were vulgar parvenus when Elizabeth I was queen. Christianity first took root in Rome as a vulgar faith flourishing among the soldiers and trade organizations (*sodalitates*). History decides what is vulgar; it also decides what is merely absurd. Culture is not lace at the cuffs, periwigs, and so on; it is an alert and sensitive adjustment to the problems of working and playing with other people—or simply of tolerating them.

Consequently, those who feel most concerned about educational advance should exercise themselves in tolerance and patience. We cannot expect all to have the same methods of growing up and being refined in humanity. Neither can we expect that all nations will choose the same industrial and social methods as Victorian England or present-day New York. One thing seems certain: factual learning, value-learning, and the development of responsible human dignity will become ever more closely associated with jobs and vocational training. This is a truth that very few educators have so far admitted. Still fewer have attempted to put it into practice; or if they have they have related it only to what happens in juvenile schooling, whereas job

experience and family experience and the experience that comes from
social and political participation are the most potent influences in the
long run. The totalitarian states have here seized their advantage; the
liberal democracies have done little even in the way of realistically
studying the context of education—a living mesh that extends through
society and endures throughout life.

Moreover, we go on thinking that the schools we now know are
"schools" in some absolute sense, and we make rules and philosophies
for them as unchanging as the laws of the Medes and Persians. Most
popular thought about schools and scholars ignores the fact that the
technological and social context has radically changed, and will change
further. Children now come to their teachers from a wider range of
homes, and they go out again to a wider range of jobs. Home backgrounds do not reinforce schools' influences in quite the way they did
a generation or two ago; nor do society and industry. Therefore the
schools will have to do others things for the children. It may well be
necessary to look more closely at influences working on adults. Advertisers do. So do mob politicians and all kinds of quacks. If we affect
to ignore adults' learning situations we do not just "leave it to them";
we miseducate them by a void, or we turn them over to the tender
mercies of "subliminal" exploiters and the like. These considerations
add up to one illustration of the universal problem of adjusting homes
and schools to fit social change. Never in human history has this been
so rapid or so radical as in our day. Tomorrow the scope and speed of
change will be greater.

There is plenty of evidence that many nations have already seen
that technological change cannot be left to chance. As long ago as
the French Revolution, French educators established polytechnics,
advanced institutes, and the "central schools" to bring their country
up to date. Germany's school development in the nineteenth century
was intended to promote technical advance. Switzerland is a country
whose educational administration is highly decentralized; but there is
a famous federal university of technology, and the technical side of
education is carefully encouraged by the central government. Both
in pre-Soviet Russia and under Stalin the central government pro-
moted technical education extensively, being content to leave other
aspects to local arrangements. Wherever we look, even in the pre-
eminently decentralized United States, we see central encouragement
of practical and technical instruction. A hundred years ago this was as
true as it is today though on a smaller scale. Yet everyone seems to

pretend that technical instruction is something apart from personal "education," which in many cases the central government of democratic countries is well-nigh forbidden to touch. Far be it from me to recommend more centralization or uniformity; but it does seem necessary to point out (a) that industrial or commercial training and activity *are* profoundly educative for better or worse, and therefore cannot be divorced from "education"; (b) that modern industrialized life has its own tremendous drive toward centralization and uniformity; (c) that technical advance in any country depends on an efficient preparation not just of the top men and women but of all the citizens; and (d) that no system of schooling or of rearing children at home can be considered any longer as a little local game. The world is its criterion. The next generation will be its justification.

What is this next generation we so calmly talk about? And what will its living conditions be like? Will words like "school," "education," and "public opinion" have either the same dimensions or the same perspectives even in our own countries? We cannot accurately answer these questions separately. It is harder still to reckon them together. Yet that is precisely what we must do if we are to make any sense at all of our plans for our own families. Let us try and envisage some of the material changes affecting our decisions.

Since about 1925, one thousand million people have been added to the human race. That is roughly a 50 percent increase in the whole human family. About eight hundred million of these were born in Asian, African, and Latin American countries—the very places least able to cope with rapid population growth in any way at all, and least of all in terms of conventional schooling. When we consider that this population *increase* in less developed countries is more than double the entire population of the USA and the USSR put together, it becomes strikingly obvious that ancient answers to educational problems based upon manageable numbers of children and an adequate supply of teachers fulfilling time-honored roles are just as socially outmoded (if not pathetic) as Bostonian Brahminism or Victorian caste punctilio. For all the newcomers mentioned in this paragraph, education is an emergency need, just as if they were victims of some natural cataclysm or wartime refugees. For them, therefore, education cannot wait. It is a bread-and-butter business; it *is* the means to food and drink in the most basic terms. Teachers' textbook concepts and pious priorities are impatiently swept aside by those who see education as food, living standards, emancipation, and the factory for the future.

The state, and only the state, can provide education on such a vast scale in the developing countries. How sharp a contrast this is to our own assumptions is obvious from two historical facts: Britain did not even have anything as "official" as local school boards until 1870, and did not devise a comprehensive public system of school organization until 1902. Respect for existing institutions and prerogatives (both educational and governmental) has everywhere hindered recognition of the patent fact that in well developed countries too education is already the main business of local government. In very many cases it now accounts for more than half of the local expenditure. Yet plain arithmetic is making it increasingly clear that reliance on local resources, though sometimes beneficial and efficient, can never guarantee overall efficiency—much less equality. Apart from the increasing concern of all major states to improve their technological efficiency for strategic and market purposes, the very mechanics and mobility of modern living make any local educational deficiencies as great a risk to *national* well-being as is malnutrition or dietetic imperfection to one's health. Education is therefore a national defense, to be nationally safeguarded. Not enough is done if the nation is lucky enough to have top-level scientists, research departments, and cultural pinnacles, for the simple reason that the ordinary business of the community can not now be done unless school-induced proficiency is characteristic of all activities.

The totalitarian countries seem at first sight to be exempt from some of the special difficulties inherent in a more freely organized system. It looks as though orders can be sent down from above, in accordance with their governing philosophy or party handbook rules. Of course, there is always the temptation for those basically reorganizing a country's way of life to try to act in this way. But sooner or later the most tightly organized of countries comes to recognize the impossibility of ensuring automatic compliance—even in the daily fulfillment of production quotas and the like. Therefore the USSR, having long set its face against training in business administration (for fear of a "technocracy" not easily contained within official planning or ideology), has acknowledged long-standing embarrassments by deciding to found a central academy of business administration in 1962 and extended this kind of training downwards to all appropriate levels. That is to say, party prescription and the drive of the enthusiastic activist will no longer be a substitute for the expert; expertise must evidently be devolved downwards. The present is the era of the *trained* person in all countries.

It was once supposed that an "educated" person was equipped for all contingencies; and by the word "educated" people meant traditionally schooled in certain forms of juvenile exercise. Severe doubts have been cast on this notion in the most conservative countries. College courses in the United States (not so conservative) are traditionally "liberal"; yet the great majority of first degrees are now vocational, and the tendency toward greater purposefulness in many studies is accelerating. Those countries which still have a somewhat protracted "general" education are expanding and at the same time intensifying their applied "further" education in one way or another. There is a world-wide search for talent. Moreover, the sheer amount of knowledge to be acquired and the extremely rapid change overtaking all industries necessitate not just a system of preparatory training at one period in life, but one which brings back *mature* learners again and again to reconsider jobs and human relationships in a never-ending reappraisal. This is all done in the name of on-the-job efficiency, of course; but, for the reasons already given, it is more widely re-educative for better or worse. And, in all of it, it is impossible to think any longer of an isolated operative down below or an Olympian pinnacle of "really educated" demigods. The whole enterprise is either skilled or ineffective together.

Therefore not only at the national level, or at the top directive level of the great corporations, but in ordinary and uncountable daily situations, it is increasingly true that education is a *business* to be efficiently organized. Moreover, life's ordinary daily business is not merely bristling with occasions for adding this item of knowledge or acquiring that skill; it also provides a whole vista of perspectives on life, a whole range of occasions for assuming or declining responsibility, and (because modern production and consumption are so "rationalized") a network of common concerns, common techniques, common language, common images, and common tastes. This kind of corporate habituation can be evocative or it can lead to automatism. It can be commercially exploited for consumer entertainment, advertising, and similar purposes not primarily intended to be educative. But there can be no escaping from the truth that increasingly centralized organization is taking place. Our only uncertainty is about its purpose, or about who does the organizing.

Living as they do in the society that is technologically most advanced (and therefore most elaborately organized), Americans have long been extremely anxious about their own acculturation by forces and requirements that are ostensibly not "cultural" or humane at all.

Some of the serious scholarship published in recent decades on this and related problems by David Riesman, William H. Whyte, Vance Packard and Martin Mayer deserves the most earnest attention of anyone alive to the phenomena of industrialization and urbanization. These writers' penetrating analyses are none the less profound for being sometimes presented with that flair and zest that characterize the best of North American writing. Unfortunately, some "professional educators" are still so ignorant that they dismiss this kind of scholarship, or completely miss its implications for their profession. It is very often quite outside formal education that the most significantly formative (i.e. educative) influences are to be found.[1]

In the communist countries, too, the centralizing and other implications of industrialization for education have long been recognized, theorized about, and given an ideological justification. The entire school system and the still more formative para-curricular activities are designed to contain all perceptions and endeavors within the purpose of the "collective." Within this frame of reference, they are capable of imparting conviction, securing devotion and contentment, and stimulating enterprise. Therefore the huge underdeveloped part of mankind is fascinated both by the manifest achievements of the communist world and still more by its persistent and glossy publicity. Communist countries, whatever their drawbacks, do not represent themselves externally in contradictory terms. They do not export trashy television programs or hideous film portraits of themselves to be endlessly relayed over the world's networks. Outside the major countries of the western world, as well as in them, the efficient organization of our entertainment business ensures that a very colossus of communication emphasizes just those aspects of our life that have least in common with civilization, religion, or humane aspirations. There is not a corner of the world into which this portrayal is not thrust, and into which the alternative interpretation of the nature of man fostered in the communist world does not equally push to underline our message. The receptive audience is already half of mankind, and will soon be more than that. The children being born in those countries are our children's contemporaries. They are the "next generation" we asked about a few pages ago. Their parents or national leaders are comparing systems, making critical decisions, and above all are building up educational programs without any hindrances or inhibitions. What can the little red schoolhouse or the little old school board do about that?

---

[1] Dr. S. de Grazia's *Of Time, Work and Leisure*. New York: Twentieth Century Fund, 1962, gives remarkable and up-to-date documentation.

It is questions like this that sharpen our realization that within a lifetime education has passed from being a domestic or parochial matter to a world-wide public concern that must have international perspectives if it is to be valid at all. The role, scope, and effect of the school are changing like a chameleon under our eyes, taking on new color to suit the background. Let us consider but two factors which must affect our reappraisal: television and the "youth problem."

In 1961 public television programs were just 25 years old. It is already impossible to think of amusements, advertising, or even teaching without them. In many countries a great number of children (not to speak of adults) daily spend the equivalent of half a school day looking at the television programs or at the comic papers associated with them. I am not suggesting that the effects are necessarily deleterious, but merely comparing the relative evocation of showy television and of a rather dull school. Moreover, where television is not of itself harmful in any way, it undoubtedly portrays life from another angle than the school. Its popularity is undoubted. In Britain in 1951 only 5 percent of households had television sets; in 1961 well over 90 percent of schoolchildren had sets at home. In Italy, illiteracy is rapidly being reduced by nightly TV lessons—during which time no alternative program is shown! All over the less developed part of the world, television's effect is like a bombshell. And when we also consider that in those very countries industry and commerce make unquenchable demands on the well-schooled minority from whom potential teachers might otherwise be recruited, it is obvious that the functions of teaching must be largely transferred to other agencies, and that the whole relationship of the person taught to these new educative agencies must be different from anything we know.

In these unfamiliar circumstances (which, in a contracting world, are already certain to be part of our children's circumstances) what rules can we lay down? The answer clearly is that we cannot lay down any rules with finality, if only because of our own ignorance. Vast new nations have come into being since the first edition of this book; but there is flux at home too. Time and again, for example, high-powered government surveys in a number of countries have tried to assess the number of scientists required in a given period of time. Time and again they have underestimated because they have ignored: (a) increasing government demands; (b) unrecognized but already emergent needs; (c) the growth of new enterprises to cope with those needs; and (d) structural changes both in existing enterprises themselves and in the personnel of their managements. Sitting at home, or (what is much the same thing) holding a conference with obsolescent terms of reference, we cannot see the world changing about us. The older and the more respectable we become—that is to say, the more like parents and teachers we become—the less easy it is for us to envisage the pressures and priorities of our children's world-to-be. Some comparative study of other contexts, if undertaken as objectively as possible, may help. But, by the same token, these studies dispel any idea that educational prescriptions cherished by us have some canonical permanence.

This consideration of our foreignness in our children's world brings us directly to the "youth problem"—too big a problem by far for us to do more than acknowledge here. From time immemorial, every family has had something of a "youth problem" when the children became old enough to question parental authority. Yet that very challenge so familiar to us is mitigated in more static societies, in societies with "extended" families, in social systems with recognizable initiation phases, and in places where early marriage and economic self-sufficiency are usual. The "youth problem" we face is more acute because of the absence from our midst of these by-passes to conflict with parental authority. Technological and social changes too have widened the gap between the generations, if only because of different worlds of awareness and different planes of expectation.

Furthermore, the extended period of dependence necessitated by our children's protracted schooling and the postponement of "fully proficient" status has brought about a completely unprecedented patchwork of maturity here contrasting with juvenility there, all together in the same person's different social relationships. (This is very often accentuated by the mechanisms of educational selection). But at bottom our "youth problem" is the same as that the world over—youth's possession of powers and perceptions that cannot be fully acknowledged and utilized.

To an unprecedented extent today's "social migrants," or indeed whole emergent populations, also find themselves in a comparable position, introducing many educational problems; but at this point it is more convenient for us to consider the relatively clear-cut problem of our own youth. We have still to devise an effective and overall provision for our young people, genuinely taxing their undoubted powers, improving their competence, and strengthening constructive responsibility, while keeping them at the long business of training for work, parenthood, and life. It therefore seems quite clear that the whole concept of "once and for all" schooling as a juvenile, preparatory, and sheltered experience under neatly recognizable agencies needs radical re-thinking. The world is at present a workshop for the elaboration and testing of suitable expedients, involving many things much bigger than a dwindling supply of teachers and relatively diminishing scholastic influences.

These world experiments belong to us, if we are wise. Like everyone else, we have more to do than blandly observe our neighbors. Setting our own house in order entails at least the following new kinds of provision: arrangements to supplement continuously the cultural background of pupils and students; supplementation and correction of the shortcomings of specialists; preparation for new types of jobs (with new human relationships in all jobs, and a new international orientation); and some substitute for the largely broken-down continuity of family occupation or of "sense of context." These and many other needs can be studied at length; but our basic need immediately is to recognize that every problem or experiment surveyed is indirectly an examination of ourselves.

We began by looking over the garden fence. Nothing ever really happens entirely in our own back yard any more. The smoke from our barbecue is grievously tantalizing to the hungry; alternatively, the fumes of our garbage fire make our neighbor's life a misery. In these times when a day's flying takes us halfway around the world, and when radio, films, and press foreshorten time and distance, it is obvious that anyone's answers to the old questions must be different. The aims are essentially the same—the offering of a full and happy life to our children. Other people's children want that too. Unless they get it, in a way that suits their readiness and idioms, our own children's prospects will be impaired. Educational opportunity, like public health, is something we cannot afford to stint. Thinking very seriously about other people's children may be ultimately the best service we can offer our own.

Selected Bibliography

STANDARD WORKS IN COMPARATIVE EDUCATION:

CRAMER, J. F., and G. S. BROWNE, *Contemporary Education*. New York: Harcourt, Brace & World, Inc., 1956.

HANS, N., *Comparative Education*. London: Routledge & Kegan Paul, Ltd., 1950.

KANDEL, I. L., *The New Era in Education*. Boston: Houghton Mifflin Company, 1955.

KING, E. J., *World Perspectives in Education*. London: Methuen & Co., Ltd., and Indianapolis: The Bobbs-Merrill Company, Inc., 1962.

MALLINSON, V., *An Introduction to the Study of Comparative Education*. London: William Heinemann, Ltd., and New York: The Macmillan Company, 1957.

ULICH, R., *The Education of Nations*. Cambridge, Mass.: Harvard University Press, 1961.

DENMARK

DIXON, W., *Education in Denmark*. London: George G. Harrap & Co., Ltd., and Copenhagen: Centraltrykkeriet, 1959.

Various pamphlets by the Ministry of Education, Copenhagen, by the City of Copenhagen Education Authority, and by *Det Danske Selskab*, Copenhagen. The pamphlets give excellent information in English on Danish education and social services.

FRANCE

BROGAN, D. W., *The Development of Modern France*. London: Hamish Hamilton, 1939.

———, *The French Nation from Napoleon to Pétain*. London: Hamish Hamilton, 1957.

GAL, R., *Histoire de l'Education*. Paris: Presses Universitaires, 1948.

———, *La Réforme de l'Enseignement*. Paris: Presses Universitaires, 1947.

KOHN, H., *The Making of the Modern French Mind*. New York: Doubleday & Company, Inc., 1955.

MILES, D. W., *Recent Reforms in French Secondary Education*. New York: Columbia University Press, 1953.

MINISTRY OF NATIONAL EDUCATION, *L'Organisation de l'Enseignement en France*. Paris, 1957.

GREAT BRITAIN

ALEXANDER, W. P., *The Educational System of England and Wales*. London: Newnes, 1959.

BANKS, O., *Parity and Prestige in English Secondary Education*. London: Routledge & Kegan Paul, Ltd., 1955.

BARNARD, H. C., *A Short History of English Education from 1760*. London: University of London Press, Ltd., 1961.

DENT, H. C., *The Educational System of England and Wales*. London: University of London Press, Ltd., 1961.

FLOUD, HALSEY, and MARTIN, *Social Class and Educational Opportunity*. London: Routledge & Kegan Paul, Ltd., 1956.

LOWNDES, G. A. N., *The British Educational System*. London: Hutchinson & Co., Ltd., 1955.

UNITED STATES OF AMERICA

BEREDAY, G. Z. F., and VOLPICELLI, L., eds., *Public Education in America*. New York: Harper & Row, Publishers, 1959.

KANDEL, I. L., *American Education in the Twentieth Century*. Cambridge, Mass.: Harvard University Press, 1957.

LERNER, M., *America as a Civilization*. New York: Simon and Schuster, Inc., 1957.

THISTLETHWAITE, F., *The Great Experiment*. Cambridge: Cambridge University Press, 1955.

WHYTE, W. H., *The Organization Man*. New York: Simon and Schuster, Inc., 1956.

THE SOVIET UNION

BEREDAY, BRICKMAN, and READ, eds., *The Changing Soviet School*. Cambridge, Mass.: Houghton Mifflin Company, 1960.

COUNTS, G. S., *The Challenge of Soviet Education*. New York: McGraw-Hill Book Co., Inc., 1957.

DE WITT, N., *Education and Professional Employment in the U.S.S.R.* Washington, D.C.: National Science Foundation, 1961.

KING, E. J. ed., *Communist Education*. London: Methuen, & Co., and Indianapolis: The Bobbs-Merrill Company, Inc., 1963.

SIMON, B., ed., *Psychology in the Soviet Union*. London: Routledge & Kegan Paul, and Stanford: Stanford University Press, 1957.

INDIA

KABIR, H., *Education in the New India*. London: George Allen & Unwin Ltd., 1956.

MINISTRY OF INFORMATION AND BROADCASTING, *The Future of Education in India*. New Delhi, 1953.

NEHRU, J., *The Discovery of India*. London: Meridian Books, Inc., 1951.

NURULLAH, S., and NAIK, J. P., *A History of Education in India*. London and Bombay: The Macmillan Company, 1951.

PANIKKAR, K. M., *Hindu Society at the Crossroads*. Bombay: Probsthain, 1955.

YEARBOOKS AND OTHER SOURCES

INTERNATIONAL BUREAU OF EDUCATION, *The International Yearbook of Education*. Geneva.
Gives an annual catalogue of educational events and changes as reported by official organizations.

UNESCO, The *Compulsory Education* series.
Provides good accounts of the statutory minimum of education in various countries. This compulsory minimum, however, is not usually related to the highly significant sectors of education that are not compulsory.

UNESCO, The *Problems in Education* series.
Reviews separate topics of international importance such as *The Education of Teachers in England, France and the U.S.A.; The Education of Women for Citizenship*; and *Adult Education: Current Trends and Practices*. These books are authoritative and very well written.

U.S. DEPARTMENT OF HEALTH, EDUCATION, AND WELFARE, The *Comparative Education* pamphlets. Washington, D.C.: Government Printing Office.
They are monographs on individual countries or regions.

UNIVERSITY OF LONDON INSTITUTE OF EDUCATION and TEACHERS COLLEGE, COLUMBIA UNIVERSITY, NEW YORK, *The Year Book of Education*. London: Evans Brothers, Ltd., and New York: Harcourt, Brace & World, Inc.
For particular problems or factors affecting educational development. It is published annually. Despite its title, each year's issue deals with a single theme reviewed from the standpoint of particular countries or institutions which especially illustrate the theme. It is, therefore, a cumulative encyclopedia of essays written by specialists, usually contributing firsthand knowledge about their own countries. The issues in the revised series from 1953 on are the most valuable. For example, the 1957 publication surveyed philosophies and theories of education

in practice throughout the world; the 1958 volume dealt with the secondary school curriculum; the 1959 volume dealt with higher education; the 1961 volume treated the concept of excellence; and the theme of the 1963 volume was the education of teachers.

PERIODICALS

COMPARATIVE EDUCATION SOCIETY, *Comparative Education Review*. New York.

UNESCO INSTITUTE FOR EDUCATION, *International Review of Education*. Hamburg.

The above periodicals provide topical information and comment on world events or problems in education. They also review problems of method in research and teaching, as they concern the study of Comparative Education.

Index

[247]